D0466926

THE
HURRICANES

THE HURRICANES

One High School Team's Homecoming After Katrina

Jeré Longman

PublicAffairs
New York

Book Design by Linda Harper

Library of Congress Cataloging-in-Publication Data
Longman, Jere.
The Hurricanes : one high school team's homecoming after Katrina /
Jere Longman.
   p. cm.
 Includes bibliographical references and index.
 ISBN 978–1–58648–673–0 (hardcover : alk. paper)
 1. Football—Louisiana—Plaquemines Parish—History—21 century.
 2. High schools—Louisiana. I. Title.

GV959.53.P53L66 2008
796.332′620976337—dc22
                                                                    2008018421

First Edition

10 9 8 7 6 5 4 3 2 1

CONTENTS

1

STORM WARNING

"COACH, YOU GOT TO GO."

"Go where?"

"You got to go, the storm is coming."

"Man, we not gonna get nothin'. It's gonna turn."

"Coach, we need to get out of here," Wayne Williamson Sr., a sheriff's deputy, told Cyril Crutchfield Jr., the football coach at Port Sulphur High in Louisiana's Plaquemines Parish.

It was Saturday, August 27, 2005, at nine in the morning. The Port Sulphur players had gathered to watch video in the team's locker room, which was painted purple and gold and fitted with latticed metal lockers. Williamson could see in Crutchfield's eyes that the coach was not convinced of approaching danger. The night before, Port Sulphur had defeated nearby Buras High 24–0 in an exhibition football game known as a jamboree. The 2005 high school season was due to start in six days. Port Sulphur played in Class 1A, the smallest of Louisiana's five football classes. Crutchfield and the Bronchos had won the state championship in 2002 after finishing as runners-up in 2001. Now they talked confidently again of "goin' to the 'Dome," shorthand for the five state-title games that were played each December at the Superdome in New Orleans.

Hurricane Katrina was heaving in the Gulf of Mexico, churning toward the vulnerable crescent of New Orleans. In two days, the storm would peel off sections of the Superdome roof and render it a hellish evacuation center, but Crutchfield was in no hurry to leave. He was in the middle of a workout. After the Bronchos lifted weights and reviewed video of the jamboree, they would run a series of short sprints to flush the soreness and exhaustion from their legs.

"Man, that thing'll turn," Crutchfield said.

"Coach, it's not looking good," Williamson said.

"How bad is it?"

"It's bad."

"Naw, it'll turn."

Katrina had raked across southern Florida three days earlier, weakening over land but reclaiming its strength in the warm, fuel-injected waters of the Gulf. It had become the third major hurricane of the season. Now, the storm had metastasized like a tumor, nearly doubling in size. On television, its clouds spread across the Gulf with a familiar, threatening, cotton-candy swirl. In a few hours, Katrina would reach Category 5 strength with sustained winds of 175 miles an hour.

It was now on a course for Plaquemines Parish, a rudderlike peninsula that took its name from a Native American word for persimmon. It was here, below New Orleans, that the Mississippi River began a final winding run of seventy-five miles to its bird-foot delta. The river bisected the parish, flowing past villages with whimsical, buoyant names like Phoenix, Bohemia, Davant, Pointe a la Hache, Diamond, Happy Jack, Grand Bayou, Port Sulphur, Homeplace, Empire, Buras, Triumph, Sunrise, Boothville, and Venice. With each mile, the city receded further into country. The prairie land narrowed and dissolved into marsh and the water, both fresh and salty, began to press in, taking hold, increasingly unimpeded to reward with its bounty or disrupt with its caprice.

Residents of lower Plaquemines lived surrounded by water, earned their incomes from its shrimp and oysters, and also understood their susceptibility to its destructive power. Highway 23 provided the asphalt spine of the river's narrow west bank. One side of the four-lane was shouldered by the river levee. The other side was protected by the so-called back levee, which kept out water from fishing-rich marshes and bayous that buffered the Gulf. Down here, Highway 23 was the only road in or out. The only two directions were "up the road" and "down the road." The southern tip of the parish was sometimes referred to as the end of the world.

Plaquemines (pronounced PLACK-uh-mins) remained as vital as it was isolated and vulnerable. The parish was a hub of Louisiana's commercial fishing industry, which was second only to Alaska's. About four hundred million pounds of menhaden, shrimp, oysters, and crabs were hauled from the waters of lower Plaquemines each year, ranking the county among the nation's top five fishing ports. The oil and gas industry made Plaquemines the state's "energy golden goose," according to a study by Louisiana State University. Eleven thousand wells operated in the parish; another 1,100 operated in federal waters off the Plaquemines coastline. Together, they were responsible for about half of the Gulf's oil production and a third of its natural gas production. The energy industry accounted for 2,600 jobs in the sparsely populated parish, which had contributed two billion dollars in mineral revenue to state coffers over the previous decade. Now the entire lower end of the parish sat in Katrina's shattering path.

This was hardly the first time that Plaquemines Parish had faced a watery upheaval. The hurricane of 1915, a Category 4 storm, killed 275 people, including 100 from Myrtle Grove to Buras in Plaquemines. Miles of levees were washed away. The *Times-Picayune* of New Orleans told of stranded men and women in small boats and skiffs who pleaded to those in passing vessels, "Throw us a crust of bread, a biscuit, anything."

That storm also resulted in the county's most singular given name. Depending on who told the story, Clara Pinkins either gave a doctor-assisted birth just as the wind and water pounded her home or climbed into a cistern made of cedar planks, and was blown from Ostrica on the east bank of the Mississippi to Buras on the west bank, where she remained until a Red Cross worker heard the crying of a baby. All parties were so relieved that the child was named Relief Jones, and the name was later passed on to Relief II and Relief III.

During the Great Mississippi Flood of 1927, Plaquemines was sacrificed as a fail-safe plan for New Orleans. A levee was dynamited below New Orleans and both St. Bernard and Plaquemines parishes were inundated. Parts of lower Plaquemines were also swamped by Hurricane Betsy in 1965 and Hurricane Camille in 1969. People knew how to live with water. Old-timers told of building trapdoors in their houses or drilling holes in the floor as a kind of pressure valve, so that water would rise without destroying their properties. Some hoisted their furniture, left the doors and windows open, and simply sprayed the mud out when they got home. Others placed axes in the attic in case they had to chop their way through the roof. A few lashed themselves to trees or poles so that if they drowned in a storm, at least they could be found and claimed by relatives.

Yet there was less natural cushioning against hurricanes than there once had been. Plaquemines Parish, along with other parts of southeastern Louisiana, was sinking from the natural settling of soils and the extraction of millions of tons of oil and natural gas. Also, coastal erosion in southeastern Louisiana had eaten away 1,900 square miles of marshland since the 1930s; the equivalent of a football field was said to disappear every half hour. The Mississippi was harnessed and channeled to the Gulf by levees, halting the deposit of replenishing silt in the wetlands. As marshland and barrier islands became denuded, southeastern

Louisiana lost its buffer against the churning wind and surge of a major storm.

Nowhere was the geographic susceptibility of lower Plaque-mines more evident than at Port Sulphur High School, which sat on a sliver of land, not half a mile wide, flanked by the Mississippi and the marshes. Port Sulphur had escaped the worst floodwaters of Betsy and Camille, but, like New Orleans, it sat between levees in what amounted to an exposed bowl.

About nine thirty on this Saturday morning, Williamson drove fifty yards from the Port Sulphur football field to a parish jail that sat in the same block as the library, the fire station, and a small cemetery. He was a gregarious, stocky man whose build suggested that he was a former lineman on the team. Before he reached the lockup, the deputy received a phone call. Parish administrators had just concluded a meeting. There was a mandatory evacuation from Belle Chasse at the northern end of Plaquemines to Venice on the lower end. A few minutes later, Williamson made the short drive back to Port Sulphur High.

"Coach, we got the call," he told Crutchfield. "It's a mandatory evacuation. We got to go."

"What you think?" Crutchfield asked.

"I think you need to go. We all need to go."

"I'll call you when I decide."

Crutchfield would never make the call. Williamson had not expected him to. The coach thought the storm would swerve to-ward Mississippi or Alabama. They always seemed to take a jog at the last minute. In September 2004, a year earlier, Hurricane Ivan had menaced Louisiana, only to turn and wreak its destruc-tion on Gulf Shores, Alabama. The residents of Plaquemines Parish had left ahead of Ivan, but it turned out to be a false alarm, and they were all back home in two or three days. Many of those who left ahead of Katrina would pack nothing more than a couple of changes of clothes.

At the same time, Williamson noticed apprehension in the eyes of some Port Sulphur players, including his own son, Wayne Jr., who was a sophomore defensive back. This was a huge storm. The night before, Big Wayne and some of the other deputies at the Port Sulphur jamboree noticed storm birds coming out of the marsh, heading inland. They had pointed wings and long bodies, probably magnificent frigate birds, and the locals knew they signaled the arrival of tropical weather. By the dozens, seemingly hundreds, they had flown over the football stadium at Fort Jackson, south of Port Sulphur, flocking like pelicans during migration.

"I believe we'll be evacuating tomorrow," one of the deputies had said, looking at the sky as the birds headed north.

He had been prescient in his forecast. Now people would be following the storm birds, trying to find shelter inland. Everyone would begin leaving this Saturday morning, or Sunday at the latest. Everyone but hardheads like Crutchfield. He was a native not of Plaquemines Parish but of Covington, in the piney area beyond the north shore of Lake Pontchartrain. For him, hurricanes meant rain and wind, but flooding for someone else. He was beginning his seventh season as head coach at Port Sulphur, but he still possessed a newcomer's naïveté and hubris, believing he and the small community were somehow invincible to bad weather.

"Coach, you need to get these kids home," Williamson insisted.

Reluctantly, Crutchfield turned off the television in the locker room and shut down practice early. The players had not even taken the field to stretch and run the fatigue out of their legs. They had been watching video of Port Sulphur's first regular-season opponent, Belle Chasse, a Class 4A school and a bitter parish rivalry.

"Don't let your momma and daddy take you all across the country," Crutchfield told his players. "The thing'll be through here Sunday or Monday. We'll be back in school Wednesday or

Thursday. We're gonna play Belle Chasse on Saturday; if we've got to, we'll play on Sunday, but we're gonna play 'em."

Then the players gathered in a circle, holding hands, and said the team prayer that they repeated each day of every season:

Dear Lord,
The battles we go through in life
We ask for a chance to be fair,
A chance to equal all our strife,
A chance to do or dare.
If we shall win, may it be by the code,
With our faith and honor held high.
If we shall lose, may we stand by the road
And cheer as the winners go by.
By day by day, get better and better.
A team that won't be beat, can't be beat.
In Jesus' name, one, two, three Bronchos.

As he spoke to Crutchfield, Williamson began laughing. He liked the coach's courage, even if it seemed misplaced this morning. The deputy had grown up in Port Sulphur, had played on its football teams in the late 1970s, and had escorted the team bus to games for sixteen years. He appreciated Crutchfield's confidence, the way he always believed that he and his team would prevail over their opponents. But this adversary was a hurricane, not a football team, and it was time to make serious preparations to leave the parish. If Crutchfield had no intention of evacuating, his players and their families would not be so recklessly cavalier. They would want to get on the road before Interstate 10 toward Texas became jammed, and gasoline grew as scarce as hotel rooms.

The Port Sulphur players piled into a school bus and Crutchfield dropped them at their various homes. While their parents spent all that money on hotel rooms, he told them, he would be home playing dominoes.

"See you in a couple days," a young lineman named Sal Cepriano told him.

Crutchfield parked the bus at a depot two miles from school, picked up his Ford Explorer, and returned to the apartment house where he lived, just beyond the east end zone at Port Sulphur High. The sunny sky did not hint of an approaching storm, even as Katrina reached Category 5 by one in the afternoon. Crutchfield checked on the weather occasionally, saw that southeastern Louisiana was directly in the hurricane's path, but still felt no pressing need to leave.

He had a football game to plan. Belle Chasse had defeated Port Sulphur two seasons in a row, and now it was payback time. On its own level, the rivalry was no less impassioned than Ohio State versus Michigan.

There were race and class divides between the northern end of Plaquemines Parish and the southern end. Belle Chasse, more than 90 percent white and located seven miles from New Orleans, had more than a third of the parish's prestorm population of twenty-seven thousand, as well as its highest property values, educational level, and average household income. Forty miles to the south, Port Sulphur was racially diverse, but the high school was predominantly black. Once, Port Sulphur had flourished as a company town for the Freeport Sulphur Company. But as the price of sulphur dropped, the company ceased local operations in 2000, and Port Sulphur lost its economic ballast. "A dying town," Jiff Hingle, the parish sheriff, called it.

It was football that now provided Port Sulphur, population 3,115, with its most visible sense of achievement. And there could be no more satisfying way to start a season than to defeat Belle Chasse. "We're going to pound 'em," Crutchfield told his players, thinking to himself, *There's gonna be an ass-whuppin'.*

On Sunday morning, August 28, Crutchfield awakened about five thirty, took a quick ride through town, and saw people packing to leave. It seemed panicky, unnecessary. *They're stupid,* he told himself. He lay down for a nap, awakened about eight or eight thirty, and took a walk outside his apartment, which stood only a block from Highway 23. All the cars were headed north.

Hollie Russell, a French teacher at Port Sulphur High, drove past with her family, starting what would become a twelve-hour drive to southwestern Louisiana. Crutchfield was sitting on his steps in shorts and flip-flops.

"Where you gonna go?" Russell asked him.

He would ride it out in the school, Crutchfield said.

"I'll be okay," he said.

"Don't be stupid," Russell told him.

An acquaintance, Wade Gabriel, rode by as Crutchfield stood outside, talking on his cell phone. He was staying, too. He would pass back by in a little bit. Later, Anthony Anderson, whom everybody called Cobb, stopped by.

"You ain't leavin'?" Cobb asked.

"You know I ain't leavin'," Crutchfield said.

"Okay," Cobb said. "I'm coming back. I ain't leavin' either."

The sky was cloudy, and around noon, rain began to fall. The hurricane was still headed directly for New Orleans; it had not turned as Crutchfield had predicted. He began to gather his belongings in case the wind blew the roof off his apartment or shattered the windows. He put most of his clothes, his television, and his computer in his Explorer. Then he drove the short distance to the two-story brick school. He returned home, loaded the floral mattress from his bed, and drove back to school, placing the mattress on the floor of the industrial arts classroom.

He also grabbed his barbecue grill and flashlight. The electricity would surely go out, but he would use the flashlight to finish his game plan for Belle Chasse. By the time his players returned, the plan would be in place. He already knew exactly what he wanted to do.

At thirty-eight, with a shaved head and dressed in a white T-shirt and blue-jean shorts, Crutchfield still possessed the wide shoulders and narrow hips of the all-American defensive back that he had been in the 1980s at Northeast Louisiana, now renamed the University of Louisiana–Monroe. He was obsessed with football, and it showed in Port Sulphur's results on the field. Only once in his six previous seasons had the team failed to advance as far as the state quarterfinals. When he coached track in the spring, Crutchfield said he might schedule eight meets each year but only attend about three. The others, he would tell his athletes in a ruse, had been canceled. This left them free to practice spring football or lift weights in anticipation of the coming season.

Rodney Bartholomew Sr., a sheriff's deputy, drove by the school to check on Crutchfield, Cobb, Gabriel, and another man named Russell Smith. The deputy found them sitting outside the industrial arts building, preparing to barbecue hamburgers and sausage. He was eating an ice-cream bar, and the others wanted one, too, so Bartholomew drove to the nearby parish jail and returned with a handful of treats. He stayed about an hour. The talk was all about Katrina and Belle Chasse.

"What you think?" Crutchfield asked.

"If it takes a turn, we're gonna be playing ball Saturday," Bartholomew said.

"I'm hoping for Saturday, too."

"If it doesn't make a turn and still misses us, we'll be playing Sunday," Bartholomew said.

"One of these days, we'll be playing ball," Crutchfield replied.

"Yeah, Crutch," Bartholomew said, "we gotta whip they behinds."

They kept talking about the game, and finally Bartholomew said, "All jokes aside, coach, if the hurricane don't turn and you see the weather getting real bad, man, you oughta get up and go. It's nothing to play with."

"Okay," Crutchfield said to assuage his friend. He had no intention of leaving.

Bartholomew was headed up to Belle Chasse, where the sheriff's department had set up its emergency operations.

Crutchfield said he would stick it out.

"I ain't going nowhere," the coach told the deputy. "Port Sulphur is my home. I'm going to live and die in Port Sulphur."

"Y'all be careful," Bartholemew said, and he drove off.

About five p.m., Crutchfield and his friends took a ride on a pair of four-wheelers along the marsh levee behind Port Sulphur High. Crutchfield saw something he had never seen before. The water seemed low, about fifteen feet short of the normal shoreline, as if it were being sucked out into the Gulf.

At eight o'clock, the sheriff's department made one final plea for Crutchfield to leave. Colonel Charles Guey, operations chief for the department, drove by the school and said, "You need to get out; we're leaving and shutting everything down."

"I'll be all right," Crutchfield said. "I don't think it'll be that bad."

"It will be," Guey said.

"You think water's coming in here?" Crutchfield asked.

"Yeah, it's coming," Guey said. "It's gonna come from Barataria Bay faster than you can blink your eyes."

After Guey pulled out, Crutchfield and his friends were on their own. Gabriel pulled his pickup near the industrial arts building and placed a battery-powered television on the hood of the truck. The men sat amid the table saws and ripsaws and wood lathes and talked and watched WVUE in New Orleans, Channel Eight. Gabriel later remembered the station's weatherman, Bob Breck, rolling up his sleeves and saying that anyone remaining in Plaquemines Parish should buckle down. It was going to be bad.

Crutchfield remembered Breck being more blunt: "Anyone still left in Plaquemines Parish is crazy."

The group had now expanded to six men. While a couple guys watched television, Crutchfield lay on his mattress and tried to sleep. An alarming noise awakened him. It sounded like the whistling of tornadoes. Rocks began to hit the windows. The hissing and howling whistles kept coming, from one side of the school then the other, outside this window then that one, as if some mischievous trick were being played by a meteorological prankster.

Lord have mercy, Crutchfield told himself.

He went back to sleep but awakened again around ten thirty p.m. Projectiles kept slamming into the windows of the industrial arts classroom. A gust of wind blew the television off the hood of Gabriel's pickup. One of the classroom windows broke, and Crutchfield and the others made a run for it, sprinting into the main section of the high school. Using his flashlight, he saw someone sitting on a chair in the hallway. Another man sat on a sofa in the teachers' lounge. These were new arrivals. Now eight of them would ride out the storm together.

They headed for the cafeteria, and finding apparent safety in numbers, the men began to laugh and talk about football again. Sure, the school might get some water, but probably not a lot of damage.

"You think you gonna play Belle Chasse?" Gabriel asked.

"Yeah, we gonna play," Crutchfield said.

One of the windows in the cafeteria broke. A panel above another window seemed to begin breathing as it sucked inward and outward in the wind. Crutchfield had left his mattress in the industrial arts building, so he took a spot on the floor, placing his head on a duffel bag, trying to shield himself from the possibility of flying glass. About three a.m., Gabriel received a call from a friend on his cell phone. More windows had fissured and the wind was shrieking. "You standing outside?" the friend asked.

No, Gabriel said. He was in the cafeteria. Some of the men slept, while others kept watch. Between three and three thirty, Crutchfield awakened on the floor and felt wet. He climbed on a cafeteria table and fell asleep again until about four thirty, when Cobb began to shake him.

"Coach, wake up. Water's coming in," Cobb said.

"Quit playin', Cobb," Crutchfield said. "You trippin'."

No, Cobb insisted, he was serious. Crutchfield shined his flashlight into a school courtyard. Water had reached the second of four steps leading into the cafeteria. Crutchfield could see a small wave cresting from the industrial arts building. The wind pushed the wave with such force that it hit the steps and splashed against the cafeteria door.

Katrina was scything toward landfall at 6:10 a.m. on August 29, weakening slightly but still bearing winds of 120 miles an hour and pushing a twenty-foot-plus storm surge. The hurricane would slam into Plaquemines Parish only thirteen miles to the south, near Buras.

Crutchfield hurried out of the cafeteria, down a hallway to a special education classroom on the first floor, where he had stored his clothes, his television, and his computer. He began carrying the items to his second-floor classroom. By the time he had made several trips up and down the stairs, water on the lower floor of the school had risen to his midcalf.

"Man, let's go to the gym," someone said. "It's higher than the second floor."

It was a short distance from the cafeteria, but Crutchfield was nervous now, and he began fumbling with his set of master keys. By the time he unlocked the safety bar on the gym door, the water inside was up to his waist. The door opened and a piano pushed outward with the swirling force. Crutchfield jumped out of the way, but another of the men, a guy who must have weighed four hundred pounds, got pinned against a wall.

Others tried to free the piano, but Crutchfield was terrified of what might be in the water. He kept running to his left toward the gym's bleachers, high-stepping along the baseline of the hardwood floor as if he were in the surf trying to reach a beach. Water splashed into his mouth and tasted salty. Something floated past and brushed him, a rug, maybe, or a floor mat. Crutchfield thought it was a snake. Instead of walking up the steps to the bleachers, he grabbed a railing and slung himself over the top.

Later he would apologize to the trapped man and would consider his actions selfish, but at the time he never thought, *Oh, he's back there, I'm leaving him.* All he knew was that the water held hidden, dangerous things and if he had to save anybody, it was himself. Another man, Cobb, did free the piano, and he suffered a deep gash in his leg. The others would later joke that Crutchfield was the only man besides Jesus to walk on water.

Eventually, all of them made it safely to the bleachers. Across the hardwood court sat a stage adorned with purple velvet drapes. From the ceiling, purple and gold banners hung in the school colors, commemorating Port Sulphur's athletic greatness: state championships in football in 1979, 1981, and 2002; a state championship in track in 1974; state championships in baseball in 1974 and 1978; a state title in basketball in 1982.

Eleven rows of bleachers led upward to a bank of windows below the ceiling. A wall of water had formed in Breton Sound to the east. Pushed by Katrina's counterclockwise winds, the storm surge had swamped the east bank of lower Plaquemines, crossed the Mississippi River, and topped and breached the river levee on the west bank, pouring into Port Sulphur. To the men in the gym, it seemed now that the school was in the middle of the Gulf. Water rose steadily. In the semidarkness, it was brown black, like the Skoal that Crutchfield dipped, and it rose steadily, up one row of bleachers, then the next.

The 2002 state-championship trophy drifted by, a large wooden plaque in the shape of Louisiana, attached to a figurine of a man carrying a football. Crutchfield slapped at the water with a stick until he could grab the trophy. Then he spotted his duffel bag, containing a Bible and some clothes, which he had used as a pillow. Apparently, it had floated outside of the school from the cafeteria and circled back into the gymnasium.

The wind sounded like a freight train but louder, a great metallic whooshing roar. Debris slammed into the walls of the gym, and the men began to fear that water would rise above the windows, cutting off their only escape route. They might have to swim outside if the water kept coming up. Maybe they could make it to the roof of the gym. They broke into a concession stand above the bleachers and searched for anything that might keep them afloat. One man found an ice chest. Somebody else grabbed a football. Gabriel was the only one with a life jacket. His brother had given it to him before the storm.

"If I don't make it, at least they'll find my body," he told his friend, Russell Smith. Gabriel tried to convince his friend to slip into the water and grab the padding around a volleyball net, but Smith seemed scared and distracted.

Water kept coming up, submerging the rims of the backboard ten feet above the court. It climbed until it had claimed seven or eight rows of bleachers. Only three or four rows remained dry. The men moved higher and higher and began to pray. They held hands and said the Lord's Prayer. Crutchfield told himself, *Man, I shoulda left; damn, I shoulda left.*

And he made a vow: *Lord if you get me out of this one, I'll never stay again.*

Gabriel began to fear that the other men might panic and strip him of his life jacket. Then things seemed to grow calm. It felt as if the eye of the hurricane had passed over Port Sulphur. "I'll go check things out," Gabriel told the others. He tied a fire hose around his waist, climbed out of a window in the gym, and plopped into the water. It was full of oil and chemicals and logs and ice chests. He dog-paddled toward the library on the second floor of the school. It seemed to be taking forever. *Please don't let a shark bite me,* he told himself.

Using an oyster hatchet, Gabriel broke a window in the library, pulled himself inside, walked down a hallway, and found some dry clothes in Crutchfield's classroom. The others remained in the flooded gym as wood and other debris circled slowly along the stage, then meandered toward the bleachers. A black Labrador retriever floated in on what looked like a school bulletin board. One moment the dog wasn't there, and the next moment it drifted past, both angry and stunned by fear.

The surge began to recede, row by row in the bleachers, seemingly as quickly as it had risen. Cobb, who was six foot five, jumped into the water to gauge its depth. He found himself submerged nearly to his neck. Cobb kept his eyes on the Labrador retriever. He knew that some people trapped alligators with dead dogs, and he figured if a gator came into the gym, it might go after the Lab first. He also remained alert for water moccasins, fearing that one of the tired snakes might try to rest on his head or shoulders and bite him when he flung it away.

As the water kept retreating, Crutchfield grew afraid that the backside of the hurricane would trap the men again. This time they might not make it out alive.

"We better get out," Crutchfield told the others.

"I ain't gonna make it," the four-hundred-pound man said.

"You can stay your big ass in here, but I'm gettin' out," Crutchfield said.

"Man, come on, come on," the others pleaded.

"Fuck him, I'm gone."

With the water between their chests and waists, the men began to leave the gym in single file. This was the scariest time for Crutchfield. He stepped on things, unknown objects, that terrified him, and he conjured images from a movie he had just seen about giant anacondas. Carrying the trophy inside his duffel bag, he half ran and half swam, splashing his way out of the gym. He passed one of the other guys in line and bounded up a flight of stairs into a classroom that was dry and safe on the second floor.

While separated from the others, Gabriel grabbed a video camera and began filming from a second-floor classroom. At first the wind was docile. Port Sulphur appeared to have become a lake. Houses had floated free of their foundations, sliding into each other like bumper cars. The football locker room was completely submerged. Much of the cafeteria remained under water. Gabriel lamented the fate of an elderly aunt who had been too stubborn to leave and had surely drowned.

"Old Teece had a hard head," he said, his voice captured on the video. "God knows when they gonna find her."

A gasoline storage tank bobbed lazily in the water. Then the wind kicked up again with the rear side of the storm. It blew with the scouring sound of sandblasting and the rat-a-tat-tat of automatic-weapons fire. Part of a Coke machine hung in the top of a tree. Swells began to roll through the schoolyard, and sheets of white rain blew like snow over the surface of the water. A desk floated outside the school, along with a miniature American flag in its stand. The top of Gabriel's white truck poked through the surface. So did the roof of Crutchfield's Explorer. The windows were down, and the ruined vehicle became nothing more than a four-wheel-drive reef for whatever fish might swim by.

Eventually, the others reunited with Gabriel in the library. The men found chips and sodas from snack machines. Some scavenged bottles of water from teachers' desks. Crutchfield located some alcohol to pour on the deep cut on Cobb's leg.

It dawned on Crutchfield that a second, smaller bag of his was missing. This one had his wallet inside, along with some papers to grade for his social studies class. Crutchfield had taken five hundred dollars out of the bank before the storm. Now, he feared it had floated away. Maybe it was in the cafeteria. The water was now just below his knees, but he was afraid of snakes. Suddenly, the money didn't seem to matter so much. Crutchfield stood on a table in the cafeteria and looked around quickly and said, "It ain't here, let's go."

Another man in the group, Jody Mackey, sloshed down a hallway past the principal's office and called out, "Come here, man." When Crutchfield skittishly rounded a corner, he found that Mackey had grabbed his bag before it floated out of the school. Relieved, Crutchfield wanted to give him half the money.

Gabriel panned his camera to the Port Sulphur football field. The purple press box stood like a buoy in the water. Only the top of the metal bleachers was visible. Small whitecaps crested over the playing surface. Waves flowed just beneath the crossbars of the goalposts.

The scoreboard was gone. Crutchfield grew momentarily confused. He couldn't get his bearings. Buildings seemed to have shifted positions with other buildings as if in some cruel game of pinochle.

"Oh, look over here," Crutchfield said to Gabriel.

The coach's apartment house had cracked open like an eggshell. Part of it was snagged on a stadium fence. The other part drifted the length of the field and rammed into a civic center behind the west end zone.

As the wind began to subside a final time from hurricane force, the men climbed to the roof of the school. An hour later, maybe two hours later, they spotted a Coast Guard helicopter. They waved a yellow curtain as a signaling flag. The chopper paused, then kept going. Apparently, the pilot was spotting survivors and radioing to others who would carry out the rescues.

At the Plaquemines Parish emergency center in Belle Chasse, Big Wayne Williamson urged his fellow deputies to check the school for survivors. A boat was on the way, he was told. About four thirty in the afternoon, Colonel Guey arrived at Port Sulphur

High in an airboat. The men looked haggard. "Don't say anything," a chastened Crutchfield said to the man who had warned
him to leave.

The eight survivors were whisked from the school and de-
posited a couple hundred yards away on the Mississippi River
levee. There they awaited a larger rescue boat that would
transport them upriver.

Crutchfield stood atop the levee, arms folded across his chest,
as Gabriel asked on camera, "Would you ever stay again for a Category 5?"

"I'm going back to Covington," Crutchfield said of his hometown.

"Think we gonna play Saturday, or anytime this week?" Gabriel
asked. "How we lookin' coach?"

Crutchfield bent over in rueful laughter.

"Ain't lookin' too good," he said.

He shook his head in disbelief.

"Man."

The hurricane had eaten away at the levees, leaving sheet piling
exposed. Telephone poles leaned in the wind. The roadway that
had been Highway 23 now resembled a canal.

"Water as far as you can see," Gabriel said on the video.
"Twenty foot of water in lower Plaquemines."

The levee was littered with paper, sticks, wood, part of a door.
Then Gabriel shot a close-up of a white casket splattered with mud
and leaves. And he found something else in the high grass. "Several
caskets," he continued in his elegiac monologue. "Uprooted. Bodies
all alongside the levees, caskets."

Then, to Crutchfield, "Main thing, we survived it."

Crutchfield walked toward him, the levee path rutted, the
wind still rippling his T-shirt, and smiled a survivor's smile. "Yeah,
I left on my back and on your back, too."

Finally, in late afternoon, a forty-foot rescue boat arrived and
took the men upriver to a shelter at Belle Chasse. Along the way,

Crutchfield saw more caskets on the levee, coal barges stranded with their cargo, houses scattered like driftwood.

There wouldn't be a game the first week, he told himself. Maybe three or four weeks. He was so hell-bent on a season, an atomic bomb could have hit and he would have said, *We have to play some ball.* He just didn't know when.

Days later, Crutchfield made his way back down to Port Sulphur to retrieve his duffel bag and his championship trophy. More than a year later, sand would still be encrusted in the folds of the figurine's uniform.

All over lower Plaquemines, there were astounding signs of dislocation. A pickup truck sat on a fifteen-foot compressor unit at the parish government building. A recliner perched on the roof of a bank. Shrimp trawlers were stacked against a bridge in the village of Empire like toys in the drain of a bathtub. Just across the bridge, two commercial fishing boats straddled all four lanes of Highway 23. Cows hung by their necks from trees. A refrigerated truck was backed into the branches of an oak, its rear wheels high off the ground, as if delivering rations to the squirrels.

Wade Gabriel also soon returned, with his camera. From the window of a moving car, he completed his travelogue of annihilation: oak trees scalded by the salt water and stripped of their leaves by the wind; gnarled limbs draped with paper and plastic that fluttered like prayer flags; houses stained brown with water lines; other houses spray-painted with the circles of those who had come in search of the dead; front steps that led to nowhere; double-wides splintered or jumbled at odd angles like cars of a derailed train; aluminum buildings peeled like fruit.

Only four parish residents had died in the storm, but almost no structures survived intact. Nothing was where it was supposed to be. Everything was something that was no longer. The school board office in Port Sulphur had its ribs exposed, as if it had starved as well as drowned. A house sat on a car.

Gabriel and his passengers ticked off a list of what had been:

"Where you see Deshawn's truck?"

"Upside down."

"Amy used to live here."

"The little bait shop used to stand right here."

"That's D&T."

"That was D&T."

"Dr. Ross office used to be right here. It's gone."

"Mom, this where y'all used to live at."

"This is my daddy car, the Marquis, in my front ditch."

"That's Raymond Bailey house way across the street in the churchyard."

"Mom, this is y'all's property. Remember the oak tree in the back?"

"This was my mom and them's property, right here. And it look like they house."

"I remember what she said about them steps. Betsy came as far as the second step. It's worser than Betsy, mom."

"We not gonna be down here for six months to a year. I couldn't even find out where Flamingo Lane was at first."

"The (church) hall still kickin'."

"Yeah, the church in the middle of the street, though."

At the football field, a life preserver was tethered to one goal post. The carcass of a needle-nosed garfish hung in the stadium gate, rammed through the chainlink fence by the force of the water. When Crutchfield first noticed the fish, it startled him. As much as he had hoped, there would be no game against Belle Chasse. There would be no football season. There would be no more Port Sulphur High School.

2

A TIDE OF EXTRAORDINARY CIRCUMSTANCES

ON JANUARY 16, 2006, NEARLY FIVE MONTHS AFTER KATRINA, the football field at Port Sulphur High was buried under four inches of crushed stone. A tent city for the National Guard and contractors covered the playing surface, leaving it muddy and rutted. In the early afternoon of an overcast day, Cyril Crutchfield wore jeans and a yellow polo shirt, dipped tobacco, and sipped on a frozen soda. It was a federal holiday, Martin Luther King Jr. Day, but there was no school to cancel in Port Sulphur. The high school's former students were either enrolled in Belle Chasse in northern Plaquemines Parish or spread across Louisiana or windblown from Texas to Tennessee. Crutchfield's Ford Explorer still sat abandoned in the school courtyard. An armadillo skittered across the empty concrete. The school hallways smelled of mold. The cafeteria carried the whiff of rancid meat. Marsh grass and driftwood and a chair sat on the roof of a breezeway. An outside wall was missing from an entire section of classrooms, whose contents were spilled outside. A tree trunk remained in the science lab like a shipwrecked pirogue.

In the second-floor classroom where Crutchfield taught civics and world geography, drawings of the nation's presidents had begun to fall from the back wall. A final prestorm geography lesson remained on the blackboard, the latitudes and longitudes of cities around the world—Manila, Jakarta, Los Angeles, Mexico City—with their own exotic vulnerability to disasters of wind and rain and shifting earth.

In the gym where Crutchfield rode out the storm, the basketball court was warped and crusted with mud. Trophies, with their drowned figurines, littered the stage and the floor. Outside the football locker room, waterlogged helmets and shoulder pads were piled on a sidewalk. A rusty, discarded blocking sled rested in front of the school where Katrina had pushed it. In Crutchfield's ruined coaching office, water dripped with a hollow acoustic sound of desertion.

After lunch in a trailer with two sheriff's deputies, Crutchfield borrowed a hammer. He wanted to retrieve a football from a locker in his office but was reluctant to enter, frightened by the possibility of a lurking snake.

"I'm not going in there," he said. "I'm scared."

Finally, he went inside, and turning his head away, he broke a lock on one of the narrow metal lockers. Quickly, he grabbed the brown and white football inside. It had been autographed by the players on Port Sulphur's 2002 state-championship team. The ball was covered with a briny layer, but the signatures were remarkably well preserved on the smooth surface. Crutchfield spun the ball in his hands. Not much else had been salvaged, except this ball and the state-championship trophy fished from rising water in the gym during the hurricane's fury.

"I had to," Crutchfield said. "I lost everything else. I wanted to make sure I saved something." And then: "If it was a choice between saving a person and that state-championship trophy, it was a no-brainer. I was saving that trophy."

Crutchfield had coached two football games in the weeks after the hurricane, but under awkward circumstances. Belle Chasse High was the only high school that reopened in Plaquemines Parish in 2005, and Crutchfield served as an assistant coach there during the rump season. But he had nothing beyond a professional relationship with the head coach, Bob Becnel, and it chafed him to live in a Federal Emergency Management Agency (FEMA) trailer behind Belle Chasse High.

On this day in mid-January, Crutchfield spoke hopefully of a regional school that was scheduled to open in lower Plaquemines in late summer of 2006. What Crutchfield did not yet know was how many of his former players would return.

Five of his Port Sulphur stars had evacuated on a tide of extraordinary circumstances, three hundred miles north to Bastrop, Louisiana, a paper-mill town near the Arkansas border. The best of those players was Randall Mackey, already a splendid quarterback at age fifteen, even though he stuttered slightly and was so reticent that other players had to call "hut" before the ball was snapped.

He was not tall for a quarterback, only five foot eleven, and he weighed but 165 pounds, but Randall had started as an eighth- and ninth-grader at Port Sulphur High before Katrina struck. One day, Crutchfield noticed him slinging a ball at summer practice in the way that coaches have of recognizing that a player's skills would bloom along with his height and weight. Soon after, Randall became the starting quarterback. He might have played as a backup on the varsity as a seventh-grader, too, as Port Sulphur won the 2002 state title, but his mother, Carla Ragas, had refused to let Crutchfield put Randall on the field. Her eldest son Josh Mackey, a running back, was named most valuable player in that 2002 championship game. But Carla thought Randall was too small. He was ninety pounds at the time, if that.

"Those big boys gonna crush my baby," Carla told Crutchfield.

"He'll be all right."

"Unh, unh, he's not playing. Give him some time."

Early the next season, Carla missed a couple of games because she worked at night. She mended nets for commercial boats that caught the smelly fish known as menhaden, or pogies, whose oil was extracted for use in perfume, cosmetics, health supplements, and paint, and whose meal was used for animal feed. She also inspected grain at a giant grain elevator north of Port Sulphur in Myrtle Grove. Next thing she knew, Randall was the starting quarterback as an eighth-grader.

People would approach her. "Your son's got an arm on him. Where'd that boy get that arm?"

One night, Carla got a call at work. Randall had gotten hurt on the field. A concussion. But he wouldn't stay out of the game. Some people around town thought that moment changed him, made him reluctant or superstitious about signaling the start of play out loud. Still, the people who came up to Carla were right. Her son did have an arm on him. He could throw the ball sixty, sixty-five yards. When Randall was a ninth-grader in 2004, he threw for 24 touchdowns and 2,062 yards as Port Sulphur reached the state quarterfinals. The Bronchos might have gone farther if he had not suffered a broken ankle during the playoffs. In July 2005, Randall had bruised his ribs and punctured a lung while riding an all-terrain vehicle. But he had fully recovered as Katrina and the season opener approached.

Four days before the hurricane struck, Crutchfield told the *Times-Picayune* of New Orleans that Randall had grown bigger and more mature. Many other starters were also returning. A great season was forecast in 2005.

"Our goal is to win a state championship," Crutchfield told the paper.

Then Katrina intervened, and Randall left ahead of the storm with a friend, carrying nothing but a shirt and two pairs of shorts.

In Port Sulphur, he had lived in a cluster of family trailers about a football field's distance from the Mississippi River. After Katrina, all that was found of Randall's mobile home was its twisted frame and a couple of photographs.

Four days after the hurricane, Carla finally reached Randall by phone. He was in Lafayette, Louisiana. She was farther west on Interstate 10 at the Ford Arena, an evacuation shelter in Beaumont, Texas. Apparently, Randall had been on the Internet and had seen the destruction of Plaquemines Parish.

"Ma, we under water," Randall said.

He wanted Carla to come and get him. She had sent her two daughters to school in Beaumont, but the girls said there had been fights, even pregnant girls scuffling. They were afraid to go back. There was talk of gangs. Still, Carla didn't want her kids in a shelter all day with thousands of people. They belonged in school. Randall had to attend classes somewhere if he wanted to play football. After a series of cell-phone calls and text messages, Randall said he learned that a Port Sulphur teammate had transferred to some place called Bastrop in northern Louisiana at the urging of a family pastor. By chance, D'Carlos Holmes, a former assistant coach at Port Sulphur, had also joined the staff at Bastrop High only days before the hurricane hit.

Where the hell was Bastrop? Carla wondered. Neither she nor Randall had ever heard of it. Still, Randall thought, perhaps Port Sulphur's destroyed season could be salvaged in this unfamiliar, beckoning place.

"I wanted Randall in school, and he wanted to play football," Carla said. "He didn't know anybody in Texas. He knew somebody on that team in Bastrop."

Eventually, five Port Sulphur players, including Randall's cousin James Brown, wound up in Bastrop and moved into an apartment with Holmes, the assistant coach. The displacement for Randall was severe. His whole life had been twisted out of shape, like the metal frame of his family's trailer. From a school with two hundred students, he had ended up in a strange place with nearly nine hundred students. Northern Louisiana and southern Louisiana might as well have been separate states. In the middle of the state, around Alexandria, everything began to change: the food, the color of the soil, the sound of the voices, the vigor of the coffee, the drive-through availability of alcohol on Sunday. The flat land began to buck and roll. Catholicism gave way to Protestantism. In Plaquemines Parish, "three" was pronounced "tree" and "boil" was "berl" and you went to the supermarket "to make groceries." In Bastrop, the language was not so florid. The Cajun and New Orleans accents gave way to a twang that sounded more like the piney woods of eastern Texas.

A kid in lower Plaquemines could hunt rabbits in the backyard, ride a four-wheeler on the levees that ran along the Mississippi and the marshes, or walk a couple of blocks and catch redfish and speckled trout in some of the most abundant waters in the United States. Bastrop was landlocked by timber and sidewalks and strip malls. The people were welcoming, though. And in time Bastrop's neighborhoods and Wal-Mart and fast-food commerce would lend the place a kind of small-town heft and sophistication lacking in Port Sulphur, which had neither a red light nor a McDonald's. But Randall's adjustment was difficult. He played little in Bastrop's first few games and missed his family enormously. He appeared to teachers and coaches to be acutely homesick and depressed. He suspected that people were solicitous of him only because he played football, said Coach Holmes, who taught world geography. When adults spoke to Randall, it was difficult to coax a response or even eye contact. Some of the Bastrop officials wondered if he were a special ed student.

His mother would call his cousin, James Brown, and ask, "What's Randall doing?"

"That boy like a zombie."

Even before Katrina struck, Randall was a quiet homebody, often content to sit around and play video games. Now he wouldn't say a word.

"That boy actin' retarded," Brown told his aunt.

From Beaumont, Carla moved to Winnie, Texas, taking a room in a hotel found for her by a church pastor. But she was forced to evacuate again when Hurricane Rita came buzz-sawing through the Louisiana–Texas border in late September 2005. Eventually, Carla returned to Plaquemines Parish, settling with a sister in Belle Chasse.

She traveled five hours each Friday to Randall's games in Bastrop, but he seemed discouraged, ready to go home, even if it meant giving up football, something that would have been unthinkable weeks earlier. Randall had skipped a few school days and practices and was in jeopardy of being kicked off the team, his mother was told.

Some days, instead of going to practice, Randall would lay in the bed of Holmes's pickup truck, mute, disconsolate. He seemed shell-shocked. Holmes tried to bring him around. He bought Randall a football video game, took him out to eat and to get his hair cut, admonished him not to waste his future. Still, he worried that he had lost Randall to some inconsolable melancholy.

"I was close to taking him back to his momma," Holmes said. "I didn't know what to do with a fifteen-year-old who wouldn't say anything."

Randall's mother and Crutchfield advised him to remain in Bastrop. The team was ranked first in Class 4A. He might win a state championship, after all, even if it wasn't in Port Sulphur.

"I want to go home," he told his mother.

"There's nothing to go home to," she answered. "We lost everything."

One weekend in late October 2005, Randall finally visited Port Sulphur for the first time since Katrina. His mother had been right. "A graveyard" is what he called his hometown.

The next month, as a last resort, Carla decided to relocate to Bastrop to be with her son. She moved into a modest yellow home near the high school with Randall and three other children. "I knew I had to come up or I'd ruin his career," she said.

A community fund was set up, and Carla received help paying her utility bills. Furniture was provided by two Baptist churches. The people seemed friendly, respectful. The students who arrived at Bastrop High in 2005 as evacuees had school fees waived and received donated school uniforms. Displaced residents received food and clothing.

"I think this is home for us," Carla, who was thirty-eight, said. "I don't think I could find a bad person here."

It seemed, she said, "like they knew us before we got here."

One family had been particularly hospitable, Carla said. Van E. Lee Jr., a local pharmacist, and his wife, Pam, were boosters whose son had played quarterback at Bastrop High in 2003. The Lees owned the house in which Randall and his family lived. Van Lee said that Carla had signed a year's lease and was paying monthly rent. The cost of the rent, Carla said, was being covered by the Federal Emergency Management Agency. For employment, Carla cleaned the Lees' home and also cared for elderly residents in Bastrop.

At first, Randall had seemed reluctant to play quarterback, preferring a spot as a defensive back. But the Bastrop coaches quickly saw what Crutchfield had long known—the kid had a terrific arm.

"One game he watched from the sideline," Holmes said. "He said, 'I can do better than that.' Once he put his mind to it, saw everyone else playing, it made him get back to reality."

Gradually, Randall began to feel that he belonged, gaining assuredness as his playing time increased. And Bastrop was a convenient place. At least he didn't have to drive forty-five miles to see a movie, as he did from Port Sulphur to suburban New Orleans. Randall became more outgoing, and his mother began to joke, "What are y'all putting in my son's drink?"

Bastrop's opponents were not always so welcoming. Nasty messages began appearing on Internet message boards, including a rumor that Randall was nineteen, not fifteen. During one game, he said, a rival player sneered, "You stupid nigger, go back down south."

Randall said he brushed it off. If he appeared reticent off the field, on the field he was poised and calm. "His vision downfield under pressure is as good for a sophomore as anyone I've been around," said Brad Bradshaw, the Bastrop coach, a thickset man who, like Crutchfield, spit tobacco into a Styrofoam cup.

For a Bastrop team that had lost three consecutive years in the state quarterfinals, the arrival of the players from Plaquemines Parish became the final pieces of an unsolved puzzle. The Rams had not won a state title in nearly eight decades. A new passing offense had been installed, but the team's starting quarterback had left school as the 2005 season began, and the backup soon injured a knee.

On December 9, 2005, Randall threw two touchdown passes as Bastrop High won its first state championship since 1927. Still too young to drive, he was voted most valuable player of the title game as a sophomore. He was also named to the Class 4A all-state team, having started 8 games and thrown 23 touchdown passes with only 4 interceptions.

"You don't want to say a hurricane is a blessing for anyone, but everything has turned up roses for a kid who struggled when he first got here," said Charles Porter, who oversaw the athletic facilities at Bastrop High.

ON THE SURFACE, RANDALL'S STORY WAS ONE OF GREAT resilience and indomitable spirit. Yet his arrival in north Louisiana also exposed the increasingly mercenary nature of high school football and the anything-goes atmosphere that existed post-Katrina, when humanitarianism collided with opportunism. After the hurricane, the Louisiana High School Athletic Association (LHSAA) allowed the state's 4,100 displaced football players to become eligible immediately at any school in the state. At least one rival school, though, became suspicious of the presence in Bastrop of the five Port Sulphur players. In November 2005, the LHSAA investigated accusations that Bastrop had violated state rules by recruiting the Port Sulphur players from evacuation shelters.

"All coaches want to be competitive," said John Carr, the coach at Ouachita Parish High School in Monroe, Louisiana, which faced Bastrop twice in the 2005 season, including the state semifinals. "But in the case of the hurricane, I believe rules were bent and abused."

Bastrop High denied any wrongdoing and was initially cleared of the charges. School officials noted that the team was ranked number 1 in the state before the Port Sulphur players arrived and said rivals appeared jealous of Bastrop's success.

"We would never risk the integrity of our school and our program," Tom Thrower, the principal at Bastrop High, said in January 2006.

Mac Chauvin, assistant commissioner of the LHSAA, said he believed Bastrop was "on the up and up." In the frenetic days after Katrina, the state association's priority had been to get students quickly relocated and back into school. There were a lot of extenuating circumstances, Chauvin said. He was certain that there had been some illegal recruiting, but none that could be proved at the moment.

"We take people at their word," Chauvin said. "One thing you can't do is legislate integrity."

Rumors had spread to Port Sulphur and elsewhere that Randall and his mother were living in a house provided free of charge. The relationship, however compassionate, between a booster and a star athlete's mother appeared suspicious, Carr said. If the hurricane had not occurred, the arrangement might "stand out like a sore thumb," Chauvin said.

According to county records, Van Lee had bought the house shortly before Carla Ragas arrived in Bastrop. Asked to see a copy of the rental agreement, Lee checked his records at his pharmacy and said he had sent it to the LHSAA. The high school organization said the relationship appeared to be within state guidelines. It could find no evidence that Carla was living rent free or was being paid any money she had not earned.

"People scattered; they had to have some place to go," Chauvin said. "The first place they could light, they did. It happened to be a guy with a rent house. A lot of things that are normally violations are probably not violations because of what Katrina and Rita did."

Crutchfield had mixed feelings about the state investigation. He had not complained to the LHSAA. At least Randall and the other four Port Sulphur players had been given a chance to play in the weeks after Katrina. Two of those players were seniors. They did not have to miss their final season of eligibility. So Bastrop had done something for them, however self-interested.

The question was, what would happen next? Randall had two more years remaining in high school. Two of the other former Port Sulphur players had one season of eligibility left. Would they come back to lower Plaquemines for the 2006 season? Should they?

"I think it'd be great if they came back," Crutchfield said. "But they've got to do what's best for themselves. If they come back, great. If they don't, we'll survive. We'll win down here just like they win up there."

Randall said he would remain in Bastrop at least for his junior year.

"I owe it to them," he said. "They welcomed me and showed me a lot of respect."

Several weeks after the 2005 state-championship game, Randall had returned to southeastern Louisiana to see his grandmother at

Christmas. But he went back to Bastrop early, his mother said. Randall had seemed quiet, tired. "Nothing will be the same," Carla said of Port Sulphur. "Everyone is scattered. Family, close friends. It'll never be the same."

Still, for his senior year in 2007, Randall said he might return to Port Sulphur, if a new school was open as planned. According to his mother, he considered Crutchfield a father figure and did not want to be seen as having abandoned him. If Crutchfield had been the head coach at Belle Chasse instead of an assistant coach during the makeshift 2005 season, Carla said, "He woulda went back."

As Randall sat in his bedroom in January 2006, playing a football video game with his younger brother, a framed jersey salvaged from Port Sulphur hung on one wall. During each of Bastrop's games, he had worn a gray T-shirt bearing his former school's name and its purple and gold colors.

"I just gotta go back," Randall said.

It wasn't that he was shy when he first arrived in Bastrop, Randall said. He just didn't feel like talking. He didn't like being so far from home. He wasn't having fun. An expectant state championship at Port Sulphur had been swamped by a hurricane.

"I coulda been in a purple and gold uniform," he said. "I hate playing football for another school."

He wore a necklace and long-sleeve T-shirt under his striped polo shirt. He smiled broadly when he spoke of Crutchfield. "That's the man," Randall said. "He fusses all the time, but I think it's funny. He cracks jokes, tries to make you better. I feel bad because I know he wanted us to play for him. We had to make a big decision."

ON AUGUST 28, 2006, THIS UPLIFTING STORY OF PERSEVERING and overcoming long odds grew darker, more complicated. The LHSAA suspended Randall for the entire 2006 season. Two other former Port Sulphur players with eligibility remaining were also suspended for the upcoming season. And Bastrop High would have to forfeit its 2005 state championship.

A second investigation by the LHSAA found that Bastrop coaches had improperly contacted and transported the five Port Sulphur players to northern Louisiana, violating state rules against recruiting. The LHSAA accused the five players of filing false affidavits, claiming that their parents had taken them to Bastrop High from various places in Louisiana and Texas. In truth, it had been two assistant coaches. The mothers of Randall and his cousin James Brown had also filed false affidavits. So had D'Carlos Holmes, the assistant coach at Bastrop who had helped transport the players.

Recruiting had long been a hot-button issue in Louisiana, particularly with regard to two private schools, John Curtis Christian of suburban New Orleans and Evangel Christian of Shreveport. Both were football factories that appeared to violate the spirit, if not the letter, of enrollment regulations. Both won state championships at a rate that would have been extremely unlikely if they had simply relied on players from the surrounding neighborhoods, as public schools did. Post-Katrina, though, recruiting had become more brazen all along the Gulf Coast, with covetous schools making recruiting trips to evacuation shelters and some players shopping themselves around to the most attractive teams.

Not everyone did this, of course, but even Tommy Henry, the commissioner of the LHSAA, began receiving e-mail messages from schools saying, "We need a quarterback and receiver, or a couple of basketball players."

The hurricane had seemed to bring out the best and worst in people, Henry told the *New York Times* shortly after the storm. Any alleged violation would have to be proved with unassailable evidence, he told the paper, but he added, "If I do catch someone, the book will be thrown at them."

And now it had been.

Bastrop High claimed it was acting altruistically to assist the Port Sulphur kids in need. But the high school association ruled that the school had been as self-serving as it had been benevolent.

Travis Stanley was a Bastrop assistant coach when the school began attempting to contact the Port Sulphur players a day after Katrina struck. This was before the LHSAA had relaxed its eligibility rules, allowing students to enroll at the school of their choosing.

According to an affidavit later given by Stanley to the state association, the illicit recruiting of the players from Port Sulphur occurred in this manner: Brad Bradshaw, the Bastrop coach, and Charles Porter, an athletic administrator at Bastrop, had shown a copy of a Louisiana football magazine to Holmes, who had been hired from Port Sulphur only days before Katrina struck. They asked if Holmes knew any of the players mentioned in the magazine from the New Orleans area. Could any of them play quarterback?

The next day, August 31, 2005, Bradshaw instructed Stanley and Holmes to pick up a wide receiver from Port Sulphur who had evacuated to the central Louisiana town of Pineville. Bradshaw told Stanley, "If he looks like he can help us, bring him back. Do what you have to do to get him here."

The coaches reached Alexandria in central Louisiana about five p.m. and began searching shelters. After a series of phone calls and text messages, they located the receiver, Jeremy Sylve, at First Baptist Church in Pineville. They convinced Sylve's parents that he would be taken care of in Bastrop. Sylve agreed, and Stanley called Bradshaw to give him the news.

Next, Holmes traveled to Hammond, Louisiana, to pick up Jody Ancar, a defensive end from Port Sulphur. Then, on September 6, 2005, Stanley and Holmes traveled to Beaumont, Texas, to pick up two more players—the cousins Randall Mackey and James Brown. Stanley was given Bastrop High's gasoline credit card, and during the trip, Bastrop's principal, Tom Thrower, called to remind the coaches that the parents of displaced players could be provided with jobs and a place to live. After the two players were gathered, Stanley's cell phone records indicate that he made a three-minute call to Bradshaw. Next, the two Bastrop assistant coaches drove east on Interstate 10 to Lafayette, Louisiana, where they picked up another Port Sulphur player, the running back Jamal Recasner.

When the LHSAA began investigating Bastrop again in the summer of 2006, both Porter and Thrower suggested to Stanley that everyone have their stories straight, according to the affidavit.

Thrower told Stanley, "It wasn't a violation if we went and got the boys," but "we need to not have made first contact," the affidavit said.

It concluded, "Bastrop High School showed no regard for the LHSAA rules and purposely set out to recruit players."

Upon learning of the suspension, Randall began stomping angrily around his backyard in Bastrop, saying desperate things that worried his mother. He stayed up all night crying.

"If I can't play football, watch what's going to happen," Randall told his mother.

Carla Ragas worried that Randall might try to hurt himself or someone else.

"Don't do anything crazy," Carla told her son.

The next night in Bastrop, more than 350 people attended a town-hall meeting, upset that the state title was going to be stripped, seeking a way to overturn the ruling. Two state representatives vowed to use their political muscle. Bradshaw told reporters in reference to the players from Port Sulphur, "We are suffering for doing the right thing. They can take away that trophy, but they cannot take away memories of that season and that night."

Bastrop officials began to blame Stanley, who later left the school in an unrelated disciplinary matter, for coercing the false affidavits from the players and two of their mothers. Players would also blame him. Stanley's house would be egged. Holmes would dispute his story of picking up the Port Sulphur players and would later call Stanley a "Judas."

While he should have used better judgment than to falsify an affidavit, Holmes said, he otherwise had no regrets. "I think it's a shame we can't help those kids we love," he said. "When I went and got those kids, I did it in good faith. Those are my kids. They were in need."

Thrower later said he knew nothing about phone calls made to or from Stanley during the trips to pick up the Port Sulphur players. Bradshaw did not return later phone calls seeking comment. State transportation rules were ambiguous, Thrower said. Surely, he said, they were written to prevent schools from buying cars for players, not to prevent them from providing a safe port in a horrific storm like Katrina.

"When kids are living in a shelter and don't know what tomorrow holds, or they're living in a hotel room with eleven people, they're gonna call someone they know and say, 'Come pick me up,'" Thrower said. "That's not the same thing as saying, 'Will you buy me a car?'"

Stanley said it was inconceivable that Thrower, as claimed, was unaware that the Port Sulphur players had lied about being transported to Bastrop. There was no way, he added, that two assistant coaches, who were also teachers, could have been absent from school and practice to pick up players without the knowledge and approval of the principal and the football coach.

"I think those kids were exploited because of their talent," Stanley said. "I was part of it. I knowingly, willingly picked those kids up. I know it was wrong."

Not everything that Bastrop did was wrong, Stanley said. The school and the town did open their arms to the kids from Port Sulphur. It was impossible not to feel sympathy and want to help them, he said. Yet the transfers received extravagant assistance "only because they played football," Stanley said. If not for

Randall's exceptional football talent, he said, his mother probably would not have been living in a rental house owned by a team booster and Randall probably would not have received so much patient help from teachers when he appeared disinterested in class. Nor would the other Port Sulphur players have been given an apartment to live in, or free food at a local restaurant, he said.

"This little mill town was off by itself," Stanley said, noting that the mill was losing jobs, making a football championship even more urgent for community self-assurance. "Bastrop had been down so long and they finally got success. It created a monster. The only thing left was to win a state championship. They had lost three times in the quarters. They couldn't get past the hump. Bradshaw knew that. He said it would take a special player to get over the hump."

B. J. Guzzardo, the assistant state athletic commissioner who headed the Bastrop investigation, said that of the forty-seven Katrina evacuees who ended up at Bastrop High, only the five football players from Port Sulphur had been contacted by school officials and had been provided transportation. Even the sisters of the Port Sulphur players were left behind and had to find their own way to Bastrop.

"I think the coach had some good intentions," Guzzardo said of Holmes. "He knew the kids. He wanted to help the kids. But he also knew they were good football players. If a kid played trumpet in the band, I don't think they were going to go get him."

Crutchfield felt sympathy for the suspended players. On one hand, he agreed that some punishment was called for. On the other hand, he said, any player who lost everything in a storm would have been tempted by someone who offered a ride, money, a place to live, a chance to keep playing football.

"I might have taken it too," he said.

In filing false affidavits, the players were probably scared of prematurely losing their football careers and of being forced to live again in a shelter or a motel, Crutchfield said.

"The hurricane took their houses," he said. "They made a decision, influenced by adults, afraid that they would lose their comfort zone again."

Tommy Henry, the commissioner of the LHSAA, also saw this issue in shades of gray instead of black and white. The kids from Port Sulphur had been betrayed by adults. Perhaps they had lied, but it was those who were supposed to be their guardians—coaches and parents—who had goaded them into deliberate falsehoods. Henry began to wonder whether suspending the players for the entire season was too harsh a penalty. They had already been victimized by Katrina, and then they had been exploited by people who were supposed to protect them. He could understand why they called out for help and accepted it from anyone who "would reach out and pull them from their desperation and despair."

Henry spoke with a former college roommate, Billy Montgomery, now a Louisiana state representative. Montgomery told him, "These kids went through the worst natural disaster in the country's history. They were in a bad situation and when they tried to get help, what did those who helped them do? A coach lied, two mothers lied. What chance did they have to tell the truth? What would you have done if you were sixteen or seventeen?"

As the 2006 football season began, Henry reconsidered his earlier ruling and reduced the suspensions of Randall Mackey and the other former Port Sulphur players from an entire season to two games apiece. He had been troubled by the question posed by his friend, Montgomery. As a teenager, would he have told the truth if he had been backed into an ethical corner, having lost everything and having faced the loss of football?

"I'm not sure I would have," Henry told himself.

3

A NEW SCHOOL OPENS

AS THE SUN SET AND THE CICADA CHORUS ROSE, CYRIL Crutchfield checked his watch. It was August 28, 2006, nearing the first anniversary of Katrina's wrath and his foolhardy decision to ride out the storm in the Port Sulphur gym. Dressed in khakis, twirling a whistle around his fingers, the coach walked in a circle on the practice field and retreated into an awful remembrance.

"All it was doing was raining," Crutchfield said to no one in particular, recalling the storm's approach. "Everyone was gone. I was home. Things changed."

A year later, Port Sulphur High sat abandoned, sequestered behind a chain-link fence. A new consolidated school called South Plaquemines High had been set up in modular brick buildings on the wrecked campus. The school drew students from the ruined communities of Port Sulphur, Buras, and Boothville-Venice. Lower Plaquemines still operated under a state of emergency. A police checkpoint monitored traffic on the four-lane north of Port Sulphur. An estimated two thousand to four thousand of the prestorm population of fourteen thousand residents had returned to the southern end of the parish. Because the area was so sparsely settled, representing only 2 percent of the New Orleans area population, the federal government was hesitant to spend the $1.6 billion necessary to fully buttress the weakened levees.

Without such fortification, people faced questions that had no comforting answers. Should they rebuild? How high? How much would flood and wind insurance cost? Could they get it at all? Life seemed undetermined, like the fates of two caskets, sheathed in cement vaults, which awaited interment in the cemetery outside of South Plaquemines High. The vaults remained strapped to the ground so the coffins would not wander off again in the next storm. One of the vaults was spray-painted with the name of Rose Mary Williams. Did anyone know what had happened to her? Why had no one come to claim her and put her back in the ground?

The post office and pharmacy and bank had yet to reopen in Port Sulphur. Fremin's, the only supermarket for seventy miles below Belle Chasse, operated out of a double-wide trailer. But a medical center, the natural gas plant, the hardware store, Ann's Restaurant and the Cajun Kitchen were operating. Giant tankers hauled oil, coal, and grain up and down the river with renewed commerce, passing so near that they seemed to float on the highway. St. Patrick Catholic Church was back, school was back, and so was football. Some kids who had lost everything still could not afford the light blue shirts and khaki pants required for school uniforms. Still, hope was budding that a village crippled by the storm was taking its first halting steps toward some kind of recovery.

PORT SULPHUR BEGAN AS A COMPANY TOWN FOR THE Freeport Sulphur Company, which acquired the rights to a huge dome of sulphur below the marshes of Plaquemines Parish at Lake Grand Ecaille in 1932. Mosquitoes were so bothersome that airplane propellers, powered by Ford Model-T engines, were used to fend them off as the mine was being built. To supply the mine with lumber and steel, a ten-mile-long canal was dug through the marsh from Port Sulphur, where Freeport built a town site complete with schools, a hospital, a lodge, a park, a pool, tennis courts, and a baseball diamond. Eventually, a golf course was built.

"There was hardly a less inviting environment—ten miles from a drop of fresh water, in the middle of a swamp, far from highways and railroads, and with no means of building solid transportation," Donia Byrnes wrote of the mine in a history of the state's sulphur industry, published by Loyola University of New Orleans. "Furthermore, it was subject to Gulf hurricanes, and it was plagued by mosquitoes. In the history of the sulphur industry, there is no accomplishment comparable to this feat of conquering adverse conditions by Freeport."

The sulphur was extracted by sending superheated water into the ground, melting the deposit, and pumping it to the surface. Freeport expanded its operations in Louisiana, and by 1963 the state had become the world's largest producer of sulphur, which is used to make such items as fertilizer, sulfuric acid, steel, rayon, and paint. Residents of a certain age remembered the fine yellow dust that coated Port Sulphur, where the ore was loaded by conveyor onto trains and ships. Cars rusted and jewelry was tarnished, residents said, but Freeport provided paved roads, sidewalks, concrete ditches, and even a security officer to patrol the town site.

"If you needed a lightbulb changed, you called and they did it," said Lois Lejeune, an administrative assistant for the Plaquemines Parish Council who grew up in Port Sulphur.

In 1978, the Grand Ecaille mine closed, and Freeport began relocating its engineers and other professional workers. The price of sulphur grew depressed as it became cheaper to produce as a by-product of oil refining than as a product of mining. By 2000, the company had ceased operations in Port Sulphur.

According to the 2000 census, more than 20 percent of Port Sulphur's 3,115 residents lived below the poverty level. The per capita income was $13,553, and average household income was $30,188. That median household income had risen to $34,200 by the time Katrina struck, but that was still below average in one of the country's poorest states. Parishwide, more than a third of black residents lived below the poverty level. Yet for locals, census figures represented only an official skin that hid a community's heart and sinew and connective tissue.

"It's peace of mind," said Theresita Ancar, the principal at South Plaquemines Elementary School, located adjacent to the high school, and formerly the principal at Port Sulphur High. "We marry each other in these little towns and grandma is five minutes away and you look after mine and I look after yours. You can leave your doors unlocked. If you do lock them, you don't need three bolts and a chain."

EVEN WITH A CHANCE FOR A NEW START AT SOUTH PLAQUE-mines High, though, everything remained unsettled, temporary, vulnerable on the eve of Katrina's first anniversary. Two or three classes' worth of students were crammed into a single classroom. Books and supplies were short. Internet service was intermittent. The walkways at school still lacked canopies. Three days earlier, classes had been canceled after rainwater came up quickly and seeped into the modular brick classrooms.

Students chose the new school mascot, and a sense of unity and youthful immortality prevailed. They chose Hurricanes. A hurricane is what had brought students from three rival schools together. No other nickname seemed appropriate. Eagles and Gators sounded neither sufficiently calamitous nor defiant. The South Plaquemines football helmets bore decals of a hurricane's circular pattern. The cheerleaders devised their own battle cry, without any hint of irony: "Hurricane season never ends."

"Oh, no, I don't want to hear that," Stanley Gaudet, the principal of South Plaquemines High, had said with a laugh a few days earlier as the school played its opening exhibition game.

Crutchfield would coach the Hurricanes. Having won a 2002 state championship at Port Sulphur, he was a natural choice. But the challenge would be staggering. He would have to blend three teams into one, three teams that previously had their own coaches and styles of play. They used different formations, different names for their plays. At practice, that separateness was evident in the T-shirts that many players wore beneath their South Plaquemines uniforms. Purple and gold for those who had been Port Sulphur Bronchos. Green and gold for the former Buras Wildcats. Orange and black for the Boothville-Venice Oilers. All three teams had played each other most years, during the regular season or the preseason jamboree. Rivalries were fevered.

"They were puppies bred in different kennels to hate each other," Big Wayne Williamson, a sheriff's deputy from Port Sulphur, said of the players.

Port Sulphur and Boothville-Venice, a fishing and oilfield supply area, had competed among Louisiana's smallest schools in Class 1A. Buras, the middle-class hub of lower Plaquemines, had been a Class 2A school. Thus, for the 2006 season, state rules mandated that South Plaquemines, with only 259 kids in grades seven through twelve, would have to compete in Class 2A against schools with larger enrollments.

At the moment, that seemed the least of the Hurricanes' problems. Their newly sodded football field would not be ready for play until late September, at the earliest. The stadium lights were still dead, and the press box was still painted Port Sulphur purple instead of South Plaquemines blue. The goalposts were twisted. The scoreboard was gone. The metal bleachers would have to be replaced.

The Hurricanes had only a makeshift locker room—a double-wide trailer that was outfitted with two toilets and no showers. There were no lockers, either. Helmets and shoulder pads and shoes were scattered about the squat trailer. The season had not yet started, but already the trailer reeked of the sweat that had worked its way into jerseys and pants and shoes and shoulder pads and chin straps and the cushioning of the helmets. Practice each day required a sixty-mile round-trip to Belle Chasse Middle School on a bus with no air conditioning. The players climbed off the bus and pulled on their uniforms in the shade of an oak tree. A truckload of weight-lifting equipment would arrive at South Plaquemines High in a day or two, but it would sit unused in a storage container for the entire season because there was no weight room at school. To get ice and drinking water for practice, somebody had to make a run each afternoon to a local fishing dock with the Gatorade buckets. A trip up the road to Belle Chasse was required after each game so Crutchfield could wash the team uniforms.

It was a chore for players just to get something decent to eat for lunch. Ninety-nine percent of the students at South Plaquemines qualified for free or reduced-priced lunches. Yet the cafeteria was not yet equipped for hot food. So the kids were given sandwiches of ham and cheese or peanut butter and jelly. Some players walked a block from campus for lunch, or before practice, crossing Highway 23 to get a piece or two of fried chicken from a roadside stand. Others grabbed a sports drink and a bag of chips from the nearby Happyland convenience store.

On this blistering August afternoon, in which the humidity had a hazy presence like a damp ghost, Crutchfield became impatient with his best player, Devin Boutwell. A six-foot-two, 270-pound defensive lineman and tight end, Boutwell, who was from Buras, would probably be the only player to sign a college scholarship from this first South Plaquemines team. But in the sapping heat, he was faltering.

"Devin must not want to go to the next level," Crutchfield said to Boutwell's father, Donnie, who watched practice from the tailgate of a pickup truck. "He's moping around, tired, bending over."

Later, during a break, Donnie Boutwell told Devin, "Coach said you've got to pick it up."

"I haven't eaten anything today," Devin said.

"You can't practice without eating," Donnie said.

EACH DAY, CRUTCHFIELD DROVE SCHOOLKIDS HOME ON his bus route, then returned to South Plaquemines to pick up his football team for the half-hour drive up the road to Belle Chasse Middle School. Past the parish library with its broken spine and crippled books. Past recovered coffins that had popped up like toast and floated away. Past a wooden fishing boat nestled in a grove of trees like a bird's nest. And, unavoidably, past the levees that held out the Mississippi on one side of Highway 23 and the marsh and the Gulf of Mexico on the other. After practice, Crutchfield drove the players back down the road, dropping them at scattered FEMA trailer parks in the lower end of the parish. He had moved from Belle Chasse, where he had lived after Katrina, and now resided near South Plaquemines High in a trailer park called Cop Land, because it housed the parish's sheriff's deputies. But the players were spread over a wide area along the Plaquemines peninsula. Some didn't get home until seven, eight, or nine at night. Along the highway, there were few streetlights to illuminate the clumps of government trailers. Some players would walk off the bus, cross the highway, and disappear like apparitions into the inky darkness.

A few players commuted by car eighty or more miles round-trip to school from New Orleans, where they lived with relatives. Everybody had lost everything. Nothing was back to normal. In the community of Diamond, 450 FEMA trailers had been set up in a park. Almost no one in lower Plaquemines had returned yet to a house. One wrecked home in Port Sulphur was spray-painted with the plaintive admonition: "Rebuildin Do Not Bulldoz." Another, in nearby Homeplace, bore this spray-painted warning across the front: "Have Gun Will Use."

After Katrina, the brothers Jordan and Maverick Ancar found their house in a canal, where it still sat a year after the hurricane, sheared of its shingles, rafters exposed, water nearly up to the roof, a familiar brown line circling the house like the stain in a coffee cup.

"They got alligators watching TV in your house," Little Wayne Williamson, a defensive back, said jokingly to the brothers as they dressed for practice. "They sittin' on the couch, eatin' chips."

Everyone laughed, but the approaching football season remained as tenuous as it was anticipated. FEMA trailers were supposed to be evacuated in winds above forty-five miles an hour. A day earlier, Ernesto had flared into the season's first hurricane before deflating to a tropical storm as it pounded Haiti with flooding rain. Still, the storm was forecast to enter the Gulf, and another year of football might be threatened.

"A thunderstorm comes, those guys are cringing," Big Wayne Williamson said. "Bad weather, they get in the corner."

Devin Boutwell had begun crying at the thought of losing his senior season and any chance of receiving a major-college scholarship. He wondered if he should transfer to another school.

Nervous, fearful, other players began to pray.

"We can't withstand nothing here," Little Wayne Williamson said. Referring to the federal government, he added, "I don't think they would pay for us again."

TWENTY-SEVEN PLAYERS WERE DRESSED OUT AT PRACTICE for the Hurricanes, some as young as seventh-graders. At that age, Crutchfield had been forbidden from playing. His mother, Annie Mae, a Pentecostal, spent her time raising five children and praying at the First Church of God in Christ in Covington, Louisiana. Football she found to be dangerous and frivolous. Crutchfield never attended a prom, never went to a movie before his senior year of high school. He had to sneak into the car to listen to music other than gospel music. He could remember few friends coming over to play. He was allowed to watch television, and he became enamored of a game that his mother would not let him play.

The New Orleans Saints, who played their games just on the other side of Lake Pontchartrain, were desultory in the early 1980s. They lost a consonant, became the "Aints." Fans wore bags over their heads. Crutchfield instead became a devoted fan of the Dallas Cowboys, America's Team. On Sunday mornings, he would attend church from nine until just before noon, rush home for a football doubleheader, leaving before the second game ended to return to church for four more hours. There was Bible band on Wednesday night and church again on Friday night, which snuffed any chance he had to play high school football.

The only football he was allowed to play was in the yard, by himself. He would come home from school, put on his play clothes and imagine his own games, throwing the ball to himself, diving and catching the self-tossed passes, even tackling himself on the lawn. Sometimes he ran for eight hundred yards in an afternoon, and he always caught the winning touchdown. But it was all in his head, until he reached the tenth grade in 1981 and forged his mother's signature on a parental consent form allowing him to play at Covington High School.

When his mother found out, she made him go in the yard and get a switch and she whipped him. She told Crutchfield he had to quit, but his dad convinced her to let him go out for the team. Covington reached the state championship game that season, the first time Louisiana's title games were played in the Superdome. An obscure school named Port Sulphur High won among the state's smallest schools. But there were no heroics for Crutchfield that season. He barely played.

His father, Cyril Sr., worked for a golf course in Covington and owned a landscaping business. Around home, Cyril Jr. sometimes felt that his first name was "Dummy." "Why did you do that, Dummy?" his father would say to him. Or if he played a game in the yard, trying to jump over a wooden sawhorse, his dad would say, "You can't jump that, Dummy." Crutchfield would keeping jumping, falling, or scraping his leg, and when he would finally clear the obstacle, his father would say, "'Bout time, Dummy. I coulda jumped that easy."

"My father believed in one thing," Crutchfield said. "Giving you a whuppin'."

His father did not offer much praise, but he attended his son's football games faithfully. And Crutchfield had never seen a man work so hard. His father had not advanced beyond the fourth grade, but he repaired his own truck and built his own house even though he couldn't read a floor plan. And he kept repeating a saying that held a larger truth about how to live a life of integrity: "Never say what you ain't gonna do. Say what you ain't did."

What might have curdled into resentment of the father was instead harnessed into motivation by the son. Crutchfield never missed a day of class in high school. Never missed a practice. Made the honor roll. In college, he was on the all-American football team, the all-American strength team, and the all-conference academic team.

"WHEN MY FATHER CALLED ME A DUMMY, I WAS GOING TO prove him wrong," Crutchfield said. "I think he did a great job preparing me for life."

He became a two-time all-American safety at Northeast Louisiana. His team won the NCAA Division 1-AA national championship in 1987. Nearly two decades later, Crutchfield still ranked fifth in school history with a dozen interceptions. His photo was in the trophy case from the university's championship season, wearing number 42. In a few weeks, South Plaquemines would play in Monroe, and the Hurricanes would dress at the stadium where Crutchfield had played his collegiate career. He would walk on the field by himself, head down, remembering some moment whose memory was like an errant pass, just beyond his fingertips. His girlfriend, Micquella Sylve, would call out, "Forty-two, forty-two," but he would not hear. Or, if he did, he would not let on. Even now, all these years later, Crutchfield missed the game so much that tears would come to his eyes on that empty field. College had been the best time of his life. He had arrived as a reticent safety. Then, one day in the spring of his freshman year, he put his head down and hit a receiver—busted his ass—and everyone started cheering. From that point, Crutchfield had been a ferocious hitter. "If someone came across the middle, I was really and truly trying to inflict harm," he said. By his count, he suffered eight to twelve concussions. All but one came when he knocked himself out while hitting an opponent. If he were playing today, he was convinced that doctors would make him stop. He had migraines, and though he was only thirty-nine, sometimes he forgot the names of his players. Kids he had known for years, he would have to call out, "Hey, number 21," or "What's your name, 14?" His father had died of Alzheimer's, and he wondered if his forgetfulness was related to disease or the concussions.

"It's kinda scary," he said. "I can't explain."

In college, Crutchfield had also been drawn to the lines and circles and arrows of football's brute geometry. Planning for games was as intriguing as playing them. These were his first stirrings of a career in coaching. His mother never did see him play a game or watch as he stood on the sidelines as a coach. Out of respect and deference to her religious beliefs, he did not ask. Annie Mae Crutchfield went blind from diabetes in 1994 and moved to Seattle to be near her four daughters, but she became proud of her only son's accomplishments. When Crutchfield won a state title with Port Sulphur High in 2002, she told her friends, "Junior always loved that football since he was small. He loved those Cowboys."

His father had succumbed to Alzheimer's just as South Plaquemines' inaugural summer camp was about to begin. At the time, Crutchfield was trying to mold players from three schools into one team. His mother and sisters assured him it would be okay to remain with his boys. So he stayed for a week before traveling to Seattle for a memorial service. His unswerving devotion to his players had left an indelible mark.

"It showed he cared about us, that somebody cared about us," Dwayne Ancar, a senior guard, said.

His father was a kind of mirror in which Crutchfield saw his own reflection. He was hard on his players. He called them "Dummy" and "Stupid" and did not offer much praise. Kids wanted a pat on the back too often these days, he believed. When they watched film after a game, his players would say to him, "Coach, you only tell us what we did wrong. Why don't you say, 'Great job?'" Well, because if the quarterback threw the ball to you and you caught it, that's what you were supposed to do. If you blocked the man you were assigned to block, that's what you were supposed to do. If you had to dive to catch the ball, or you blocked somebody and got up and blocked somebody else, great job. Otherwise, you just completed your assignment.

Glad your father wasn't my father, he sometimes told himself about this player or that one. *You wouldn't make it.*

Twice divorced, with three children who lived with their mothers, Crutchfield was a homebody like his father. Sometimes he lost his temper just as easily. But he also worked obsessively, the way his father had. Many coaches taught phys ed as a sinecure, but Crutchfield taught civics and geography. He was popular as a teacher because he let students speak their minds in the classroom and he did not sugarcoat his remarks to them. In a place where many kids lived in single-parent homes, Crutchfield was a father figure to a number of players. Sometimes, he was a mother figure, too, letting female students put makeup and lipstick on his face. He had a master's degree in education and, years earlier, had begun work toward a master's in business administration. He drove a bus route before and after school. He coached football in the fall and track in the spring. He stayed up late after practice watching film, often sleeping on the couch, waking up early to watch video one more time before heading out on his bus route. He seemed at times to live on pork chops, sunflower seeds, and a sugar rush, shaking Red Hots candies back and forth in his hands as if they were dice.

Hollie Russell, who had taught French at Port Sulphur High, said she credited Crutchfield for the progress of her son, John, a special ed student who was the water boy on the Bronchos' 2002 state-championship team. "He always told John, 'You can do it, don't let anything stand in your way, the only barrier is yourself,'" Russell said.

In speeches to his players, Crutchfield quoted everybody from Malcolm X to Goldilocks to the Wizard of Oz. He also teased his players about their mothers and spanked the boys at practice on their birthdays. (He gave his own mother's name as Annie Mae, but it was a pseudonym because he feared his players would ride him mercilessly if they knew her real name.)

Yet he was also a primary figure of authority at South Plaquemines; when Crutchfield walked into a classroom or a locker room, it grew silent immediately. If players misbehaved, he disciplined them with his own exotic methods. Those who made Fs on their report cards would have to do a series of dizzying forward rolls, from one goal line to the other and back again. Some who misbehaved in class would have to get into a position for push-ups, hands on the ground, arms extended, and hold it for three excruciating minutes as their arms trembled and biting gnats swarmed about their faces.

Stanley Gaudet, the principal, said that he did not have much respect for Crutchfield before Katrina. They had been at rival schools. Gaudet, bearded and given to dry humor, had been the principal at Buras High. Crutchfield had not wanted his Port Sulphur team to continue playing Buras, Gaudet said, adding, "We had words."

Working with Crutchfield changed his opinion.

"You can't help but respect him," Gaudet said. "You see his work ethic and how much he gives to the kids. He gets the most out of them. He teaches tenacity."

Still, Crutchfield's style would not be welcomed everywhere. He used sophisticated offenses and defenses, but he was also a throwback to a time when neighbors disciplined each other's kids and the football coach held ultimate power and a player was under his full control. He could yell at a kid, or curse operatically. He could push a player or hit him. "Tick tock," Big Wayne Williamson called Crutchfield, because you never knew when he was going to go off. Still, he could be counted on. After Katrina, he stayed in lower Plaquemines while many left. He provided a sense of security and familiarity when everything was insecure and unfamiliar. He remained composed when everything was shattered, assured when everything was uncertain. Even before the storm, many thought it would be difficult—or even impossible—to convince another coach of his caliber to move to such a remote place. So his sometimes harsh manner was accepted. Because football coaches held tremendous influence in a rural, isolated county like Plaquemines Parish. Because this was a hard place that did not shrink from hard methods.

"A lot of kids don't get the discipline at home," Big Wayne Williamson said.

Elouise Bartholomew, the aunt of quarterback Ridge Turner, would give Crutchfield written permission to spank her nephew if he clowned around in class. "If he has to spank him in front of the class, that's all right," she would write. "Do your business."

When his team won, fans would chant, "Whose field? Crutchfield!" Some parents who had known him previously at Port Sulphur thought he had mellowed, if only slightly. "Now at least you can see the expressions on his face," said Jeanitta Ancar, who had two sons among the Hurricanes.

His players learned to take Crutchfield's excitable personality seriously but not personally—most of them, anyway. Many regarded his methods with a cockeyed fondness. Behind his back, they impersonated the way he said "garbage" when he became upset and bit his lip and walked around mumbling privately. He could be as hard on himself as he was on his players, which granted him a certain authenticity.

"Bridge, just fall on my head and kill me," he had said while driving the team bus home from a preseason scrimmage.

And after another: "Instead of playing football, we were on the beach with the ladies in bikinis, sipping mai tais. Hello, what's your name? I'm Coach Garbage."

SOUTH PLAQUEMINES' FIRST REGULAR-SEASON GAME WAS four days away. The opening opponent was Belle Chasse High, the team for whom Crutchfield had been preparing when Katrina struck. The longtime coach at Belle Chasse, Bob Becnel, was also the school's athletic director. He was a seventh-generation member of a prominent family of citrus farmers, who shipped their sweet, juicy produce to markets across the South and Midwest and stocked local roadside stands with navel oranges, satsumas, Creole tomatoes, and Cajun boiled peanuts. Now a Class 4A school, Belle Chasse had reached the state-championship game in

Class 3A in 2001. Because Becnel coached the biggest school in the parish, his team was the one the others most wanted to beat.

Long before Katrina, Belle Chasse had been a fierce parish adversary of Port Sulphur, Buras, and Boothville-Venice. Old antagonisms had transferred collectively to South Plaquemines. Some from lower Plaquemines had played a truncated, two-game season for Belle Chasse High after Katrina in the fall of 2005, or had enrolled later and participated in spring football practice in 2006. It was an awkward merger. Those from Port Sulphur, Buras, and Boothville-Venice continued to wear letter jackets from their devastated schools. Many were simply biding time until South Plaquemines High opened in late summer.

Caileb Ancar, an all-district tackle from Port Sulphur, found the practices at Belle Chasse less intense than what he was accustomed to. "It was like a joke to them," he said.

His cousin, Little Wayne Williamson, had planned to play at Belle Chasse, but quit. "It didn't feel right," he said. "It felt right with Crutchfield."

The chasm grew early in the spring of 2006 as players began to declare their football allegiances for the upcoming season. Crutchfield wanted to practice separately with players who planned to attend South Plaquemines in the fall. Belle Chasse officials disapproved. Technically, it was still one school, and separating players might constitute a rules violation. Players from lower Plaquemines said that Crutchfield was prohibited from practicing with them as long as a ball was being thrown or kicked. Sometimes, they said, he sat and watched from a bus.

When spring practice started in pads, a number of players said that Becnel did not want them around if they were planning to leave Belle Chasse for South Plaquemines in the fall. He did not want them at practice, in the weight room, or in a football phys ed class, and he sometimes gave them inferior equipment, players said.

"He said, 'I'm not going to train the enemy,'" Sal Cepriano, the South Plaquemines center, said.

Becnel denied that he gave substandard equipment to players from lower Plaquemines. In fact, he said, he gave athletic shorts and shirts for free to those players and did all he could to accommodate them.

"I felt like we bent over backward," said Becnel, a friendly man with a shock of dark hair.

Still, he did acknowledge that it was tense in the spring of 2006, with essentially two competing teams at the same school. After a devastated 2005 season, Becnel was getting Belle Chasse prepared for the fall of 2006. He was trying to determine which players would remain at Belle Chasse and which would be leaving for the opening of South Plaquemines. It did not seem practical to him for those who planned to leave to practice with those who planned to stay.

When some players from lower Plaquemines went out for spring football at Belle Chasse in 2006 and then quit, Becnel said, "I didn't appreciate that."

He also said that his words were twisted into unintended meanings in lower Plaquemines. When he told kids that they would play before big crowds at Belle Chasse, the translation was that no crowds would come to South Plaquemines. When he talked of possible college scholarships at Belle Chasse, this became a put-down of the chances to get a scholarship at South Plaquemines.

"These were all planks in the fire that became this rivalry," Becnel said. "That's why the fire gets so hot."

During the summer of 2006, the South Plaquemines players were allowed to work out at Belle Chasse High because their own field was not ready. Everyone walked on eggshells, Becnel said, but he felt he had been as hospitable as possible.

"Coach Crutchfield does a great job; I have a lot of respect for him," Becnel, who was forty-nine, said. "He's a great motivator. His teams play, by far, the hardest from whistle to whistle. They play tough and smart. I don't know if they respect us. I know they want to kill us."

4

A CHANCE TO EQUAL OUR STRIFE

ON SEPTEMBER 1, 2006, CYRIL CRUTCHFIELD WOULD FINALLY get to play against Belle Chasse. Tropical Storm Ernesto had veered off toward Florida before threatening the debilitated Louisiana coast and causing another postponement. After school, the South Plaquemines players met in Crutchfield's classroom for a pregame meal of spaghetti and meatballs. It was a rule that they eat in silence, their minds on the game. Each player had his own ritual. Some listened to music on their headphones. Rory Jones, a receiver, padded around in green Shrek slippers. Rodney Bartholomew Jr., another receiver, sucked on a pacifier.

Jones had attended Boothville-Venice High before Katrina struck. Now he commuted to South Plaquemines daily from a relative's home in suburban New Orleans. It was comforting to be back among friends, and oddly liberating. Lower Plaquemines had been obliterated by Katrina, but it was the one place where Jones could escape the storm. Everyone had suffered from its destruction. He did not have to explain the ruination, what he had seen, how much he had lost.

"When you're an evacuee, everyone wants to talk about Katrina," said Jones, who had evacuated to Lafayette, Louisiana. "They think you have it easy because everything is free. Or they think you're from New Orleans and they say, 'Our school will be better when you leave.'"

The players loaded their equipment and made the forty-mile bus trip up the road to Belle Chasse High School, home of the Fighting Cardinals. As Crutchfield parked the bus outside one end zone, Marcelin and Jeanitta Ancar met the players. Their sons, Jordan and Maverick, were on the team. Marcelin Ancar had been an all-state center at Port Sulphur High in 1984. He had lost his letter jacket when Katrina shoved the family's home in a canal. Several months later, his wife provided him with a replacement. It was too hot and muggy for anything but T-shirts today, but tears formed in Marcelin's eyes as he recounted the story of the replica jacket.

"It was like seeing my kids born, that's how much it touched me," he said.

The crowd was standing room only, the visitors' side thick with supporters from the smashed communities of lower Plaquemines. Fans of South Plaquemines had their faces painted silver and blue, the school colors. Some wore T-shirts that said, "The Hurricanes Are Coming. Mandatory Evacuation." One man sported a tattoo of praying hands holding a ribbon that said, "Katrina" and "Port Sulphur." The game had become a meeting place for people, some of whom hadn't seen each other since the hurricane. They traded stories about coming home and rebuilding, and there was both hope and uncertainty in their voices. They waved at familiar faces and called out nicknames and hugged friends they had not seen in months. They complained about FEMA and the insurance companies and laughed about having someplace to go again on a Friday night. They sat and stood in the bleachers united against a common enemy—Belle Chasse.

Two days before the season opener, the South Plaquemines players had huddled in the shade of a live-oak tree draped with Spanish moss at Belle Chasse Middle School. They stood quietly in their black and white practice jerseys, the silence broken by the trilling cicadas and a voice as solemn as a jazz funeral.

"This is bigger than us," Roger Halphen III, an assistant coach, said to the players. "We've been kicked in the mouth the last year. I done seen people crying. I'm seeing people lose hope. They're moving away. They don't certify our levees. Businesses don't open up. We win this game, this is going to give hope to people. This is for the hope of south Plaquemines."

ACCORDING TO THE 2000 CENSUS, THERE WERE JUST UNDER ten thousand people living pre-Katrina in Belle Chasse, tucked at the northern tip of Plaquemines Parish between the Intracoastal Canal and the west bank of the Mississippi River. It suffered some wind damage and flooding from the hurricane, but Belle Chasse had been sufficiently north and west of the eye of the storm to avoid crippling harm. From the bridge over the Intracoastal Canal, the skyline of New Orleans shimmered seven miles in the distance. Along Highway 23 from the north, motorists entered Belle Chasse through a tunnel that served as both an architectural and a cultural transition from urban to rural, land to water.

Belle Chasse had a few red lights beyond the tunnel and the homogeneous fast food of McDonald's and Popeye's and Burger King. It was home to the relocated parish government and a naval air station. But this was the beginning of an amphibious place whose lifeblood flowed from the river and marshes and bays and the Gulf. A ferry ran between the east and west banks of the Mississippi every half hour. At Salvo's Seafood, shrimp was scooped by the pound and crabs sat like doughnuts by the row in a glass case. At Li'l G's Kajun Restaurant, the walls were adorned with alligator heads, a blue marlin, and the snout and claws of an alligator snapping turtle. White plumes drifted from the stacks at the Chevron Oronite plant, whose maze of pipes manufactured lubricating oil and fuel additives. Farther down Highway 23, 247,000 barrels of oil were processed daily into gasoline, heating oil, and jet fuel at the white baseball-shaped domes and squat circular tanks of the ConocoPhillips Alliance refinery.

Pickup trucks rumbled through Belle Chasse, often with boats attached to their hitches. A freight train bisected the town around noon each day, and roosters crowed behind a few of the houses that abutted the Mississippi River levee. South of the naval air station, the prairie began to narrow into rustic stillness. Post-Katrina, there were no red lights, no movie theaters, no banks, no appliance stores, one supermarket, and one medical center along the final seventy miles of Highway 23.

The people of Plaquemines Parish were wary of outsiders, but they were amiable and generous and possessing of an aptitude for working hard without appearing to be hurried or impolite. They greeted strangers with a welcome of "Whatcha need, my baby?" and sent them on their way with an urging to "Take care, my darlin'." Even pre-Katrina, the county remained a sparse place, with twenty-seven thousand people scattered along a peninsula that was as much water as land. It was often said about Plaquemines that people were outnumbered by alligators. Still, there was a remarkable diversity to such a small population, the oil and fishing and citrus industries having attracted an ethnic jambalaya that included Native Americans, blacks, Creoles, French, Spanish, Italians, Irish, Filipinos, Croatians, Vietnamese, and Cambodians.

Casual interaction between races and ethnic groups occurred with a regularity and a tolerance often absent in bigger urban areas. Even with such shared cultures, though, Plaquemines remained a divided place. It was separated east and west by the Mississippi, split north and south by class and race, and further partitioned in the lower end by community tensions and rivalries that were played out most visibly on the football field.

The divide was starkly evident in the parish's inability to move the county seat from thinly populated Pointe a la Hache on the east bank of the Mississippi. The parish courthouse burned in 2002, and the east bank suffered severe damage from Katrina, but residents had three times rejected a plan to move the government seat, each vote falling short of the needed two-thirds majority. Meanwhile, parish government had been temporarily relocated to Belle Chasse, with the district attorney operating out of a triple-wide modular unit, the courthouse annex located in a remodeled electrical services company warehouse, and the parish council offices situated in a refurbished tomato co-op shed.

There had been an attempt to consolidate the three high schools in lower Plaquemines in the 1990s, school officials said, with school-board approval granted, some eleven million to fifteen million dollars allocated, and architectural plans drawn up. Then anti-consolidation forces prevailed, the decision was reversed, and the schools remained separate until Katrina struck, even as it became increasingly difficult to attract qualified teachers to such a remote area.

Some school officials and residents feared that a community that lost its school would also lose its identity. There were other reasons for the separation. Primarily, according to the current parish school superintendent, Eva Jones, residents of Buras did not want their kids going to school with kids from Port Sulphur. Buras had been a white, middle-class center of lower Plaquemines, while Port Sulphur had a nearly even mix of white and black residents before Katrina, but a predominantly black high school. There were concerns in Buras about diluting the quality of education. Some residents were put off by what they considered overly boisterous football fans at Port Sulphur. And some prejudice lingered, as if trapped in amber from the 1920s to the 1980s, when the parish was run by the notorious segregationist, Leander H. Perez Sr. and his family.

Among some in Belle Chasse and in Buras, there appeared to be a particular dismissiveness of blacks from Port Sulphur. Belle Chasse was an accepting place, but it was also a place where a white man could feel free to wear blackface on Halloween. And both there and in Buras, stereotypical remarks by some, offered in private, depicted blacks from Port Sulphur as "a different class of people" or "animals" who acted civilly in small numbers but not in groups, shiftless types who were lecherous for white girls and wanted only to "fish, fight, and fuck."

Resentments hardened in 2000, when several Port Sulphur High football players were accused of raping a student there during school, even though the case never went to trial and the charges were eventually dropped.

More frustration and bitterness surfaced after Katrina, when schools were placed in Boothville-Venice and Port Sulphur. Buras had received no school, and there had been almost no sign of rebuilding. All that remained open were a bar and a marina. The Delta Food Mart resembled a movie set, only its facade standing. Katrina collapsed the water tower and flooded the high school, whose windows were canted open as if the building had exploded from the inside.

How could Buras not get a school? Some residents saw malign intent: The movers and shakers in Belle Chasse didn't want Buras to recover, so the southern end of the parish would lose its political clout. Eva Jones was from Port Sulphur and she wanted South Plaquemines in her hometown. She was black and her constituency in Port Sulphur was black.

The truth was more prosaic, said Paul Lemaire, a school-board member from Port Sulphur who pushed to have a school in the lower end of the parish. South Plaquemines was placed in Port Sulphur, not thirteen miles down the road in Buras, to accommodate students who lived in the 450 FEMA trailers in a nearby park. The parish sheriff's deputies and their families were also housed in another park in Port Sulphur. The high school's location gave students and teachers a shorter commute from their FEMA trailers in Belle Chasse and elsewhere in northern Plaquemines. Buras had its sewer and water systems destroyed. Port Sulphur was the only place with the available space and infrastructure to put a temporary high school. Eventually, the school board would vote to move South Plaquemines High permanently to Buras, but things were not moving quickly enough in the fall of 2006 for those who had lived there before the storm.

"They killed our town," said Roger Halphen, who was from Buras. "There's no business. It's dead. Sometimes, you feel like giving up. When people you were born and raised with don't come back, you feel pretty lonely."

NO ONE MORE SKILLFULLY OR RUTHLESSLY EXPLOITED THE divisions of Plaquemines Parish than had Leander H. Perez Sr., the political boss and segregationist whose family ran the county like a dictatorship from the early 1920s until the early 1980s. Serving briefly as a judge, then as district attorney, Perez held a law degree from Tulane but gave the appearance of a casting-call autocrat, with silver hair and a white hat and thin-framed glasses and a long cigar. His birthday became a parish holiday. According to his biographer, Glen Jeansonne—author of *Boss of the Delta*, published in 2006 by the University Press of Mississippi—Perez would not have succeeded in a place that was more urban and sophisticated, where the populace had the time and inclination to get heavily involved in politics. In places like New York, Washington, and London, "People would have laughed at him," Jeansonne said in a 1982 documentary called *The Ends of the Earth*.

"Instead, in Plaquemines, he was greatly admired," Jeansonne explained in the documentary. "The people were poor and desperate and very dependent and knew very little about politics, were apathetic, and he used them."

Plaquemines had been known as pliant territory since at least the presidential election of 1844, when James K. Polk received 970 votes, a remarkable total considering that only 272 voters had been listed in the previous census. It was said that a Plaquemines politician chartered two boats out of New Orleans and carried 350 men down to Plaquemines in what amounted to floating voting booths. Not to be outdone in chicanery, Perez, in controlling both Plaquemines and neighboring St. Bernard Parish, was reported to have placed on the voting rolls such nonresident names as Babe Ruth and Charlie Chaplin.

Oil was discovered in Plaquemines in 1933, and it became known as the Golden Parish, one of the richest counties in the state. Perez appointed himself the personal lifeguard of these pools of black gold. Through a family-owned company called Delta Development Inc., he leased land from the parish and state and re-leased it to oil companies at a huge profit. Decades later, the Perez family was accused by the parish of stealing as much as eighty million dollars in oil royalties. In 1987, the suit was settled for ten million dollars and parish control of the land.

Leander Perez held virulent racial attitudes, viewing blacks as "burrheads" who were "fundamentally immoral." There were only two kinds of blacks, he said; "The good ones are darkies, and the bad ones are niggers." A saying developed around the parish: "If you're black, stay back, if you're brown, stick around, if you're white, you're all right." This seemed particularly applicable in the minority community of Ironton, which did not receive running water until 1981.

The Perez machine went to extraordinary lengths to keep the voting rolls as segregated as the schools. According to *Boss of the*

Delta, not a single black voter was registered in Plaquemines from 1936 to 1953, and only forty-three by 1962—despite a minority population of about six thousand. No black candidates appeared on the ballots, and because of their dependence on the parish for jobs, many blacks were reluctant to push for representation. Those who did faced consequences that were absurd and grim. The Reverend Joseph Taylor, a civil-rights activist who was currently eighty-one and pastor of the Greater Macedonia Baptist Church in Port Sulphur, said the registrar of voters sometimes stole out a back door of the courthouse when blacks came to register. When his own activism persisted in the 1950s, Taylor said, a cross was burned in his yard, his car was set on fire, and a portion of his house was set ablaze.

Integration, in Perez's view, was a conspiracy by Communists and Jews to dilute white superiority. Separate schools were established in Plaquemines for whites, blacks, and mixed-race students, which echoed the apartheid system of South Africa. In 1963, concerned about the potential onslaught of "national race agitators," Perez transformed decaying Fort St. Philip, built by the French in 1724 and accessible only by boat or helicopter, into a prison with electrified barbed-wire fences. Under increasing pressure from the federal government to integrate parish schools, Perez claimed that the Fourteenth Amendment had not been legally ratified, then supported a system of private schools. According to *Boss of the Delta,* when Plaquemines schools were forced to integrate in 1966–67, textbooks were taken from public schools for use at private schools, most of the athletic equipment was removed from Boothville-Venice High, and a coach at Belle Chasse High locked students out of the gym.

White flight was such that by 1968, only five students graduated from Belle Chasse High, according to Bennie Rousselle, the Plaquemines Parish president at the time of Katrina, whose father had resisted Perez. Years later, Rousselle joked that he had been such a good student, he graduated third in his class.

Eventually, the private schools closed in Plaquemines Parish. And, as *Boss of the Delta* noted, integration, while far from ideal, functioned better in the parish than in urban centers, particularly New Orleans. Leander Perez died in 1969, but not before ceding power to his sons, Chalin, who became the president of Plaquemines Parish, and Leander Jr., who became district attorney. They began to feud, though, and the family political machine ground to a halt in the early 1980s, as the first open elections in Plaquemines in fifty years were held for the school board and the parish council, or county commission.

Still, the divisive effects of the Perezes seemed to linger. And after Katrina, some nostalgia persisted for Leander Perez Sr. One of his aging acolytes still took out advertisements in the *Plaquemines Gazette*, railing against the American Civil Liberties Union. And there was a vague feeling by some that Plaquemines might have climbed to its feet more quickly after the storm with the assistance of a strong-handed leader.

"He might have been racist to an extent, but if you were from Plaquemines Parish, you got taken care of," said Mark Cognevich, president of the parish historical society.

Many offered harsher assessments, variously blaming Perez for creating dependency, cynicism, or despair about government. Some also faulted him for the problems of coastal erosion, believing his cozy relationship with oil companies had played a central role in the drilling of miles of marsh-destroying canals through the marshes.

"How would we be better off if he was around?" asked Ernest Johnson, who was currently seventy-one and had become in 1983 the first black elected to the parish council, eight years after filing a lawsuit seeking the apportionment of single-member districts. "He stole how many millions? We have a wetlands problem. He didn't like whites or blacks. He liked having whites on his side, but all he was, was a dictator, a mean man."

IF ANYTHING SEEMED TO UNITE THE PEOPLE OF PLAQUEMINES Parish as South Plaquemines traveled to Belle Chasse to open the 2006 football season, it was mutual suspicion. Wariness was based on this stereotype: Residents of lower Plaquemines wore white fishing boots, called Cajun Reeboks, and were not in tune with modern times, while the people in northern Plaquemines were wealthy and condescending. Bennie Rousselle explained the north–south divide thusly: "People in the north think people in the south are uninformed and less educated. People in the south think that people in the north get everything, that they're snobs and well to do."

Rousselle was convinced that the only reason a high school opened in lower Plaquemines was to restart football. Meanwhile, Paul Lemaire believed that some parish officials resisted South Plaquemines High because they wanted to hoard all the county's athletes at Belle Chasse.

Residents of lower Plaquemines had crowded into Belle Chasse after Katrina. By some estimates, the population, which had been more than 90 percent white, had jumped from ten thousand to as high as fourteen thousand after the storm. The homes were nicer in Belle Chasse, land much more expensive, the stores more upscale, the shelves more plentiful. A plot of land that sold for $28,000 in Port Sulphur might go for $70,000 to $90,000 in Belle Chasse. While few houses remained in lower Plaquemines and most people lived in trailers, McMansions in the Jesuit Bend and Spring Wood subdivisions in Belle Chasse sold for $350,000 and up. If the people were richer, though, their wealth did not endear them to their southern neighbors.

Attending school in Belle Chasse after Katrina seemed only to reinforce perceptions by residents from lower Plaquemines that they were unwelcome in upper Plaquemines. People from down Highway 23 thought that people up the road lacked a kind of authenticity and believed snootily that they were as refined as the oil that came upriver.

"We actually use our stoves," said Lorne Landry, whose foghorn voice carried distinctively from the stands of a South Plaquemines football game. "Some of those people eat out every night."

Perhaps this was the normal tension between city and country, spawned by a feeling of pastoral insecurity or resentment. Still, this perception of Belle Chasse's arrogance had been hardened by ferocity of belief—if not by unassailable fact—into an impregnable truth. Some in lower Plaquemines saw this as a racial divide, others as a class division.

"It's like we're garbage, trash," said Mike Barthelemy Sr., a French-and-Indian oysterman and shrimper from Port Sulphur. "Even the white people aren't white enough down here."

After Katrina, this mistrust of Belle Chasse expanded into a wider suspicion of outsiders. Many saw conspiracy at work: The U.S. Army Corps of Engineers wanted to submerge lower Plaquemines, letting the Mississippi run its natural course to replenish sediment along a disappearing coastline. The military wanted the lower end for its purposes. Or the oil companies did. Or land-grabbers who would build upscale fishing camps, creating a Cajun and Creole Key West.

Many residents of lower Plaquemines felt their kids got a second-hand education, while students at Belle Chasse got the top schools, the newest books, the best teachers, the newest sporting equipment, even the finest lunchroom tables. Students and teachers at South Plaquemines looked skeptically upon the school board's using a one-million-dollar donation from ConocoPhillips to rebuild the aging science lab at Belle Chasse High when the South Plaquemines lab lacked test tubes and slides for its microscopes.

The parish school superintendent said that per capita spending was the same at all schools. Still, everyone in lower Plaquemines seemed to have an example of a slight, big or small, to illustrate this north–south schism.

During the 2005–2006 school year, some South Plaquemines students said they had picked up signals in things said and unsaid that confirmed their outsider status: The way the Belle Chasse kids walked past them and seemed to look down their noses at them. The way they bragged and seemed inconvenienced by the presence of kids from down the road. Devin Boutwell, the defensive tackle and tight end from Buras, refused to wear the red shirts that were part of the Belle Chasse school uniform. He remembered a girl telling him once in the school parking lot, "Go home, y'all are overcrowding us."

Once, the students from lower Plaquemines acted provocatively against this feeling of ostracism, walking in a group across the courtyard at Belle Chasse High to a pavilion where Belle Chasse seniors gathered. Just to see what would happen, they said. The response? A school official, they said, urged them to get back on "their side" of the courtyard. "I didn't know we had a side," said Sal Cepriano, the starting center at South Plaquemines. "It was supposed to be our school, too. We were supposed to be one parish, united. But it was still segregated."

Paul Lemaire was in Balestra's, the supermarket in Belle Chasse, and heard a woman complaining after the storm about having to stand in line with people from down the road.

"Excuse me," Lemaire said. "Did you just say what I thought you said?"

"I'm not talking to you," the woman said.

"Well, I'm one of those people from down the road," Lemaire said.

He had returned to Port Sulphur only a month before the season opener, all the while praying at night, "Lord, don't let me die in Belle Chasse."

Jeanitta Ancar had been in Balestra's, too, one day when the cashier told a customer, "I wish those people would go back where they came from," only to have the store owner tell her, "It's because of the people down there that you have a job."

Such comments were particularly chafing because a number of residents in Belle Chasse had formerly lived in lower Plaquemines, coming north after the destructive swamping of Hurricane Betsy in 1965 and Hurricane Camille in 1969. There was a feeling by those from down the road that people in Belle Chasse had forgotten where they came from. While some in Belle Chasse considered it the Emerald City, residents from Port Sulphur, Buras, and Boothville-Venice eagerly pointed out that the oil and fishing wealth was generated primarily at the lower end of the parish, not the upper end.

So was the football success. Buras won a state title in 1966 and 1990 and finished second in 1991. Port Sulphur took state in 1979 and 1981 and 2002 after finishing as runner-up in 2001. Boothville-Venice reached the state quarterfinals in 2002 and the semifinals in 2004.

Not surprisingly, school officials at Belle Chasse felt they were being unfairly portrayed. Monica Wertz, the principal at Belle Chasse High who had grown up in Port Sulphur, acknowledged a feeling of smugness by some in upper Plaquemines. "Some have forgotten when they walked barefoot," she said.

Yet Wertz also said that Belle Chasse High had opened its arms to students from lower Plaquemines for the 2005–2006 school year. She said she shared her office with Theresita Ancar, who had been principal at Port Sulphur High. Some teachers from Belle

Chasse shared classroom space with as many as two teachers from down the road. School uniforms were bought for students who had lost their clothes along with their homes.

Sure, there had been tensions in the chaos after Katrina, Wertz said. At first, she broadened her morning greeting to students over the public address system from, "Good morning, Belle Chasse High" to "Good morning, Plaquemines Parish." A supervisor told her to stop, she said, because she was perceived to be showing favoritism and there were concerns that Belle Chasse High would lose its sense of identity.

Even so, Wertz said, "I think we did something that many people thought was not possible. We pulled together."

AS TONIGHT'S INAUGURAL GAME FOR SOUTH PLAQUEMINES approached, however, Crutchfield drew on separateness, not commonality, during his pregame speech. "I'll never forget what they did to me in Belle Chasse," he told the Hurricanes. "I'll never forget what they did to you. I'll never forget they think people down the road are trash. The Bible teaches us that what you shall sow, you shall also reap. Well, the bad seeds are going to grow up and choke the shit out of the good seeds. I'll never forget the ass whuppin' you 'bout to unleash on them. Never forget how you felt when you were at Belle Chasse. Never forget."

As the Hurricanes entered the cramped locker room at Belle Chasse High, Crutchfield carried a folded American flag with him. The flag had been draped on the coffin of his recently deceased father, Cyril Sr., a Korean War veteran. To honor his father, some players scribbled "Cyril" on the patches of eye black worn on their cheeks.

South Plaquemines would play its first official game in white uniforms, silver helmets, and light blue leggings that matched the numerals on the jerseys. The Belle Chasse Fighting Cardinals wore red and black.

"This is what we've been waiting for," Crutchfield told his players. "Some of us have waited for two years. Let's take advantage of the situation."

The players gathered for a team prayer. The one used previously at Port Sulphur had been reworked for a new school, a new team of players from all over lower Plaquemines:

Dear Lord,
The battles we go through in life
We ask for a chance to be fair.
A chance to equal all our strife
A chance to do or dare.
If we shall win, may it be by the code,
With our faith and honor held high.
If we shall lose, may we stand by the road
And cheer as the winners go by.
By day by day, get better and better.
A team that won't be beat, can't be beat.
In Jesus' name, one two three 'Canes.
Ohhhhhh, break it down! Offense!
Break it down! Defense!
Break it down! Hurricanes!
Spell it out! H-U-R-R-I-C-A-N-E-S.
'Canes, 'Canes, 'Canes.
'Canes on three, 'Canes on three!
One, two, three 'Canes!

Belle Chasse had four times the enrollment of South Plaquemines, but Crutchfield preferred to play much bigger schools in the early weeks of the season. Aside from getting a chance to defeat a parish rival in the opener, he would gain strength-of-schedule points for seeding in the play-offs. In playing bigger schools, though, Crutchfield risked crucial injuries or demoralizing losses. He would take the chance. This is the way he had always done it. And just to show that he wasn't afraid of Belle Chasse, that he planned to attack from the beginning, he called for an onside kick to open the game.

He had boldly predicted victory to the *Times-Picayune* of New Orleans, saying, "We're going to be like wild dogs." But everything went wrong from the beginning. The onside kick failed; Belle Chasse took possession and soon scored on a forty-yard touchdown pass that was tipped into the hands of a Cardinals' receiver. Just before halftime, Belle Chasse added a field goal to take a 10–0 lead. South Plaquemines was a new team, awkwardly joined from disparate parts. Neither the enthusiasm of its players nor the confidence of its coach could bring coherent play on the field.

The South Plaquemines quarterback, Ridge Turner, a five-foot-ten, 160-pound sophomore, was making his varsity debut at the position. Before Katrina, he had been a cornerback at Port Sulphur. After the storm, he had attended Helen Cox High in suburban New Orleans, where he had been a reserve defensive back. Tonight, he appeared rattled, hurried. There was enormous pressure on him to replace Randall Mackey. Sometimes Ridge seemed to grow distracted, pitching the ball prematurely to no one, and it fell dangerously to the ground. Other times he did not hold the ball firmly on the seams when he threw a pass, or he tossed it awkwardly while leaning on his back leg. This was his first official game. He could hardly be an expert at reading defenses. By halftime, Ridge had thrown three interceptions, and South Plaquemines had fumbled three times. His legs had also begun cramping in the heat. Twice, Ridge crumpled to the ground, wincing.

"Totally embarrassing," Crutchfield said to the Hurricanes at halftime. "Get some manhood, some balls and some heart and some character, and make a play."

"Don't give up," he told his players. He certainly wasn't giving up. The Hurricanes were down by only ten points. They had thrown three interceptions and fumbled three times. How much worse could it get? The players from Belle Chasse were soft, he said, accustomed to having "mom and dad give them everything."

"We've been experiencing loss for the whole last year," Crutchfield said. "Get an attitude and make a play. We have nothing to lose."

He had promised a victory to himself, to his team, to everyone in lower Plaquemines. "I promised it to my father," he said. "I don't want to let him down. When that clock strikes zero, I'm going to get on my knee and pray to my dad and say, 'Are you proud of your son?'"

But this was not going to be Crutchfield's night. Ridge Turner was struggling in his first start. Players seemed confused about where to line up. South Plaquemines would end up with seventeen rushing yards on sixteen carries. Ridge would throw two more interceptions in the second half. Then, with one minute, forty-five seconds remaining, running back Avery Riley outran the South Plaquemines defense for a sixty-three-yard touchdown, giving Belle Chasse a 16–0 victory.

This made the loss sting even more. The Hurricanes had been defeated primarily by players who had grown up down the road but had not returned after Katrina. Riley was from Port Sulphur. Rocky Duplessis, a safety from Buras, had picked off one of Turner's passes, and Blake Matherne, who was from Boothville, had swiped another.

"That's pathetic," Crutchfield said of South Plaquemines' six turnovers.

Ridge leaned his head against a door frame in the locker room and sobbed. Becnel had now defeated Crutchfield three games in a row, twice versus Port Sulphur and now versus South Plaquemines. The seniors from lower Plaquemines would never get another shot at Belle Chasse. Several cried softly.

Sure, Crutchfield's pregame bragging had played a part in the Belle Chase victory, Becnel told the *Times-Picayune*. "Our kids have been hearing that all summer," he said.

In the South Plaquemines locker room, Crutchfield told one of his players not to bother showing up next week. Keven Smith, a running back and defensive lineman from Boothville-Venice, had talked back to the coach after being reprimanded. "That never happened before, and it's not going to start now," Crutchfield said.

Eventually, Crutchfield's anger and disappointment softened.

"We did a lot of talking, but talk is cheap," he said. "I feel silly and stupid. But I'm not going to give up. As bad as I feel right now, I feel a hell of a lot better than I did a year ago at this time."

5

"SON OF A GUN,
WE'LL HAVE BIG FUN ON THE BAYOU"

STANLEY GAUDET CAME OUT OF THE PRINCIPAL'S OFFICE AT South Plaquemines High holding a can of bug spray. He had ordered two cases of insect repellent for Homecoming. Anyone wanting a shot of OFF!® could get it for free tomorrow night near the ticket window.

"West Nile," Gaudet said. "You've got to be prepared in south Plaquemines."

It was October 19, 2006. School had been open for two months, but the cafeteria still wasn't preparing hot meals. Students still had to share books. The band had no instruments. There was no gym for a pep rally. The Hurricanes had lost four of their first five games. Then the season had begun a fundamental pivot.

Ridge Turner awakened in a way that happens when football can be played with instinct and anticipation. Playing quarterback for the first time could bring on a blindness of indecision. Ridge was asked to see everything. Was the cornerback playing man to man? Was the safety cheating over? Was the linebacker blitzing? Sometimes there was so much to look for that it became a confusing blur. Now, it was as if a cataract had been removed and everything milky and obstructive was gone. Ridge was only a sophomore, in his first varsity season. Early on, he sometimes seemed to throw the ball indiscriminately, in hopes that one of his teammates would catch it. But now he understood how to read a defense, and he was playing assuredly. He had a whip of an arm and a graceful stride, knees up, elbows tucked, the ball cradled in the crook of his arm.

As South Plaquemines entered league play, against teams from the New Orleans suburbs with similar enrollments in Class 2A, Ridge became one of the state's leading passers. Against St. Martin's, he threw for 291 yards and four touchdowns and ran for two more touchdowns—all in the first half—as the Hurricanes won 53–27. A week later, he passed for 314 yards and two touchdowns, and ran for another score as South Plaquemines defeated Fisher High by 41–15. This was his team, its fate in his hands.

"He's starting to get that swagger," Crutchfield said. "He's got a long way to go, but he's come a long way, too."

Ridge credited his improvement to Crutchfield's simple refusal to abandon him.

"He breaks everything down and explains it," Ridge said. "He's got this confidence. He never gives up."

Now, in late October 2006, Ridge and his teammates would finally get to play a home game, the first in lower Plaquemines since Katrina struck. Forty thousand dollars' worth of new sod had finally taken root. New goalposts and a new scoreboard were in place. The press box had been painted sky blue for South Plaquemines High, covering up the purple and gold of Port Sulphur High. It was Homecoming. Two nights before the game, Big Wayne and Little Wayne Williamson had noticed the lights on at the field. They lived a couple of blocks away, in a trailer camp for sheriff's deputies, and they drove up to the stadium and walked around its perimeter. The field was empty, but it didn't matter. The football lights were back on.

"I just had to go look," Big Wayne said. "It was like the Second Coming. We home now. We home."

Big Wayne escorted the team bus and was also the stadium cook. On Homecoming day, he began barbecuing at noon, filling the grill with burgers and hot dogs and sausages. Parish workers finished lining the field. A teacher and a school-board employee helped spray-paint the final touches on a hurricane logo astride the fifty-yard line. But only the lights on the visitors' side of the field would stay on. The lights on the home side flickered and went out.

"It's going to be a race to the finish," Gaudet said. "Everything around here has been a race to the finish."

He had taken it upon himself to order a set of first-down markers because the parish's purchasing agent had been called as a juror in a murder trial. But the markers still hadn't arrived.

"I don't want one of those flimsy, flip-up markers," Gaudet said. "I want a Dial-a-Down."

About two in the afternoon, Highway 23 began to shut down for two and a half miles. The bulldozers and oil-field trucks and double-wide trailers sat in traffic while the first South Plaquemines Homecoming parade ran its restorative course. Sirens and flashing lights led the procession. Someone popped a wheelie on an all-terrain vehicle. A deputy sheriff blared rap music from the speakers of his squad car. Maids on the Homecoming court wore fitted suits and corsages and rode on the backs of convertibles. They tossed beads, candy, and stuffed animals. To the most familiar faces, they handed out roses and drinking cups bearing their names. Kids ran along the shoulder of the two-lane, gathering the spray of candy in plastic bags. Drivers pulled over and watched the parade from lawn chairs or the tailgates of pickup trucks. A few brought their barbecue grills.

"Katrina took this place from us and now we want it back," said Frances Lacross, a groundskeeper at Belle Chasse Middle School, explaining why she attended the parade. "If we don't support the lower end, nobody else will."

Even before Katrina, there had been little around here but football, church, and fishing. Now football was the anchor that kept the place from floating away completely.

"This is another step of saying, 'We're here and we're here to stay,'" said Theresita Ancar, the principal at South Plaquemines Elementary.

Wearing a black tuxedo and white velvet crown, Dwayne Ancar, the Homecoming king, rode past, tossing plastic footballs from a red convertible driven by his mother. He was a starting guard, but he had nearly quit the team earlier in the season. Life was hard enough without football. His family scattered ahead of Katrina and one of his uncles died of cancer before Dwayne got to see him again. When the family reconvened again in Belle Chasse, seventeen or eighteen relatives shoehorned into a single house. Dwayne's grades slipped. His lost his temper easily. "I couldn't get comfortable," he said. Football was supposed to be an oasis from these troubles, but players began bickering with each other in practice, on the sidelines during games.

"I didn't think the team cared about winning," Dwayne said. "Everyone was selfish."

A few victories had caulked the fissures in the team. And now, about three o'clock on this cool, azure afternoon, the stadium lights finally came on in full. Near the end of the parade route, Gaudet placed a yellow rose in his mouth as if he were a flamenco dancer. It was possible for a moment to forget about the FEMA trailers and vulnerable levees and crumbled buildings. "We need this like New Orleans needs Mardi Gras," he said.

An hour before game time, the new first-down markers appeared on the sideline. While his teammates warmed up, Ancar remained in his tuxedo for the naming of the Homecoming queen. Then he hurried into his light blue jersey and silver helmet.

"Seniors, this is your last Homecoming," Crutchfield told his players. "I've been waiting for this a long time. We're back home. Let's make it count."

South Plaquemines mishandled its first snap against McMain High of New Orleans but quickly regained its composure. Ridge threw four touchdown passes. With half of the third quarter remaining, he tossed a twenty-yard scoring pass and the Hurricanes went ahead 38–0.

"It feels good that everyone has come together," said Rodney Bartholomew Sr., a sheriff's deputy who had helped Big Wayne escort the team bus for years. "It's not Port Sulphur. It's not Buras. It's not Boothville-Venice. It's South Plaquemines. People said they could never play together. But it didn't take 'em long."

Ridge threw another touchdown pass, this one for seventy-seven yards, and a zydeco version of Hank Williams's "Jambalaya" blared on the public address system—"Son of a gun, we'll have big fun on the bayou"—as the home crowd of more than a thousand danced in the stands.

The Hurricanes kept scoring until they went ahead 57–0. By then, the maids on the Homecoming court, in their suits and hats and high heels, had joined the cheerleaders, celebrating in the thick sand on the sideline. Later, after his players had gone, Crutchfield sat in the doorway of the trailer that served as a locker room. He ate a sandwich and watched as the cars continued to exit the stadium, bumper to bumper. Headlights ringed the field like lights on a movie marquee.

"This is what people have been waiting for," Crutchfield said. "A year ago, there was nothing. People have been wanting to come home, looking for some place to go on Friday night."

WITH FOUR VICTORIES IN THEIR LAST FIVE GAMES, THE Hurricanes (4–4) would now play for the championship of District 11 in Class 2A against the Isadore Newman School of New Orleans. The winner would receive an automatic berth in the state play-offs. The contrast between the schools could not have been more pronounced. It was a game of subtexts: rich versus poor;

city versus country; private versus public. Newman, located in Uptown New Orleans, just off St. Charles Avenue, was one of Louisiana's elite private schools. It was the alma mater of Peyton and Eli Manning. The school had received some wind damage from Katrina but had reopened in January 2006. Its enrollment was approaching prestorm levels. This was a game Crutchfield desperately wanted to win.

Two days before the game, he wore a camouflage hat at practice and was in full throat against overconfidence.

"This ain't fuckin' P.E.," he yelled at his players. "Ya'll think we beat everybody? We're four and four. We ain't beat nobody. We beat McMain. Everybody beats McMain. I could get people out the bayou and beat McMain."

He had just the motivational ploy he needed for the Newman game. South Plaquemines would serve as Newman's Homecoming opponent. This showed a lack of respect, Crutchfield told his players. A Homecoming opponent was supposed to be weak, sacrificial.

"I want to beat the fuck out of these people," Crutchfield said. "They playing us for Homecoming? Homecoming? What are they thinking?"

He was in a manic mood, excited and agitated. His team had a chance to make something of this bizarre season. He was just beginning to have fun. But practice wasn't going well. Ridge overthrew one of his receivers, and Crutchfield said, "That big monkey had that fuckin' woman on the Empire State Building couldn't have caught that one."

When Little Wayne Williamson missed an assignment in the secondary, Crutchfield screamed, "You fuck up on Friday, you better put 'em up. We gonna fight. You whip my ass, we'll fight after the game. You whip my ass again, we'll fight when we get back to school on Monday. I don't care what happens, we not losing this game. You better get it in your mind."

With a starter absent from practice, a young player named Anthony Kap was installed at linebacker. He should be able to pick up the defense quickly, Crutchfield told Kap. "You from Cambodia," Crutchfield said. "You got slant eyes. You're smart."

Then Kap missed a call and went left instead of right on a blitz. Crutchfield shouted, "Hey Cambodia, this is fuckin' America. Ringo means right. Lucky means left. We not in Japan, where they drive on the wrong fuckin' side of the road."

Then his voice went slack.

"I like you," Crutchfield said. "Don't get nervous. I fuss a lot. Relax. Do your job."

Anyone who had played for Crutchfield for any length of time knew to just let these squalls of profanity and political incorrectness blow over. The worst thing anyone could do was interrupt. "We know he's just trying to make us better," Little Wayne said.

IT WAS A LESSON THAT KEVEN SMITH HAD LEARNED AT THE expense of being suspended for a week after the Belle Chasse game. There had been an incident on the field. Crutchfield said that Keven talked back to him; Keven said he was speaking to a teammate. In either case, he had been shelved for a week.

Instead of returning, though, Keven had quit the team. His girl-friend was pregnant and his son would be born around New Year's. He felt he had to look for a job.

What am I going to do with a son? he asked himself.

His parents were disappointed "but not mad enough to put me out." Instead, they told him, "It's time to be a man and take care of your responsibility."

Keven began to speak with Julie Butler, who taught a class in adult responsibility at South Plaquemines. Teenage pregnancy was an urgent issue at the school. Four girls were pregnant or had recently given birth. Smith's best friend on the team was the father of a ten-month-old son.

"The educational level of many parents is no higher than high school, so education isn't stressed," Butler said. "Kids are raising kids, who are raising kids. With Keven, I'm hoping he'll break the cycle."

He wanted to become a licensed practical nurse and, eventually, a registered nurse. He said he planned to propose to his girlfriend on January 3, 2007, the first anniversary of their meeting. College football was now a dream deferred. Keven would not even play basketball this season at South Plaquemines. Continuing his education, not sports, would probably determine his future path, Butler said.

"Keven's a bright kid, one that makes you glad to come to work," Butler said. "He knows what he doesn't want to happen. As long as he believes in himself as much as we believe in him, he will make it. Sometimes, it's hard for kids to look up at the big picture when they're always looking down, trying to get over one hurdle or the next."

Fatherhood had once been the furthest thing from his mind. His senior year of high school was supposed to be about renewal and football, not putting baby clothes and strollers on layaway and hunting for dollar-store bargains on diapers.

"I love my son and he's not even here yet," Keven said. But, he added, "Sometimes, at home, I'll be thinking, 'What if I hadn't gotten her pregnant?' I wonder how different it would be."

He was only eighteen, but now he had adult responsibilities. His girlfriend, Whitney Allen, was sixteen. They met after Katrina, having both evacuated to Lafayette, Louisiana, two teenagers running from the storm into unintended consequence.

"Sometimes, I feel old," Keven said.

He continued to live at home with his parents in Plaquemines Parish, while Whitney lived with hers in New Orleans. Keven lived in a seven-by-twenty-seven-foot FEMA trailer with seven other relatives. He slept in a bed with his father. His mother slept on a fold-out sofa, while his sister and her four children took the bunk beds and a third bed fashioned from cushions and the kitchen table. When he needed privacy to study for a test, Keven stepped outside to read by the dome lights of his father's pickup truck.

"Peace and quiet, that's something you don't really get in the house," he said.

Otherwise, he seldom left the trailer, which was situated about thirty miles north of school, in a FEMA park situated behind a restaurant called Captain Larry's.

"Nothing but trouble outside," Keven said. "Drugs. I don't get down with that."

His family had secured a Small Business Administration (SBA) loan and hoped to move back to Boothville in lower Plaquemines by New Year's. Before Katrina, school was a five-minute walk. Keven could hunt rabbits in the backyard. His father, a crane operator, had a shrimp boat. His grandmother, an uncle, and several aunts lived in the same enclave near the Mississippi River levee. Now, he worried about his parents, both of whom suffered from high blood pressure. He worried especially about his mother and the strain of caring for four grandchildren, ages thirteen, eleven, six, and four, in a cramped trailer.

"She's about to catch a heart attack," he said.

After the Hurricanes lost four of their first five games, Keven began to miss football. He believed he had let his friends down. "I felt they needed me," he said. His mother told him not to worry about a job right away. Even with his life suddenly complicated, she wanted him to enjoy his senior year. "We'll work it out," she said.

First, Keven had to convince Crutchfield to let him back on the team. He apologized, and Crutchfield accepted. Everyone's life had been overturned by Katrina. He would give the kid a second chance. It wasn't as if Keven was trying to jump on the bandwagon of a winning team. The Hurricanes still had a losing record when he asked to return. *If he wanted to come back now, it must be for the right reasons,* Crutchfield thought. Upon his return, Keven played running back in a couple of mop-up appearances. At five foot six, 216 pounds, he was short and squat, not unlike Jerome Bettis, now retired from the Pittsburgh Steelers. If Bettis was the Bus, Smith was the Minibus.

"He was so respectful, it really touched me," Crutchfield said. "When I put him in at the end of those games, he didn't complain. He just did what he was supposed to do. He played well. I thought this was a guy we could use."

Now, with the Newman game two days away and South Plaquemines' top two running backs missing from practice, Crutchfield needed someone to carry the ball. Another back ran the wrong way on a counter, and Crutchfield said, "Get the fuck out. That's garbage. Keven, get in there."

"Run the fucking play again," Crutchfield ordered.

Then, sheepishly, "I'm supposed to give up cursing."

"Fuck."

THE NEXT DAY AT PRACTICE, WITH THE LEAGUE CHAMPI-onship game twenty-four hours away, Keven leaned over the railing of the team's double-wide trailer and threw up.

"Oh, man," he said. "I musta ate something bad."

He seemed in agony.

"If you want to be a starter," Keven said, "you gotta fight through."

AS CRUTCHFIELD DROVE THE BUS INTO A PARKING LOT AT the Newman School, something was out of sorts. The freshman receiver Dylan Boutwell wasn't playing tonight. His mother had an argument with Crutchfield involving Dylan's older brother, Devin. Devin had injured his knee in the fourth game of the season, threatening his senior year and his chance to receive a college scholarship. His mother thought Crutchfield was not showing sufficient concern over Devin's injury.

Ridge Turner was almost left behind, too. He had brought home a failing grade on his report card. His aunt told him he had to drop football.

"I can't play no more," he told the coaches.

Crutchfield had Rodney Bartholomew Sr. speak with Ridge's aunt. You should have kept on top of this, the deputy told Crutchfield. Then Rodney tried to convince Ridge's aunt to let him play. It was an important game. The team needed him. They would make sure Ridge picked up his grades. Finally, his aunt relented.

"I'd rather him have a good education than play football," his aunt, Elouise Bartholomew, later explained. But, with Katrina, she added, "We already lost our home. Losing football would be losing everything."

The deputy went to Ridge's home to pick him up for the trip to New Orleans. Ridge didn't believe him, thought he was kidding. Rodney called Ridge's aunt again, confirmed her permission, and told Ridge to grab his gear.

The Hurricanes dressed in the opulent weight room at Newman. LeRoy Neiman prints adorned the wall. Roger Halphen peered in the training room. "Looks like a doctor's office," he said.

South Plaquemines was down to twenty-two available players.

"Homecoming," Crutchfield said. He kept repeating the word, as if each pronouncement were a paper cut. "Homecoming."

South Plaquemines whiffed on an onside kick, botched a punt, and fell behind 7–0. Then Keven began to bull his way through the Newman defense, scoring from fourteen yards, and again from one yard. Then he bowled over the goal line from three yards and the Hurricanes led 28–14 at halftime.

Finish this game off, Crutchfield exhorted in the dressing room. "Kick their ass," he said. "At birth you were better athletes than those sumbitches."

South Plaquemines fumbled the second-half kickoff. Newman recovered and scored. Now the game became as slippery as an eel, writhing out of one team's hands into the other's. Each lead was brittle, unsustainable. South Plaquemines played a daring defense, blitzing furiously but not leaving a traditional safety to play center field. The Hurricanes applied little pressure, and Newman kept throwing slant passes through the vacant middle. With six minutes remaining, Keven plowed into the line one more time, but he wrenched his left ankle and had to be helped to the sideline. He lay on the ground in pain as a doctor examined him. His night was finished.

South Plaquemines swept into the end zone with two and a half minutes left and went ahead, 40–35. But the middle of the Hurricanes' defense remained vulnerable. Seconds later, Newman threw another slant pass, this one for sixty yards, and the Greenies prevailed on Homecoming, 43–40. South Plaquemines had one final chance to win the league championship, but Ridge threw twice into a suddenly upwelling wind and both passes fell incomplete. Many of the Hurricanes dropped to their knees on the field.

Crutchfield sat inside the dressing room, his head in his hands. Keven stood on crutches. There was no sound except for sniffling and coughing and the tearing of tape from wrists and ankles. Crutchfield stood to address the team, but he moved away and turned his back. Tears ran down his face.

When he was a kid, his dad had told him repeatedly, "You just can't stand prosperity." Now the league championship was within his team's grasp, and it had slipped away. All that work, everything overcome since the hurricane, and for what? To lose a game like this? Crutchfield drove the bus home but did not sleep. The game kept playing in an agonizing loop in his head. He cried.

A WEEK LATER, IN THE REGULAR-SEASON FINALE, AN ODD season grew only more peculiar. Patrick Sylve, South Plaquemines' leading rusher, quit the team. As the Hurricanes loaded up for their trip to the sugarcane fields of Reserve, Louisiana, west of New Orleans, Sylve did not like the bus he was assigned to ride. He had missed practice, and an irritated Crutchfield put him on the bus with the backup players. Sylve just walked off the bus and quit. Mike Nguyen, a backup defensive tackle, was absent, too. He had been suspended after fighting for a friend's right to use a certain fishing hole.

From the beginning, South Plaquemines appeared indifferent against Riverside Academy. By the end of the first quarter, the Hurricanes trailed 28–0. By halftime, they were behind 41–8. "That is really sad," Crutchfield told his players. "Pathetic."

It was a chilly night, and only a small group of South Plaquemines fans had made the ninety-minute trip. Cindy Ancar stood along a fence behind the bench, watching her son, Dwayne, play his final regular-season game. The family had received an SBA loan to purchase a modular home. They hoped to move in by Thanksgiving. Still, the daily struggle with insurance and FEMA was wearying.

"It's one disappointment after another," Cindy Ancar said. "It's like they don't know we exist. They say, 'Come home,' but when will it really be home?"

Sometimes, Cindy said, she thought you had to be crazy to rebuild in lower Plaquemines. Now that the weather was getting colder, she got up at four thirty on school days and boiled water so that the family's FEMA trailer would be heated when Dwayne awakened for school.

"It seems like prehistoric times, the Flintstones," Cindy said with a rueful laugh. "Soon, I'll be driving my car with my feet."

As she talked, the Hurricanes continued to play timidly in the second half, losing 47–14. In the first season of its existence, South Plaquemines had finished with four wins and six losses. Given the expanded play-off format in Louisiana, the Hurricanes still qualified for the postseason as the twenty-first seed among thirty-two teams in Class 2A. It was the kind of season that would be appreciated in retrospect. Four wins did not seem like much, but this was a team formed from scratch, composed of bitter rivals, based at a school that had no locker room or weight room or even a home field for most of the season, which forced players to travel sixty miles round-trip to practice each day.

On the other hand, team unity and confidence had been fragile. Some of the best players had been unresponsive at crucial moments. By the end of the regular season, South Plaquemines was hardly able to field a complete offense and defense for practice each day. Unable to lift weights, the Hurricanes seemed to wear down as the season progressed. Linebacker Trey Stewart, the strongest player on the team back in August, had lost twenty-five pounds.

"At least we made the play-offs," Dwayne Ancar said. But, he added, "There is so much stress and strain, a person can only take so much."

Wrestling season was starting, and mats were set up for practice in an auxiliary cafeteria. Basketball was under way, too. Lacking a usable gym on campus, South Plaquemines held its practices and games twenty-five miles south in Boothville. This meant some players had to travel sixty or more miles back home at night to northern Plaquemines or suburban New Orleans. The school cafeteria was still not fully functional. Until the kitchen was built to code, hot food had to be cooked elsewhere on campus and carried in for lunch. Carpenters were still working to place canopies over the school's sidewalks. Power blackouts were common in bad weather. Some school supplies remained insufficient.

"Every time I ask for a pencil, they start fussing," said Maverick Ancar, an eighth-grade lineman.

Most local businesses in Port Sulphur had returned or were rebuilding. Since the football season began, the post office had opened and some streetlights had been installed on Highway 23. Yet three months into the school year, there was still no place at South Plaquemines High to hold P.E. classes outdoors. Only a few weeks earlier had the football team finally gained the use of blocking sleds. Roger Halphen, the assistant who also taught phys ed, said he felt misled.

"We had the idea the school would be ready in a week or two after it opened," he said.

SOUTH PLAQUEMINES WOULD BE ON THE ROAD FOR ITS 2006 play-off opener. Its opponent would be Pickering High, located in west-central Louisiana, near the Texas border. But Crutchfield faced a more urgent contest three days before the Pickering game. He was in a runoff election for a seat on the Plaquemines Parish Council. The parish communities were unincorporated and thus not governed as municipalities. Instead, the parish was divided into nine districts and administered by a council, similar to a county commission. Crutchfield was running in District Six, the Port Sulphur area. He had been considering a run for office for a couple of years, and now Katrina had spurred his entry into politics.

On Tuesday, November 7, Crutchfield took a day off from school to get out the vote. An extremely low turnout was expected for the runoff. It was a weekday; people had to work. And many residents of the lower end were still scattered about the state and the Gulf region. A vote here or there could make the difference. Dressed in jeans and a light blue South Plaquemines windbreaker, Crutchfield drove his SUV around the Port Sulphur area, visiting trailers and the Riverbend Nursing Center, urging residents to get out and cast their ballots.

"You nervous?" Mallory Alexis, a former student, asked him.

"Yeah, I'm nervous," he said.

"You got it," she said, standing outside her family trailer.

"It's gonna be close."

From place to place Crutchfield went, saying, "Don't forget, I need that vote."

Almost everyone wanted to talk football.

"Who we got this week?" a woman asked.

"Pickering. You going?"

"Nah, too far."

Someone else wanted to know whom Belle Chasse was playing in the first round of the Class 4A play-offs.

"Bastrop," Crutchfield said.

Randall Mackey had returned from his two-game suspension to lead Bastrop through another undefeated regular season. He would be facing a familiar rival in Belle Chasse. At one trailer, Crutchfield knocked on the door and was met by Dorita Black, whose son, Jamal Recasner, was another of the five Port Sulphur players who had left for Bastrop after Katrina. She could not wait for the end of football season, Black said. She was tired of living three hundred miles apart from her son. As soon as the season was over, Jamal was coming home, she said.

"I can't sleep," she said. "I'm about to have a heart attack."

Before football practice began, Crutchfield cast his vote in a trailer behind the parish government building in Port Sulphur. Recovery in the lower end of Plaquemines seemed to be growing stagnant, he said. Kids needed places for recreation. People needed help to come home. One man told him that his home-owner's insurance had risen from $800 to $3,200 a year—a fourfold increase. Who could afford that?

Someone from the lower end of the parish had to step up and go to bat for the people, Crutchfield said. Make sure they wouldn't be forgotten down here. "What they have in Belle Chasse is no comparison," he said.

Above all, Crutchfield said, the federal government needed to spend whatever it took to make the levees safe against another storm. The government believed that $1.6 billion was too much to spend in an area where so few lived.

"If the levees aren't certified, it's going to prevent people from coming back," Crutchfield said. "I don't care if we have fifty people in the area, or five hundred, we deserve the same protection as every other city in the United States. I'm for the war in Iraq. We spend billions and billions of dollars outside our territories. What they gonna do for the homeland citizens?"

Practice ended at six o'clock, before the polls closed. Later, Crutchfield walked from his FEMA trailer to the parish government trailer where the results were being posted. Quickly, it became apparent that he would not win.

"I'm behind sixty-seven votes," he said glumly, walking with his hands in the pockets of his jeans. "Sixty-seven."

In the open primary, Crutchfield had finished second among five candidates in District 6, only forty-four votes behind the leader. He was especially disappointed in a downturn of votes from the community of Diamond, where 450 trailers were placed in a FEMA park. His total from the primary to the runoff seemed to drop by half.

"I can't believe this," said Micquella Sylve, Crutchfield's girlfriend. She worked in a school cafeteria and was known as Mickey. Her son, Bradley, an eighth-grader, was a cornerback and South Plaquemines' top sprinter. When Crutchfield and Mickey returned the short distance to their FEMA trailer behind the high school, she went into the bedroom and began crying. Crutchfield turned on the television and watched election returns on a New

Orleans station. In the end he lost to Burghart Turner, whose family had been in Port Sulphur for many years, 537 votes to 366.

"I'm disappointed in the numbers," Crutchfield said. "You'd expect to get the same votes you got the last time."

A day later, Mickey Sylve was still distraught. The election defeat seemed like a betrayal. Crutchfield had done so much for the lower end of the parish, she said, winning a state championship. Still, he had been rejected at the polls. This was a parochial place, and Crutchfield was not from here, as Turner was. He was from Covington, north of New Orleans. It might as well have been north of New York. He was a terrific football coach, but he was an outsider.

"An outcast," Mickey called him.

He had a forceful personality. Maybe some people thought he was too arrogant, she said. With a master's degree, he was also far better educated than the average resident of lower Plaquemines Parish. Crutchfield taught school, he coached, and he drove a school bus. His father had always worked more than one job, and so had he. But he made an estimated seventy thousand dollars a year, and in such an insular community, some people thought he was greedy for wanting the additional eighteen-thousand-dollar salary of a parish councilman, Mickey said. It was the crab-in-the-barrel theory: When one tries to climb out, the others pulls him back in.

Racial politics might also have played a part, Mickey thought. Previously, Crutchfield had dated a white woman, which apparently alienated some voters. Also, the communities of Diamond and Happy Jack and Pointe a la Hache were largely populated by mixed-race residents who considered themselves French and Indian or Creole. Many were light skinned, and Crutchfield was dark skinned. He was the football coach, a charismatic and popular man. But in some of those French-and-Indian homes, he would not be welcomed, according to a friend of his, Romel Barthelemy, who lived in Diamond. To certain people, Crutchfield would say later, "I'm a nigger."

Even though Crutchfield had received several job offers in northern Louisiana in recent years, he had declined them all. He would never leave Port Sulphur, he said frequently. Some of the best fishing waters in the country were just behind the high school. And he liked the kids down here. ("They grow up hard, mostly single parents, but they ball their ass off.") At South Plaquemines, he could coach the way he wanted. ("I get on the kids, cuss 'em out. You can't do that everywhere. You can't grab kids and shake 'em up.") Even though he demanded excellence from his kids, and some feared him, they also respected him and loved playing for him. If he left, he felt the next coach wouldn't get as much out of the players as he did. Some people thought the team would disband if he were to go to another school. But this election defeat seemed like an act of community disloyalty, Mickey said.

"If something good comes along, I think he's gonna go," she said. "Even though he loves Port Sulphur, because of what happened, that's really sad."

6

"CALL EVERYBODY!
CALL THE WHITE HOUSE!"

BY THE TIME THE SOUTH PLAQUEMINES TEAM BUS BEGAN ITS five-hour trip across southern Louisiana to Pickering, Cyril Crutchfield's attention seemed to have fully returned to football. There was no more talk of leaving South Plaquemines. The Hurricanes arrived about ten p.m. the night before the play-off opener. The players gathered in the tiny lobby at their hotel near Fort Polk. Dressed in an olive suit, Crutchfield spoke for thirty minutes. He began with a poem, reciting "The Bridge Builder," by Will Allen Dromgoole (1860-1934):

> *An old man, going a lone highway,*
> *Came, at the evening, cold and gray,*
> *To a chasm, vast, and deep, and wide,*
> *Through which was flowing a sullen tide.*
> *The old man crossed in the twilight dim,*
> *That sullen stream had no fears for him;*
> *But he turned, when safe on the other side,*

And built a bridge to span the tide.
"Old Man," said a fellow pilgrim, near,
"You are wasting strength with building here;
Your journey will end with the ending day;
You never again must pass this way;
You have crossed the chasm, deep and wide,
Why build you the bridge at the eventide?"
The builder lifted his old gray head:
"Good friend, in the path I have come," he said.
"There followed after me today
A youth whose feet must pass this way.
This chasm, that has been naught to me
To that fair-haired youth may a pitfall be.
He, too, must cross in the twilight dim;
Good friend, I am building the bridge for him."

This was South Plaquemines' inaugural season, its first play-off game. This team would build a bridge for next year's team and for other teams to come, Crutchfield explained. He had traveled that road, like the old man. If his players listened to him, he would guide them across this chasm of the play-offs. This was the best time of their lives, he told the seniors. There was no worse feeling in the world than taking off a uniform for the last time, he said. "If we lose tomorrow, I ain't gonna lie," he said. "I'll be crying like a baby."

But if the Hurricanes trusted him and played as aggressively as they had practiced all week, if they played with heart and emotion, they would win.

"Get it in your mind that you have to be cocky, you have to be arrogant," Crutchfield said as his players crammed onto a sofa and chairs and stood around the lobby. "People say that about me all the time. I like it. Being cocky, talking shit, that's the player I was. I miss it. If you get it in your mind that you can't be denied, I promise you, your day is coming."

His voice became insistent, his words gathering force. It was a quintessential Crutchfield moment, excitable, encouraging, profane. His players would talk about it for a week.

"This is your first play-off game; you should be high like you on that dope," Crutchfield said. "You should be running around, yelling, screaming, 'Aaaaah, motherfucker!' They'll think your ass is crazy. You may not be good, but they won't know."

After a half hour, he walked out of the hotel and into the parking lot. Still in his suit, hands jammed in his pockets, Crutchfield paced the length of the building, juiced with the adrenaline of his own words. He waved off a visitor, said he wanted to be alone and kept walking. Back and forth he went on this humid night, everything silent but the scrape of his shoes on the concrete.

LATE THE FOLLOWING AFTERNOON, CRUTCHFIELD AGAIN walked by himself, this time on the field at Pickering High. He was dressed in jeans and a light blue polo shirt. The day was over-cast, and Crutchfield felt the odd sensation that he was looking up at his deceased father in the clouds. What seemed like a rainbow appeared, and it hadn't been raining. *My dad's here,* Crutchfield thought to himself. *It's going to be all right.*

In this spiritual moment, he thought he heard his father's voice: *What you worried for, Dummy? You gonna win the game.*

Oh, man, Crutchfield said to himself. *We're gonna win.*

After less than seven minutes, South Plaquemines trailed 21–0.

Pickering ran a veer option and kept slicing through the Hurri-canes with dive plays. Its backs ran to the end zone untouched. After the first quarter, Pickering led 27–6. Early in the third quar-ter, South Plaquemines trailed 34–12. It was a familiar pattern of self-destruction. Only this time, the Hurricanes did not succumb. Crutchfield pinched his defensive tackles closer to the center. The players kept encouraging each other instead of bickering. Ridge

Turner calmly rescued his team. He threw a slant pass for a twenty-seven-yard touchdown. He kept on an option for a touchdown run of seventeen yards, then zigzagged into the end zone from nineteen yards on a quarterback counter.

With ten minutes, forty-eight seconds remaining, South Plaquemines drew to within 34–32. Then the rain began. Earlier in the week, rain had come down in silvery sheets at practice and seemed to wash away a season's worth of frustration. Players began whooping and hollering and wrestling in the mud. They were just kids again, playing football in sopping-wet merriment. It was the best practice of the season. And now it was raining again, and the South Plaquemines players began screaming along the sideline.

"It's hurricane weather!" Sal Cepriano, the center, yelled.

A cold front was sweeping through, and thunder crackled, and the sky spidered with lightning. In northern Louisiana, some playoff games were halted briefly, but in Pickering they played on. Fans ran to shelter at a concession stand, but the South Plaquemines cheerleaders began to chant, "Wash 'em out, 'Canes, wash 'em out!" The home team began to fumble. With six and a half minutes remaining, the Hurricanes finally went ahead, 40–34.

Nothing was secure in this rain, though. Guard Dwayne Ancar came to the sideline with a throbbing headache and lay face down on a runway near the stadium track. While others shouted encouragement, he found the gathering noise excruciating, and screamed, "Shut up. I have a migraine!"

Both teams kept dropping the wet ball. Desperate to hold its lead, South Plaquemines took an intentional safety. As the rain continued, Pickering kept driving toward what would have been the winning touchdown. Then, with twelve seconds left, the ball was fumbled again, and the Hurricanes recovered. It was the most improbable moment of an improbable season. Somehow, South Plaquemines had won. Two fans scooped Crutchfield up and carried him across the field. Keven Smith kissed Crutchfield on the cheek. Then he kissed Ridge.

"Whose field?" the fans chanted. "Crutchfield!"

"Call everybody!" yelled Andria Barthelemy, whose son Lorne was a seventh-grade lineman. "Call the White House!"

In the jubilant locker room, someone shouted, "A hurricane hit tonight!" and linebacker Trey Stewart answered, "Category 5." It was not until the players had stopped at a McDonald's on the celebrative trip home that they discovered they had been robbed. Apparently, someone had entered the locker room during the game and taken a DVD player, cash, even one player's sneakers.

In what seemed a perverse joke, Keven said a twenty-dollar bill had been removed from his wallet and replaced with a single dollar. He had been eating sparingly on the road, trying to hoard the spending cash his mother gave him.

"With the baby coming," he said, "I need all the money I can get."

SEVERAL DAYS LATER, PARENTS GAVE THE HURRICANES A steak dinner. It was done out of gratitude for their perseverance, but Crutchfield became upset. To him, this signaled a culmination, a sense that everyone was satisfied after one play-off victory, when four potential rounds remained.

In the second round, South Plaquemines drew a home game against fifth-seeded Clinton High School, located north of Baton Rouge. By this point, the strange had become the ordinary. So it hardly seemed unusual when the stadium lights faltered at dusk as South Plaquemines warmed up for the game. A backhoe had rammed a power line in the area, and electricity went out for miles along Highway 23.

Power outages were regular disturbances since Katrina. So the players did what they had done frequently in the past fourteen and a half months—improvise. Coolly, the South Plaquemines players taped their ankles in the red and blue glow of lights from a sheriff's cruiser. Crutchfield studied his game plan by the white lights of another police car. Inside the trailer that served as a dressing room, Sal Cepriano changed the visor on his helmet with the illumination from two cell phones. Lights from an ambulance shined on the ticket booth.

For two hours, the stadium lights remained dead. Players gathered in the warmth of the trailer to escape the evening chill. They spread out along the floor, resting on equipment bags, using shoulder pads as pillows. Eventually, the Hurricanes became impatient, fidgety. Occasionally, someone shouted a curse. Dwayne Ancar pounded a wall with his gloved hand.

"We're ready to go," he said. "This is taking too long."

The game was delayed by an hour. When it finally started, South Plaquemines seemed listless, confused. Players lined up improperly on offense and sometimes forgot to call defensive signals. They spoke to each other, bewildered.

The Hurricanes lost 48–16. Perhaps they were overmatched. Perhaps they were sated, or spent, after the unlikely victory against Pickering. South Plaquemines threw six interceptions; two were returned for touchdowns. When the game ended and players from both sides began shaking hands, Ridge Turner remained on his back, devastated, his hands grasping his face mask, his knees raised. Paul Lemaire, a school-board member, helped him to his feet. Ridge's breath was visible in the chill as he sobbed.

Other players dropped their helmets and went to their knees, pressing their faces to the turf. Some squatted on the field as parents and girlfriends began to comfort them, rubbing their backs, hugging them, draping their uniforms with blankets.

"Keep your heads up," Lemaire told Ridge and his teammates. "It was a hell of a year."

Mike Barthelemy Sr., whose son Mike Jr. was a linebacker, walked among the players, saying, "Stand up, get your chin up, stop crying. I thank every one of y'all. It took courage to come back and play. You've been through a hell of a lot. I'm proud of every one of y'all."

Crutchfield was too distraught to address his team. Dressed in a light blue shirt and khakis, he stood on the field, staring into the distance. He walked into the dressing room, put his head down on a table, then pulled his shirt to his face and cried. Only once in his previous six seasons in lower Plaquemines had his team failed to reach at least the quarterfinals. He was accustomed to coaching the week of Thanksgiving.

"What am I going to do?" he asked vacantly. "I should have had 'em ready. As head coach, I've got to take the blame."

He began to think ahead to next season. The team needed a weight room, he said.

"That's key," Crutchfield said. "If they add a little bit [of strength], they can get over the top."

Eating a sandwich distractedly, he reduced the season to the misery of prime numbers: five wins, seven losses.

"Seven fucking games," he said. "I ain't used to that."

He put his right hand to his cheek, crossed his hands, waved them like semaphores as he talked. His eyes watered. He grew nostalgic for all the players he had lost from Port Sulphur to other schools after Katrina.

"I like winning," he said. "I'm selfish with winning. We want to win every year. If we don't win, we want to be right there. Now what the hell am I going to do next Friday?"

Roger Halphen reminded him, "You ain't never had thirty kids that lost fuckin' everything. You ain't never started from a blank slate before, whoever showed up."

He had slacked off with discipline after the hurricane, Crutchfield said. He had taken things for granted. Now he would get back to his old self. Players would be dressed for practice ten minutes after the school bell rang. Everything would be tightened up.

Kenny Guidroz, one of his former Port Sulphur stars, now playing receiver at Tulane, came into the dressing room. He was on crutches, recovering from an injury.

"It's been a year now," Crutchfield said of Katrina and his somewhat more lax approach. "Next year, all that stuff's over with. You have weaker kids now. Different kids. You hit one of these kids now, they quit."

Turning to Guidroz, he said, "Didn't I hit you with a down marker?"

No, it was somebody else, Guidroz said.

Rubbing his hands together, Crutchfield acknowledged that his team had come a long way this season. He was proud of his players. But he looked down and shook his head and said he would have to change the collective mind-set. With everything his players had been through, they had lost their self-assurance along with their homes and the familiarity of their lives.

"When something bad happens, they put their heads down," Crutchfield said.

There was reason to be excited about the upcoming 2007 season, though. The Hurricanes would drop to Class 1A to play against the state's smallest schools, those with enrollments similar to South Plaquemines'.

"We're gonna win the state championship next year," Crutchfield said, suddenly invigorated. "We're gonna win the 1A state championship. You hear it coming out of my mouth."

His mood brightened, thinking of the possibilities of the coming season. He put his head in his hands and began to speak more fondly of the recent past.

"Look at everything those kids had to go through," Crutchfield said. "They lost everything. They were told by certain people they weren't going to have a season, they weren't going to play for the district title, they weren't going to have people in the stands. They made a choice to come down here. They're living in

FEMA trailers. They don't have a locker room, don't have a weight room. Part of the year they didn't have hot lunches. First seven weeks of the season, they had to get on a bus and take a thirty-five-minute ride to a tedious practice on a sandwich. On top of that, they had to do homework and everything. Then there were three schools that never knew each other. They didn't play for a whole season, didn't have a spring practice. There's no other kids in the state of Louisiana that had to go through that. They might have lost their school, but they didn't have to go through that. After starting oh for three, those kids hang in there and make it this far. They showed me a tremendous amount of resiliency. It lets me know they're tough. I'm proud of that."

He recounted the story of how he had been forbidden to play football as a boy, and how he had forged his mother's name on a consent form to make his high school team. That same passion was still with him, Crutchfield said.

"I live and die football," he said. "That hurts my relationship."

He was referring to Mickey Sylve, his girlfriend, who was in the dressing room.

"It really does, but you know what. I try to be straightforward with those kids," Crutchfield said. "I might have told her recently, too. The best love she ever gave me, yeah, it was pretty good, but it could never parallel that feeling when that boy caught the winning touchdown [in the 2002 state-championship game for Port Sulphur]. It's the best feeling in the world.

"I try to tell the kids. The best kiss, all you remember ten to fifteen years from now is it was a good kiss. I'm not going to get goose bumps thinking about that kiss. But I am going to get goose bumps thinking about when that clock struck zero and we won that game."

7

"THEY CAN'T CALL US PAPER CHAMPIONS ANYMORE"

"COACH, I MISS MY FOOTBALL. LAST NIGHT I HAD NOTHING to do. I was home watching Rudolph."

"You're not the only one," Cyril Crutchfield said, turning to a friend, Lorne Landry. "I watched that, and Frosty, too."

The South Plaquemines season had been over for three weeks. On this Saturday afternoon, December 9, 2006, about fifty fans from Port Sulphur had made a bittersweet trip to the Superdome in New Orleans to watch the Class 4A state championship. They had come to celebrate two kids—Randall Mackey and Jamal Recasner—who were playing for a title for Bastrop High. They had come to cheer, but they were also here to eulogize something prized and valuable that had been lost.

Crutchfield was convinced that, if not for Katrina, Port Sulphur might be playing for a third consecutive Class 1A championship. He sat in a corner of the Superdome, watching while his former players wore unfamiliar colors and were cheered on by unknown fans as they tried to win a title that would go into someone else's trophy case.

"I'm a little shaky," Crutchfield admitted before the game. "I'm happy for these kids. I want them to win a championship. But I'm disappointed things are not how we would like it to be, with everybody home, everything normal."

Of Randall and Jamal, he said, "I'm glad they got a chance to play somewhere. Do I think some things were done wrong? Yes. We're on the other end of the stick. It didn't work out for us. Bastrop benefited and possibly the kids did. The most important thing is the kids. You don't want to be selfish."

Crutchfield wore a pale blue South Plaquemines shirt, while a smattering of others in the crowd of 36,663 wore the purple, gold, and black football jackets and jerseys of ruined Port Sulphur High. The awkwardness of the moment was evident to Crutchfield's friends as he grew quiet and began shaking his legs nervously.

"I know it's hard on you," Rodney Bartholomew Sr. told the coach. "It's hard on me, too."

For Randall and Jamal, the afternoon was a chance for a redemptive conclusion to a season that had begun with both of them suspended. They had been illegally recruited to Bastrop and had lied about it. To its critics, Bastrop High was the "Katrina Rams," a team whose self-interest undermined its compassion for the displaced players. A team that ignored fair play and would not have gone undefeated for a second consecutive season if not for the two kids from Port Sulphur.

Bastrop's supporters did not doubt the team's authenticity. The 2005 state championship had been stripped, but a repeat title in 2006 would be considered legitimate.

"What they gonna say now?" Randall asked before the game. "They can't call us paper champions anymore."

He did miss wearing a Port Sulphur uniform and playing for Crutchfield, Randall said. "He just crazy," he said of his former coach. "You make a mistake, he about pile drives you. But he gives everybody a chance. He was always keeping me right in school, telling me to stay focused with my grades."

Randall backtracked on his earlier remarks that he would like to play his senior season back in lower Plaquemines in 2007. Over the summer, he had returned to Port Sulphur for a visit. Some of the South Plaquemines' fans said that he wanted to come back for good, but that his mother would not let him. Not true, Randall said. Living was better in Bastrop, he said. Bastrop afforded him a chance to play against better competition, to draw more attention from recruiters offering college scholarships. He was considering Texas, LSU, Florida State.

"I went back, it was like, 'Oh my God, look at this,'" Randall said. "I walked down my street. I seen a lot of things. Trash. Found my dog, dead. Laying behind a fence. All bones. I don't feel like going back down there. I don't want to see none of that stuff. I want to live life like it is now."

Before the championship game started, Carla Ragas came by to say hello, wearing a red and blue Bastrop jersey. "I love this man," she said of Crutchfield. Her eldest son, Josh Mackey, had been named most valuable player of the 2002 championship game for Port Sulphur. "If not for Crutch, my kids wouldn't have played sports."

Bastrop's opponent was Archbishop Shaw of suburban New Orleans. Randall played unevenly as the game opened, but threw a fifty-one-yard pass to set up Bastrop's first touchdown. Then he injured his left ankle and lay on the ground, unable to get to his feet. Crutchfield stood up, concerned. But Randall missed only a play or two before returning. He rifled a short sideline pass that eluded a cornerback and became a twenty-three-yard touch-down, giving Bastrop a 14–7 lead.

"Awesome," Crutchfield said. "He put the strength on it. A regular kid would have had it picked off."

Randall put zip on his short passes and touch on his deep throws. His first pass in the championship game, an incompletion, sailed sixty-five yards. His most elegant throw was another fifty-one-yarder, perfectly feathered but ruled incomplete in the end zone before halftime. Crutchfield smiled and shook his head in amazement.

His own quarterback, Ridge Turner, sat nearby. Ridge and Randall had lived on the same street in Port Sulphur. They still talked often. Turner sat quietly by himself, thinking, *That's gonna be me next year.*

All afternoon, Randall played with elusive grace. When Archbishop Shaw had him trapped, he escaped. He broke tackles with the balance and power of a running back. Unlike many high school quarterbacks, he threw accurately on the run, finishing an unblemished season in which he completed 107 of 185 passes for 2,067 yards, twenty-seven touchdowns, and four interceptions.

"One of the best players I've ever seen," said Scott Bairnsfather, the Shaw coach.

Jamal Recasner, who was five foot ten, 205 pounds, rushed for 143 yards and gave Bastrop a lead of 22–7 in the fourth quarter. Two defenders hit him during a sixty-nine-yard touchdown run but could not bring him down. A third grabbed his jersey but could not hold on. As Jamal sprinted for the end zone, Crutchfield stood and raised his fist, but the moment was tinged with a special poignancy.

As an eighth-grader, Jamal had played on Port Sulphur's 2002 championship team. Now he was the last remnant of that team still playing in high school. As Recasner scored, tears came to the eyes of Big Wayne Williamson, who wore a Port Sulphur jersey in the stands.

"I can't believe we lost that," Big Wayne said. "I feel good for him," he continued.

Still, he seemed melancholy. "If all our kids came back, we'd be playing here," Big Wayne said. "I believe that."

Bastrop won 28–14. The Port Sulphur fans stood and cheered as Randall received the outstanding player award and Jamal hoisted the championship trophy. It was a cathartic moment for Bastrop. Later, speaking to reporters, Randall declared that the forfeited 2005 season "was gone to me."

As he headed back to the Superdome locker room, Randall said he planned to give Crutchfield a call. "I know he's happy for me," Randall said. "I know he thought that Port Sulphur could be number 1. I feel the same way. But you can't change what happened."

Later, as he left the 'Dome to drive home to Port Sulphur, Crutchfield said he was glad that his former players had won a championship. "You just wish it was us," he said.

8

A CHAIN'S AS STRONG AS ITS WEAKEST LINK

THE 2007 FOOTBALL SEASON ARRIVED AT SOUTH PLAQUE-mines High, to be greeted by a funeral wreath in the end zone. It was attached to the fence and said, "Rest in peace, Hurricanes." Ostensibly, the wreath had been sent from Belle Chasse High, tonight's opening opponent. Actually, the wreath had been ordered by the South Plaquemines cheerleaders to toss more motivational gasoline on this five-alarm rivalry. The Hurricanes would be playing Belle Chasse at home this year and expected redemption after last season's 16–0 defeat.

"That felt like another storm had hit when we lost that game," Ridge Turner said.

South Plaquemines was ranked fourth in the Class 1A preseason poll. Among the players, there was a sense of common purpose that had been lacking in 2006. Roxanna Cepriano wanted to wear an old Port Sulphur jersey to the opener, but her son Sal, who had moved from center to guard, said, "No, Mom, I'm a Hurricane now."

Two hours before kickoff, the Hurricanes lined up at the back of one end zone, dressed in their dark blue game pants and Under Armour shirts. Each player grabbed the hand of the teammate on either side of him. "A chain's as strong as its weakest link," Cyril Crutchfield told his players. They lifted their arms in unison, brought them down to their sides, and walked silently, hand in hand, to the opposite end zone and back. A few Belle Chasse players were on the field. Someone wondered if they would try to disrupt the South Plaquemines' ritual.

"Do not let your hands go, for nothing," senior tackle Caileb Ancar warned.

For his debut at South Plaquemines, Lyle Fitte, a five-foot-eight, 190-pound running back, had written "564" on the patches of eye black worn on his cheeks. That was the dialing prefix for Port Sulphur. He had returned to lower Plaquemines for his junior season after playing for Belle Chasse High in 2006. He had been injured in the preseason and missed the 2006 opener against the Hurricanes after undergoing surgery to have pins inserted in his left elbow.

"I think it was a tough decision for him to leave," said Bob Becnel, the Belle Chasse coach. "He was treated well."

He was, Lyle agreed, as long as he was healthy. When he got hurt, the coaches had seemed vaguely distant. "You feel kind of used," Lyle said.

His primary reason for returning home, though, had been to reunite a family still splintered by Katrina. His grandparents lived on family land in a trailer in the community of Diamond, while his mother, Avis, lived thirty miles up the road in a FEMA trailer park. She worked in the permit office for the parish government in Belle Chasse. At first, she had been reluctant to return to the lower end of the parish, Lyle said, because "she thought the storms would get worse." Avis Fitte also preferred the school system in Belle Chasse, but Habitat for Humanity was building a three-bedroom home for her and her three sons in Port Sulphur. She expected to move in by the end of football season.

"I'm going to be a homeowner," she said. "My kids will have an inheritance."

Before Katrina, the Fitte clan had lived in three houses on land that had been in the family for generations. It was the way many people lived in the Port Sulphur area. Families with names like "Fitte" and "Barthelemy" and "Ancar" and "Sylve" gathered in clusters. Sometimes the streets bore the names of the families residing on them. Grandparents lived next door to their sons and daughters and grandchildren, whose homes abutted those of aunts and uncles. In some cases, the family lineage neatly followed the ascending or descending addresses between Highway 23 and the levees that held out the river and the marsh.

Two years beyond the storm, the home of Lyle Fitte's grandparents sat unoccupied. A plea was spray-painted in green on the front: "Don't Demolish." Two trailers flanked the house. A third was across the street, near the river levee. The modest wooden home had been stripped to its studs. The porch was missing, the roof sagged, the windows lacked panes to keep out the weather, the outside walls were moldy. Lyle's grandparents, Debra and Larry Fitte, had carried no flood or homeowner's insurance. And so far they had received no assistance from the state's Road Home program, which offered homeowners up to $150,000 in recovery grants.

Debra and Larry Fitte were having a difficult time proving that they owned their house. Their land had been in the family for seven or eight generations. The water bill was in one relative's name, the light bill in another. Building permits had been lost at the parish permit office. The Fittes said they had built the house themselves with cash. It rose in stages over two years as they had the money to pay for it—the roof in one stage, the siding in another, then bedrooms, a kitchen, a bathroom. It was their home all right, built with their labor, filled with family celebrations for holidays and birthdays, provable in every way but a piece of certified paper. A Road Home official had called to say he found a record of the trailer that Debra Fitte's mother had lived in before Katrina. That was well and good, except that her mother had lived in a house, not a trailer.

This was exactly why Avis Fitte did not want to return to family land. She wanted to avoid maddening red tape and disputes involving other potential heirs, whose signatures were needed under Louisiana law before anything could be rebuilt. For another home in the area, the Mennonite Disaster Service said, 108 signatures from an extended family had to be secured before the house could be rehabbed after the storm.

"I want my children to have something for themselves," Avis said. "I don't want them to have to worry about anybody else coming in."

ON AUGUST 31, 2007, TWO YEARS AND TWO DAYS AFTER Katrina, Plaquemines Parish still operated under a state of emergency. Lingering effects of the storm were not immediately apparent at the tank farms of the ConocoPhillips refinery south of Belle Chasse, or at the cottages in Myrtle Grove that rose on stilts like extravagant birdhouses, or among the piles of coal at the International Marine Terminals. But beginning just north of the Woodland Plantation Inn, pictured on bottles of Southern Comfort whiskey, Katrina's wake became evident: Telephone poles leaned as if exhausted. Arthritic trees were shorn of leaves and limbs. The roof of a parish maintenance building remained curled up like some sheet-metal crustacean.

Outside the cemetery in Diamond, a coffin unprotected by a concrete sheath lay rusted and partly opened, still unclaimed since it had washed onto the highway during the storm. The office of the Palm Terrace Motel in Port Sulphur, reduced to a door frame and a pink wall, sat untouched, a monument of rubble. In Venice, where the highway ended, the marina still lacked a hoist for the shrimp fleet, so fishermen had to jump into the water to repair their propellers and drive shafts.

Most of the small businesses had returned to Port Sulphur—the doughnut shop, Delta Drugs, the dollar stores, Guilbeau's gas and convenience store. Perhaps half the town's three thousand residents had also returned. A few homes were being repaired in lower Plaquemines, but mostly it was a double-wide recovery, everything in trailers and modular buildings. At least a third of the thirty-eight South Plaquemines players still lived in FEMA trailers. Mike Barthelemy Jr., a freshman linebacker, slept on an air mattress as his family awaited its rebuilding grant from the state. Shane Dinette, a senior running back and linebacker, preferred to commute about fifty miles each way from the New Orleans suburbs rather than live in a trailer behind his mother's restaurant, five minutes from school.

"Not much down here," he said. "Too depressing."

The continued vulnerability of lower Plaquemines was evident in a dormitory being constructed in Venice for river pilots, who guided freighters through Southwest Pass to and from the Gulf of Mexico. The bunkhouse sat on twenty-four-square-inch cement supports, twenty-five feet off the ground. This evident sturdiness only enhanced the sense of fragility and susceptibility of those who lived below in trailers.

Once a week, Lynn Holland, a mental-health therapist and family counselor, traveled to the Plaquemines Parish Medical Center in Port Sulphur. Since Katrina, she found escalating cases of acute anxiety and depression. People felt dislocated and cramped inside their trailers. An eighty-year-old woman had her land taken so that the levees could be expanded and strengthened in Port Sulphur; she was living elsewhere in a trailer now but had heard nothing from the state or the U.S. Army Corps of Engineers about where she would eventually go, and when. On the east bank of the river, a family with a handicapped child still awaited electricity and running water so they could move into their trailer.

Young children told Holland they were scared of storms. When clouds pushed through with their dark, reptilian shapes, and the wind picked up and rain began to fall in this subtropical place, kids began to hyperventilate and cry and dread going to school. They feared losing their homes again, their toys. Incidents of domestic abuse were up. People were living on top of each other in their trailers. Tensions built; tempers exploded. Children asked where they could go to get away, to escape the yelling and hitting, to find a quiet place to do their homework. Try the front steps, Holland told them, or sit beneath a tree in the yard.

At the FEMA trailer park in nearby Diamond, some parents were afraid to let their children outside because drugs were being sold openly. Teenagers were bored, Holland said, so they increasingly resorted to drinking, drugs, sex.

"Everybody is so stressed out," Holland said. "They want to know, 'How am I going to get back in my home?'"

At South Plaquemines High, the walkways were named Hurricane Alley, Katrina Way, and Rita Way. Denita Tate, who taught tenth- and twelfth-grade English, said her students still felt a piercing sense of loss. Daily, the adjacent, wrecked campus of Port Sulphur High reminded them of Katrina's damage. Many of her students seemed too distracted to do homework. A number of them lived with relatives other than their parents. Some had parents who were incarcerated or battling addictions to drugs. One of her female students walked the levees at night because her mother was not home and she had no other place to go.

Yet despite the anxiety and uncertainty, many were determined to rebuild in the area. Some could not afford to move elsewhere. Others would not consider anyplace else. Cases of high blood pressure were "through the roof," but so was a desire to regain some sense of familiarity, said Dr. Vincent Michell, a physician at the medical center. Once after the storm, he treated a woman whose husband had hooked her in the back of the head with an artificial fishing lure. "Don't throw that bait away," the husband told the doctor, retrieving the Deadly Dudley and heading with his wife right back into the teeming marshes.

Asked why people came back, the answer was simple: this was home. "You can move around down here," Beau Fitte, Lyle's younger brother and a freshman defensive end, said. Everybody knew everybody. Many people were related. What little they had, they willingly shared.

It was a place where cooks knew how to smother a raccoon in wild onions until the meat fell from the bone, and how to precisely stick a pig and catch the pulsing in a bucket to make the sausage known as blood boudin. Some picked a nonpoisonous type of nightshade, called morel, and used it with spinach, mustard greens, turnip greens, and cabbage to make a grass gumbo. A friend might drive past and drop off a sack of oysters for dinner. Or he might offer a cooler of redfish or a bag of teal and greenhead ducks.

"Where else you gonna find that?" asked Anthony LaFrance, an assistant football coach.

Only the lazy would go hungry in a place like Port Sulphur and Diamond and Happy Jack, Debra Fitte, Lyle's grandmother, said in her raspy, cigarette voice. Dinner was no farther than the end of a fishing hook or the barrel of a gun.

"Country people don't starve," she said.

She could afford to be patient while waiting for rebuilding assistance, she said. She could pull up a chair and "cop a squat on the porch" of her trailer in Diamond, watching ships roll up and down the river. If the wind was right, you could hear the music when a cruise ship passed. Otherwise, it was quiet, safe. You didn't have to put up with the neighbor blaring his radio or feel afraid to walk down the street. New Orleans remained one of the country's deadliest cities. In lower Plaquemines, there were a few knuckleheads around, but everyone knew who they were.

"I wouldn't trade it, me," Deb Fitte said. In the New Orleans suburb of Gretna, she said, "People always have a frown on their face. Like they afraid they gonna get shot. Down here, people live free."

And now her three grandsons—Lyle, who was sixteen; Beau, who was fifteen; and Evan, who was fourteen—were with her again, playing football for South Plaquemines. Everybody called her Gram, and she wore airbrushed T-shirts bearing her grandsons' names and brought them sports drinks and chips at practice each day. "My Tee Bébés," she called them in her French accent.

A junior, Lyle Fitte was an honor student, taking English, chemistry, algebra, and American history. He was already in an encouraging position to qualify for a college football scholarship, having scored a nineteen on his ACT exam as a sophomore. His mother had been valedictorian at Port Sulphur High in 1990. Avis Fitte had an associate's degree and had intended to get her bachelor's in accounting when Katrina struck. Now it was Lyle's intent to use football as a way to become the first in his family to graduate from college. As the season progressed, he would receive mail from such schools as Ohio State, Villanova, the University of Hawaii, and the University of Miami.

"I always listen to what Coach Crutchfield says: 'Your mom and dad had y'all in poverty and you're gonna have your children in poverty,'" Lyle said. "I'm going to stop that. I'm going to get my degree. I'm going to end the curse."

He was handsome and sculpted and wore braces. Crutchfield sometimes teased him about his vanity: "Hey mirror, I'm Lyle Fitte. I'm pretty." If he appeared to the coaches selfish and overly concerned about his statistics, though, it seemed to be a necessary selfishness. Football was his way out, and he seemed determined not to miss his chance. Lyle kept a set of makeshift weight-lifting equipment in his grandmother's gutted house, the rusty bar wrapped with electrical tape. He could bench-press 290 pounds and was the second-strongest player on the team. Several mornings a week, he awakened at five thirty and ran a series of sprints up the sixteen-foot river levee outside his trailer.

"I don't know if it's a lack of drive to do better, because no one else has done it, or what's holding kids back," Big Wayne Williamson said. "We have just as much talent as anyone, but most of them don't do anything with it out of high school. Maybe they're thinking, 'Well, others didn't make it, so how can I make it?' Sometimes you get the feeling they're afraid to leave home, afraid to go try."

Only 61 percent of the adults in Port Sulphur had an education level of high school or above, according to the 2000 census. Once, well-paying jobs were plentiful on fishing boats and in the oil fields. A high-school diploma wasn't necessary for a comfortable life. Now there were fewer of those jobs. The need for an education had become more urgent. Yet only 5 percent of Port Sulphur's adult residents had a bachelor's degree; parishwide, that number was just under 11 percent. Many players grew up in single-parent households. Crutchfield said that they often seemed to lack self-assurance and discipline and encouragement at home. In a place of grinding poverty and underemployment, education suffered as a priority.

"I think this culture here is a generation behind," he said.

Katrina had battered the education system as well as the homes and buildings in lower Plaquemines. It was still difficult to get a full complement of certified teachers. The first battery of post-hurricane standardized tests revealed mixed results. The students at South Plaquemines met or exceeded state averages in math and science, but only about 39 percent were reading at grade level or above.

"Kids moving place to place, some lost their fundamentals," Stanley Gaudet, the South Plaquemines principal, said. "We're starting to move on, but we might be further behind than we were then. I think we lost some of our best students overall. They didn't come back. I try to get kids to set goals, to get their parents to have high aspirations. You have twelve- and thirteen-year-olds who went to three or four schools after the storm. You lose your stability."

Crutchfield heard whispers in the parish that he cared only about football, that he used his players for his own gain. It was demonstrably untrue, but even his girlfriend's sister thought Crutchfield should not keep anyone on the team if the player's grades fell below a certain average, even though he might still be eligible for football. What was he supposed to do? Crutchfield asked. Report cards went to the parents, too. Didn't they have a responsibility to their sons? If a kid was eligible, he asked, why should he kick him off the team?

Colleen Carroll, an English teacher at South Plaquemines, said she was impressed by how much Crutchfield did for the school. "If I have a problem with discipline or grades, sometimes I just have to mention his name and kids straighten right up," she said. "He really does care."

At the same time, she believed Louisiana ought to raise the grade-point minimum above the current 1.5 average needed to remain eligible for sports.

"I feel like we're almost undermining these kids' potential," Carroll said. "They're capable. If we allow them to be complacent, they'll be complacent. If we don't challenge them, a lot of them won't seek to challenge themselves."

Crutchfield spoke to his players frequently about improving their grades so that they might be eligible for football scholarships. He set up tutoring for them after school. Some got the message too late. Terrance Jones, the star quarterback of Port Sulphur's 2002 state-championship team, told Crutchfield, "Coach, I didn't know I was going to be that good."

As far as Crutchfield knew, no players from Port Sulphur High had received a college football scholarship before he became head coach in 1999. Since then, a half dozen had received grants-in-aid. Several dropped out without a degree, but three of his former players were in college on scholarships now. Kenny Guidroz, a receiver from Port Sulphur's state-championship team of 2002, was a fifth-year senior at Tulane, scheduled to graduate. Among players from the 2006 South Plaquemines team, defensive lineman Devin Boutwell was now a freshman at Southeastern Louisiana. Rodney Bartholomew Jr., an all-state receiver, was playing basketball at Corning Community College in New York State.

"I think Katrina gave them hope that if they can come back and deal with this, they can go through anything," Crutchfield said. "I just wish kids would step up and break the cycle. I think it's coming."

Lyle Fitte was determined to be one of those players. This was the beginning of his junior season, when scouts would start to take notice. He could think of no more satisfying way to start than to defeat Belle Chasse, his former team. He kept in touch with a number of the players from up the road. If South Plaquemines won, he would be immune from their trash talking for an entire year. If the Hurricanes lost, he'd never hear the end of it. As he did before each game, Fitte wrote "GOD" on the tape wrapped over his cleats. During warm-ups, he knelt in the end zone and said a prayer. And he told his teammates, "Put the ball in my hands."

SOUTH PLAQUEMINES WON THE TOSS AND DEFERRED POSsession until the second half. Belle Chasse received the ball and fell under immediate pressure from a ravenous defense. "We gonna devour them, eat they ass up," Crutchfield had told his players. The Hurricanes were physically stronger this year. The coaches had power-washed the ruined gym on campus and had set up a weight room on the basketball court. A year ago, the weight-lifting equipment sat in a cargo container and the Hurricanes got pushed around. Not this year. Crutchfield applied relentless pressure on defense, sending at least six players charging across the line on each play. Many people said that South Plaquemines relied on speed, which was meant as a compliment but also served as a slight to predominantly black teams. Yes, South Plaquemines was fast. And the Hurricanes did gamble as they tried to rattle the opposing quarterback. But they did not take reckless chances. Crutchfield spent a great deal of time crafting his defenses. His players were sophisticated in recognizing formations, filling gaps, reading the intent of offensive linemen as they pulled and trapped.

Belle Chasse quickly became unnerved. Quarterback Blake Matherne was sacked for a seven-yard loss on the game's first play. A penalty for illegal motion followed, then a screen pass that lost a yard. A few minutes later, Matherne threw a pass that South Plaquemines cornerback Bradley Sylve should have intercepted for a touchdown. With two minutes remaining in the first half, Belle Chasse finally cracked. A snap to the punter sailed over his head for a safety, and the Hurricanes went ahead 2–0.

It was hardly a secure lead. Crutchfield stood on the sidelines, signaling plays with crisp motions of his hands. He spread the field with four and five receivers, stretching defenses thin and carving them with screens and sweeps and counters and options. But there were no secrets in a game against a parish rival. Bob Becnel had Belle Chasse prepared. The Cardinals were calling out the South Plaquemines plays before the Hurricanes could run them. They were beating the Hurricanes to the point of attack. Crutchfield feared a game of attrition. Belle Chasse, with a larger roster, seemed to be playing rope-a-dope, conserving energy, trying to wear South Plaquemines down on a hot, muggy night.

The tactic appeared to be working as the second half opened. The legs of the South Plaquemines players began to cramp. Ridge Turner was playing both quarterback and cornerback. Even his stomach began to seize up, and he grimaced in pain. With two minutes remaining in the third quarter, Ridge composed himself and threw a thirty-three-yard pass down the left sideline. Then Lyle Fitte scored from six yards to give the Hurricanes an 8–0 lead. He ran with his chest jutted forward, dipping and darting. And he had the patience and anticipation that coaches often referred to as "vision," an uncanny sense of knowing where the hole would open.

"The best I've coached at setting up his blockers," Roger Halphen said.

The two-point try failed, though, and as the fourth quarter opened, Belle Chasse tied the score. Ridge was beaten in the secondary on a thirty-four-yard touchdown pass. Pass coverage was the one weakness in South Plaquemines' defense. Crutchfield grew irritated because his cornerbacks frequently did not look back at the ball when it was in the air. Another pass on the extra point drew Belle Chasse even at 8–8. Ridge's legs spasmed again. Gaudet and Marcelin Ancar, an assistant coach, tried to massage the knots out of his legs.

More players kept cramping. With four minutes remaining, Belle Chasse reached the South Plaquemines' nine-yard line. Then the game was halted for ten or fifteen minutes by a severe injury to one of the Hurricanes. Shane Dinette fractured his left arm. He lay there as his jersey was cut away and screamed as a foam splint was placed on his arm. Crutchfield gathered his players. The game seemed to be slipping away.

"I don't feel like hearing about this for another year," Lyle admonished his teammates. "I don't."

Play resumed, and a Belle Chasse pass fell incomplete in the end zone on third down. Facing fourth down at the Hurricanes' nine-yard line, Matherne lined up in the shotgun for Belle Chasse and rolled left but Lyle intercepted his pass in the end zone. South Plaquemines had one final chance.

Three minutes, thirty-nine seconds remained. The Hurricanes went to their most reliable play, counter left, running it a half-dozen times in succession. Belle Chasse knew it was coming but could not stop it. For the Hurricanes, right guard Felix Barthelemy and right tackle Jordan Ancar kept pulling ahead of Lyle and Ridge, forming a convoy for one, then the other, until South Plaquemines had reached the Cardinals' five-yard line. Only a half minute remained now. Crutchfield wanted Lyle to throw a halfback pass, but left tackle Caileb Ancar said, "Coach, we can't risk that."

So Lyle carried again on a counter inside the one-yard line. South Plaquemines had no time-outs left. As the players lined up, confusion took hold. The umpire had spotted the ball outside the left hash mark. Before it could be snapped, the referee intervened, picked up the ball, and moved it nearer the center of the field. The mix-up bewildered the Hurricanes.

"Hey, wait!"

"You not going to call time-out?"

"You can't do that!"

On the final play, the center snap was awkward and Belle Chasse sent a ferocious blitz. Ridge was tackled back at the nine-yard line as time expired, sending the game into overtime.

Each team would get a chance to score from the ten-yard line in the extra period. South Plaquemines never regained its composure. On third down from the five-yard line, the receiver Cantrelle Riley ran a slant pattern instead of a designed route to the corner of the end zone. Ridge's pass was intercepted. Belle Chasse needed only one more play to win. On first down, Matherne threw to the back of the end zone, and there was no South Plaquemines defender within ten yards of the Cardinals' receiver. Belle Chasse won 14–8, and Matherne sprinted off the field in celebration.

"They had been calling him all week, saying what they were going to do to him," Becnel said of the South Plaquemines players.

Lyle Fitte threw his helmet in disgust. In the team trailer, he removed his jersey and shoulder pads and began shouting as many of his teammates sobbed.

"We came early in the morning all summer for this?" he asked. "The whole fucking parish was down here. Fuck. We gotta deal with that shit for a whole year. You know how many coaches and students and teachers wanted us to win? We might win the state championship, but when we come back to Plaquemines Parish we'll hear, 'Y'all lost to us.' They'll tell me, 'You shoulda stayed with us.' I don't want to hear that shit."

Crutchfield sat slumped in a chair. For the fourth consecutive time, he had lost a game to Becnel and Belle Chasse. No one in lower Plaquemines would let him forget it.

"I ain't going out the house," Crutchfield said. "I might need a police escort. They might kill me."

9

"I CAN'T SIT. I'VE GOT TO PLAY."

MARCELIN ANCAR WAS STILL THINKING ABOUT THE BELLE Chasse game: "You can win the rest of your games, but that one will still come back to haunt you." It was a week later. South Plaquemines was on the road at Hammond High, a Class 5A school. Ancar was too excited and nervous to eat as the Hurricanes pulled into a McDonald's for their pregame meal. A friendly, excitable bear of a man, he had been an all-state center at Port Sulphur High in 1984. Now he worked for the parish wastewater treatment plant. He had also received his coaching license this season to assist Crutchfield. This would give him a chance to coach his sons, Jordan, a senior tackle, and Maverick, a freshman lineman.

Almost yearly, the family visited Disney World. And except for a Port Sulphur High Bronchos mug, two boxes of Disney Christmas ornaments were about the only things recovered after Katrina pushed the Ancar home into a canal in the community of Happy Jack, just north of Port Sulphur. The family evacuated to Tennessee, outside Memphis, but there was never any question that the Ancars would return to Plaquemines Parish. "We're country folks," said Jeanitta Ancar, who traveled by ferry each day to manage the cafeteria at Phoenix High on the east bank of the Mississippi. "This is all we know."

Happy Jack provided some of the country's best sport-fishing waters. The marshes were ripe with redfish and speckled trout, and Marcelin was highly skilled in the ways of the bayou taught to him by his grandparents. His sons discovered their own wily, if unorthodox, methods. Some people used artificial bait for fishing; Jordan once used his grandfather's artificial limb. As his mother remembered, he tied a string to the toe and dropped a line into the water as a young boy while his grandfather called after him, "Jordan, PawPaw needs his leg."

THE ANCARS EMBODIED THE CULTURAL, RACIAL, AND ETHNIC diversity of southern Louisiana. One of the state's prominent historians, Carl Brasseaux, called it perhaps the most complex rural society in North America in his book *A Primer on Francophone Louisiana*. Limiting the description of Louisiana's residents to Cajuns was as dubious as describing all Texans as cowboys.

Brasseaux, director of the Center for Louisiana Studies at the University of Louisiana–Lafayette, found eighteen distinct groups of French speakers who immigrated to the state after it became a French colony in 1699. They include Acadian (Cajun) exiles who refused to pledge fealty to British rule in Nova Scotia in the 1750s; refugees from a slave revolt in what is now Haiti in the late 1790s and early 1800s; and twentieth-century arrivals such as French Jews avoiding persecution, Lebanese Christians, and Belgian war brides.

The narrow peninsula of Plaquemines Parish served as an eclectic branching of the state's genealogical tree. Its boughs were sinuous and tangled, reflecting Louisiana's Native American heritage, French and Spanish colonialism, and African and West Indian enslavement.

It was here, in the delta below Venice, that the explorer La Salle planted a cross in 1682 and claimed the Mississippi River basin for France, naming it Louisiane in tribute to Louis XIV. Plaquemines became one of the state's original parishes in 1807, four years after the Louisiana Purchase. From the 1770s to the 1980s, divergent groups arrived: Canary Islanders whose descendents, known as Islenos, preserved their Spanish dialect and narrative poems; Filipinos who built fishing villages on stilts; Croatians who introduced the oyster industry; Italians who assisted as sharecroppers in the sugarcane harvest and became truck farmers; Irish who built canals and levees; blacks who came from the Carolinas to work on menhaden boats; Vietnamese shrimpers who fled Communist takeover; and Cambodian fishermen who suffered at the genocidal hands of the Khmer Rouge.

Isolation and diversity gave identity in lower Plaquemines Parish a varied and indeterminate feel, like the marsh itself, where land met water and the place was not one thing or the other but a blend of many things. Boundaries were fluid and contradictory; labels were imprecise and risky.

Nowhere did identity appear as complicated as it did in the area from which Marcelin Ancar and his wife, Jeanitta, came in lower Plaquemines—communities like West Pointe a la Hache, Diamond, Happy Jack, and Grand Bayou, where the residents were of mixed French, Native American, Spanish, and African descent.

Although some whites in the area considered him black, and some blacks considered him white, Marcelin considered himself neither. He identified himself as Indian. In a cultural sense, he called himself French.

Marcelin's grandparents spoke French, with his grandmothers learning their English at church. When his oldest son, Jordan, was in preschool, his teacher sent a note home: Jordan was having trouble pronouncing the names of animals. As it turns out, he was having no trouble at all. He was saying the words in French taught to him by his grandfather.

Three of his grandparents were Indian, Marcelin said, and one was white. His grandmothers had high cheekbones and straight, coal-black hair, though Marcelin said he was uncertain with which tribe he was affiliated.

Some in lower Plaquemines identified themselves as descendents of Attakapa Indians, whose settlements were scattered primarily across southwestern Louisiana in the early eighteenth century and who were stereotyped as warlike man-eaters. The Attakapas were said to use alligators for meat and hides and their oil for insect repellent, to use Spanish moss for baby diapers and to believe a creation myth in which man emerged from the sea in an oyster shell.

Others in lower Plaquemines identified themselves as being from the Houma tribe. There were scattered Houma communities in places like Happy Jack and Grand Bayou. The Houma people first encountered French explorers in the late 1600s. A red stick marking the edge of their territory gave the name to Baton Rouge, Louisiana's capital. Contact with colonial settlers and planters marginalized the Houmas and forced them deeper into the bayous and marshes of southeastern Louisiana, primarily in Terrebonne and Lafourche parishes, where they adapted to their isolated surroundings as fishermen and trappers.

In the mid–1800s, according to Brasseaux, the historian, Houma people intermarried with French speakers and took Cajun French as their principal language. A small number of Houma Indians also intermarried with blacks and were known by the derogatory term "Sabines"; until the 1960s, Houma people were prevented from attending white schools in southeastern Louisiana. Federal recognition of the Houma tribe has remained elusive.

According to some anthropologists, the self-identity of modern Houmas was rooted, in part, in an effort by multiracial people to avoid being viewed as black in a state that once legalized prejudice. Marcelin Ancar said he did not consider himself to be of African ancestry. His wife, Jeanitta, said she did not believe she was of African ancestry, either, "but you never know."

"It's very confusing at times," she said. "We're just one big gumbo down here. The races, the food, everything is mixed."

Marcelin sometimes listened to Cajun music, and at other times favored the country sounds of Hank Williams Sr., Conway Twitty, and Loretta Lynn. He named Jordan after one of the members of the Backstreet Boys singing group. Maverick, his youngest son, was named after the Tom Cruise character in *Top Gun*, the movie Marcelin and Jeanitta watched just before their youngest son was born.

"Good thing we weren't watching *I Love Lucy*," Marcelin said.

When he transferred to Port Sulphur High in 1981 from St. Jude's Mission School in Diamond, which many French-and-Indian kids attended, Marcelin said that one of his teachers asked the white students to stand up, then the black students. He said the teacher asked him why he remained sitting, and he replied, "You didn't call my race."

He said he was sent to the principal's office, where he explained what happened. The teacher was later reprimanded.

"Down here, a lot of people tell you what they want you to be," Marcelin said. "They think you're white or black, nothing in the middle. The whites consider you black; the blacks say, 'You're not black but you're afraid to say you're white.' I say don't let anyone tell you who you are."

At seventeen, Jordan Ancar said half-jokingly, he based his identity on the kind of day he was having. "If I'm having a bad day, I'm black," he said. "If I'm having a good day, I'm white. If I'm having a middle day, I'm Native American."

As for an expected state championship this season, Jordan said, "I plan on being white after that game."

In addition to French and Indian, some mixed-race residents of Happy Jack, West Pointe a la Hache, and Diamond referred to themselves as Creoles. This was a complicated term whose meaning contracted and expanded like the bellows of an accordion. During Louisiana's colonial period from 1699 to 1803, it generally referred to whites and blacks who were born in the region. Later it was a term used by elites of French and Spanish ancestry to distinguish themselves from the Cajuns, who were considered lower class. Mixed-race descendants of slaves freed before the Civil War, known as free persons of color, also came to identify themselves as Creoles. Currently, according to Brasseaux, most people who call themselves Creoles are descended from French-speaking slaves freed during or just after the Civil War.

Creoles of color have generally been referred to by their separateness, as a people not accepted as white but not willing to be considered black. The anthropologist Eric Waddell described these Creoles as being "caught in the twilight zone between two ethnic movements," appearing to be black but sharing many of the cultural traditions of French Acadians, or Cajuns.

Shadings of color became an urgent issue in Plaquemines Parish during the half century that it was ruled by the political boss Leander H. Perez Sr., who held that blacks were inferior to whites. The oil boom that began in the 1930s also changed a culture in which people of various races and ethnic groups had generally worked side by side with little animosity, James Conaway wrote in a biography of Perez called *Judge*.

The discovery of oil intensified competition for jobs and brought to Plaquemines Parish white workers who carried "their own, more virulent racism" from elsewhere in the South, Conaway wrote.

"Black men who went away to war returned to find Plaquemines a changed parish, with white families moving out of their communities and old white friends pretending not to know them," Conaway wrote. "The ugly practice of proving one's white birthright became de rigueur for voting, marriage and good parish jobs. People had to account for generations of ancestors and went to absurd lengths to prove there was no 'touch of the brush' in their family, all of which created a climate of uncertainty and misery and, eventually, violence."

During the Perez rule in Plaquemines, Marcelin Ancar said, his grandfather attended a Catholic Church in the community of Myrtle Grove where whites sat in pews on one side and blacks on the other. One day his grandfather was told that he couldn't sit on the white side, so he left, returned with a shotgun, and asked, "Which side did you say I had to sit on?"

Even after the Perez family dominance ended in the 1980s, race continued to be a complicated issue in lower Plaquemines Parish, as it was everywhere. "The distinction between Creoles of color and blacks has been contentious, with some Creoles looking down on American blacks and with countercharges that Creoles are denying their African-American identity," the anthropologist James White wrote in "Cultural Gumbo?" a 1998 ethnographic overview of the Mississippi Delta written for the National Park Service.

Young players on the South Plaquemines team were overheard talking about girlfriends, saying, "If she can't use a comb, don't bring her home," and "If she's darker than a paper bag, don't bring her home." These were lingering references to the largely discontinued "comb test" and "paper-bag test" by which Creoles of color kept darker-skinned blacks from attending dances and other social events.

Mike Barthelemy Jr., a freshman linebacker and running back who was light skinned and considered himself French and Indian or Creole, said he had encountered a racial twist when he was nine or ten: The coach of his Bantam League team, who was black, did not want him to play running back. "He thought I was white and that I wouldn't be good enough," Barthelemy said.

His father, Mike Barthelemy Sr., sometimes lamented that "freestylin'"—intermarriage between blacks and those who considered themselves French-and-Indian or Creoles—would mean the demise of "my people." At the same time, Mike Sr. said, Katrina's destruction had largely blown away the importance of these distinctions along with his house.

Now, he said, "I'm just a man. I'm not black, white, Creole. I got past that."

Post-Katrina, there appeared to be a new commonality among the people who lived in lower Plaquemines. They had lost everything and had returned because this was home. And they needed validation that their decision to come back had been the right one. The football stadium provided a gathering place, and the South Plaquemines football team showed it was possible to unite communities that were caustic rivals. A state championship might signal something that a slow, sometimes seemingly disinterested, government response had not: that lower Plaquemines would not be forgotten, that the future could be inviting and familiar. Players sat with their arms around each other's shoulders, sometimes stroked each other's hair, slept at each other's houses, lay in a tangle on the floor of the trailer of a locker room, listening to music before games, quietly preparing for the evening's rough muscularity.

Once the games started, Cambodian players ran downfield on kickoffs, Indian kids blocked for black kids, white players caught passes, and Creoles made ferocious tackles on defense. This sense of multiple identity—people who were "neither nor" but also "both and"—represented a multiculturalism that could be instructive to outsiders, said Nick Spitzer, an anthropologist and folklorist at the University of New Orleans.

"In football, a guard makes a great block, an Indian guy springs a black guy and it's a nice human story," Spitzer said. "You don't have to be in Greenwich Village saying, 'I'm Bohemian, European, Arab, black,' playing with it as a personal statement of how cool you are. People just are those things."

PERHAPS NO FAMILY WAS AS HEAVILY INVOLVED IN FOOTBALL in lower Plaquemines as the Ancars. Jordan and Maverick played for the Hurricanes. Marcelin was an assistant coach. Jeanitta washed the team uniforms after each game. Their daughter, Taylor, who was twelve, kept statistics on the sideline.

Marcelin could still feel, more than two decades later, the emptiness of losing his final play-off game at Port Sulphur in 1984. He had stood at midfield, his wrists still taped, his helmet still on his head. When someone said, "Let's go," he said, "Where?" He stood there. *What just happened?* he asked himself over and over after a stinging one-point defeat.

"Don't worry," his father had told him. "It'll be okay."

"What do you mean, it'll be okay?" he had replied. "We lost and I can't play anymore."

He had tried to walk home, but his father would not let him.

He lost his letter jacket in Katrina's swamping, then cried when his wife bought him a replica. Even now, Marcelin often struggled to sleep the night before games. Sometimes, he walked up and down the street to soothe the anxiety of anticipation, or took a stroll along the river levee.

Port Sulphur had won a state championship in 1981, Marcelin's freshman season. Now he wanted his sons to experience that same exultant feeling. Jordan, who stood six foot tall, had one final chance. This was his senior year. Since last season, he had shed his baby fat through a regimen of weight lifting, dropping from 225 pounds to 205 pounds and losing four inches from his waistline. Crutchfield had once considered him soft and weak, dismissing him as a "pussy." Now Jordan was the most improved of all the South Plaquemines linemen. "He just leapt forward," Roger Halphen, who coached the linemen, said of Jordan. "He's a headhunter, always looking for somebody to block downfield." His parents expected Jordan to attend college and get a degree—they once nearly pulled him from the team because he made a C on his report card—but now his senior season was in jeopardy just as it began.

Forty-eight hours before tonight's Hammond game, Jordan had broken two bones in his left hand while blocking a punt in practice. The angle of the fractures was so severe that the bones could not be set with a cast. As the Hurricanes walked into the McDonald's in Hammond, Jordan had his left arm in a sling and his hand wrapped in a splint.

"I want to play," Jordan had told the doctor.

"You can't."

"My team needs me."

Even so, the doctor said, Jordan might be out four to eight weeks. That could sideline him for the rest of the regular season, his final season. Football was the main reason he had wanted to come back to lower Plaquemines after Katrina. Jordan started crying, and his father walked out of the doctor's office. It was too painful to watch. The Ancars called Cyril Crutchfield about two thirty in the morning to give him the bad news about his starting right tackle.

"He looked like he lost a family member," Micquella Sylve, Crutchfield's girlfriend, said.

Bubba Miller, another South Plaquemines lineman, was also out, with cartilage damage in his knee. The Hurricanes would have to use three defensive linemen for the Hammond game, instead of four.

"We're in a bind," Crutchfield said.

As the team dressed in a practice gym, he got a phone call. It was Randall Mackey. Bastrop High was again ranked number 1 in Class 4A and had won its season opener a week ago.

"What are you doing?" Randall wanted to know.

"What are *you* doing?" a startled Crutchfield asked.

He then offered some advice to his former player: Quit running so much and start throwing the ball more. They hung up after a couple of minutes, and Crutchfield said, "Boy, they must have an easy one tonight."

The South Plaquemines game would feature two teams who drew their nicknames from natural disasters, the Hurricanes versus the Tornadoes. Both had lost their opening games. The South Plaquemines players appeared lethargic during warm-ups. Perhaps they were still thinking about the loss to Belle Chasse. "They should be playing 'Taps,'" Roger Halphen said to the players. "Y'all look like a bunch of rats being fed to a snake."

The mood lightened immediately as Cantrelle Riley returned the opening kickoff for South Plaquemines to the Hammond two-yard line. Lyle Fitte took a pitch into the end zone and a two-point conversion put the Hurricanes up 8–0.

Jordan Ancar paced the sideline in his khakis and his white jersey, number 64. Then he took a seat on the bench. Impatient, he said, "I can't sit. I've got to play."

His mother came to the fence surrounding the field, and as he spoke to her, tears filled Jordan's eyes. Jeanitta Ancar hugged her son and said they would get a second opinion next week.

"I can't stand to see him crying," she said, dressed in a T-shirt airbrushed with the names and jersey numbers of her sons. "We've got to get somebody to help us. It's killing him not to be in that game."

A two-yard run on a counter put the Hurricanes ahead 16–3. Jordan beseeched his father, "Dad, they need me."

"Go by your momma," Marcelin Ancar replied.

Jordan returned to the bench, crying. His teammates came by to comfort him.

"We got your back," Riley said.

Jordan's hand was out of the sling now.

"I can't sit much longer," he said. "I'm about to take somebody's pads."

Jeremy Sylve, South Plaquemines' starting right guard, wrenched an ankle, and Jordan again approached his father.

"What are you doing?" Marcelin Ancar screamed.

"I gotta play."

"Well, you can't."

Ridge Turner threw a twenty-six-yard touchdown pass, and South Plaquemines took a 24–3 lead at halftime. Sal Cepriano, the left guard, patted Ridge on the head and said, "You run this team now. Way to get going."

In the locker room, Marcelin Ancar said, "This is the team that should have showed up last week."

With heavy rain fast approaching, the referees tried to speed up the second half. Lyle scored again on a counter, running forty-three yards to the end zone. He would rush for 250 yards in the game. Ridge completed a seven-yard curl pass for the final score in a 39–3 victory. The Hurricanes were 1–1.

"I think y'all can go deep in the playoffs," said a Hammond assistant coach, Hiram Porter, who had played with Crutchfield in college.

In the locker room, Crutchfield spoke to principal Stanley Gaudet. "Now we're gonna open some eyes," he said.

It was pouring outside. Jordan Ancar took off his jersey and laid it in a pile with the other jerseys. His return seemed unthinkably distant. "Eight weeks is too long," he said.

Crutchfield's cell phone rang. His team had won, he told the caller, then asked, "Did you hear anything about the Belle Chasse game?" And then he called out, "Belle Chasse is going into over-time."

On the bus ride home, he learned that his parish nemesis had won again.

10

"LIKE PIT BULLS ON A FRESH PACK OF PORK CHOPS"

ON LONG ROAD TRIPS, THE CRUTCHFIELD RULES APPLIED: Every player had to wear a dress shirt and tie. His belt had to be visible. Earrings were forbidden. No talking was allowed at team meals. Everybody had to leave a dollar tip. Anyone violating these rules did so at his own risk.

After a four-hour trip to Opelousas, in the Cajun country, for a game against Northwest High School, South Plaquemines stopped to eat at Ryan's, a buffet-style restaurant. The chain had locations around the state and was Crutchfield's preferred choice for pregame meals. Usually, the restaurant had hamburger steaks and mashed potatoes prepared when the team arrived. As the players ate in a group, Sam McGinnis, a freshman receiver and defensive back, apparently did not know the travel rules or chose to ignore them. He talked and giggled, not loudly but audibly, and Crutchfield seemed to cross the room in one stride. He caught the freshman off guard and swatted him in the neck and side of the head.

"You think this is a joke?" Crutchfield asked the startled freshman. "You smiling?"

Later, McGinnis would say, "It got my mind right," but in this moment, his head stung from embarrassment. It was a harsh rite of passage for many who had played for Crutchfield. Once, he had nearly ripped the shirt off of his star running back, Josh Mackey, for talking during Port Sulphur's run to the 2002 state championship.

"We got it; now it's their turn," Little Wayne Williamson, a senior safety, said of McGinnis and the younger players as the Hurricanes left the restaurant. His voice lacked any trace of sympathy.

As the players boarded the bus and waited on Crutchfield, Rod Parker, an assistant coach, admonished them: "No talking; y'all know he's on the prowl."

There was not another sound during the twenty-minute drive to the stadium, except for the shimmying of the bus on country roads as it followed the flashing red and blue lights of a police escort.

AS HE DID EACH FRIDAY, BIG WAYNE WILLIAMSON ACCOM-panied the Hurricanes in his police cruiser. Big Wayne and his escorting partner, Rodney Bartholomew Sr., had played on the defensive line together at Port Sulphur in the late 1970s. They were longtime friends who had become sheriff's deputies for Plaquemines Parish. They had worked together so many years in escorting the team, first for Port Sulphur and now for South Plaquemines, that they operated with the same deftness of familiarity that athletes did. They were especially skillful in navigating the choked streets and bridges in the New Orleans area, one of them driving ahead to block off an intersection while the other guided the team bus smoothly through traffic in a law enforcement version of the pick-and-roll. Both deputies were in their late forties, and both thought this might be their last season traveling with the team. Bartholomew's son, Little Rodney (who was not so little at six foot six), was playing basketball at a community college in New York state. Little Wayne Williamson was a senior at South Plaquemines. Big Wayne planned to keep attending games, but he wanted to ride the bus instead of escorting it.

He had other business in Opelousas on this muggy September night. He had come to check on the three-bedroom home he had bought in southwestern Louisiana after Katrina. The hurricane had shoved Big Wayne's home in Port Sulphur forty feet off the property, into a stand of hackberry trees. Pieces of shingle were found in the trees, twenty-two feet off the ground. It seemed to him that a ghost had invaded his house. His two aquariums remained upright, full of water but empty of fish. ("I guess when the water got to a certain level, they said, 'We're outta here.'") In his bedroom closet, a pair of dress loafers had floated from the floor to a hanger rack, where they remained, side by side.

At forty-seven, Big Wayne thought it too risky to rebuild another home in Plaquemines Parish, so he chose Opelousas in St. Landry Parish. It was far enough inland to absorb the force of a hurricane, and it had a feeling of rural peacefulness. Katrina had not brought so much as a breeze to the town.

Big Wayne thought he might resettle here at some point and take a job with the St. Landry Parish sheriff's department. It would be easy enough to transfer his experience teaching crime prevention, school-bus safety, and an antidrug campaign called D.A.R.E. to schoolchildren.

After the 2006 season, he had brought Little Wayne to check out schools in Opelousas, but his son told him, "Dad, I'm from Port Sulphur. I want to graduate with my friends."

Before the hurricane, Big Wayne's home had been a kind of community center on weekends, kids playing football in the yard or the street, two or three televisions going in the living room. His favorite team had always been Alabama. People didn't believe him, but when he was a kid he had opened an encyclopedia to the entry on football, and there was a photograph of an Alabama player. *He must have played on a good team if his picture was in an encyclopedia*, Wayne thought. From that point, he was a Crimson Tide fan. This drove his friends crazy. Five years earlier, when Alabama last defeated Louisiana State University, several of his buddies took revenge by using weed killer to spray the initials LSU onto his lawn.

Since the storm, though, everything seemed fractured, displaced. Big Wayne and Little Wayne now saw each other mostly on game days. Little Wayne lived in Port Sulphur with his grandparents and his first cousin, Caileb Ancar. Big Wayne lived with other deputies in a trailer encampment called Cop Land. A season earlier, the trailer park had been located beside South Plaquemines High, but the landowner wanted the property back. Now Wayne lived in Davant on the east bank of the Mississippi. Given the long trip home tonight, there was no way he would catch the last ferry crossing at midnight.

NORTHWEST HIGH WAS SITUATED IN THE SOYBEAN AND HAY fields outside Opelousas. By the time the South Plaquemines bus arrived, its windshield was crusted with the splash of small flying insects called love bugs, which spent their adult lives engaged in something even more consuming than football—mating. Northwest was a Class 3A school with three times the enrollment of South Plaquemines. For the third consecutive week, the Hurricanes were playing a much larger school. It was part of Crutchfield's plan to get a high seed in the Class 1A playoffs through a complicated strength-of-schedule formula used by the state high school athletic association.

An air conditioner rattled in the South Plaquemines locker room, providing relief from the stultifying heat. Someone had placed a pink toilet cake atop the vents. The room smelled of industrial disinfectant. As the players dressed in their silver jerseys and dark blue pants, Crutchfield sat across a plaid love seat that seemed to belong in Archie Bunker's living room.

Three of the Hurricanes' linemen were hurt, but at least Jordan Ancar had received some good news. He would not need surgery to repair his broken left hand. This was only week three of a ten-game regular season, but Crutchfield said, "I'm bored. I'm ready for the play-offs."

"I know we're the best team in 1A," Crutchfield said. And turning to McGinnis, the callow freshman, he said, "That's why I slapped you deaf, Sam. It's important. It's life or death."

It was this demand for discipline and an insatiable desire to win that Big Wayne Williamson found most attractive in the coach. When Port Sulphur lost a play-off game in 2000, fueling talk that Crutchfield might take another job, Big Wayne asked him outside the locker room to stay in Plaquemines Parish while fans chanted, "Please don't leave."

If hitting a kid seemed harsh—and some parents had previously complained—Big Wayne believed it toughened the boys up, taught them how to become men. He had been paddled by his own coach at Port Sulphur. Upset with Little Wayne's behavior early in high school, he had once yanked his son right out of center field during a baseball game. His instructions to Crutchfield about Little Wayne were simple: "If he does something wrong, don't let him come home unpunished."

TONIGHT, CRUTCHFIELD WANTED SIX HUNDRED YARDS OF total offense for the Hurricanes and zero yards for Northwest. The Northwest coach had said in the local paper that he had spotted a weakness in the South Plaquemines defense. The Hurricanes appeared to be vulnerable in the middle against the run.

"Let's change their minds about that bullshit," Crutchfield told his players. "Lock 'em down and bring that pressure."

Two busloads of fans had traveled from lower Plaquemines. Big Wayne stood on the sideline in his khakis and a black T-shirt with "SHERIFF" across the back. It was good to see so many people coming out to support the team. "Normalcy," Williamson said. "This is what's holding us together, the pin in the cog."

Under a fingernail moon, the Hurricanes deflected a punt; Ridge Turner threw a thirty-yard pass and scored from one yard to put South Plaquemines ahead 7–0. A darting run by Lyle Fitte made it 14–0 five seconds into the second quarter. Northwest would find no weakness in the middle of the Hurricanes' defense. Linebacker Seth Ancar, a sophomore who returned to lower Plaquemines after playing elsewhere in 2006, clogged the middle with thirteen tackles and three sacks. This was Homecoming for Northwest, but early on the Raiders began to capitulate.

"Are we that good, or are we playing garbage?" Big Wayne asked as the Hurricanes took a 21–0 lead early in the second quarter. "This is too easy."

For the first time in more than a year, he could relax at a game. On August 30, 2006, two days before South Plaquemines' inaugural game, Big Wayne had been traveling home to Port Sulphur when he struck a car on Highway 23. The driver had run a stop sign and crossed four lanes of traffic, and Wayne broadsided the car, killing the man riding in the passenger seat.

He had known the victim, and every night he struggled to sleep, seeing the look on the man's face, a look of finality in his eyes. "Damn!" the man seemed to be saying. It haunted Big Wayne. Every time he closed his eyes, he saw the man looking at him, knowing he was about to die.

Big Wayne attended counseling and missed four games during the 2006 season. He considered quitting his escort job. Several years earlier, he had hit a deer after a game, forcing it off the road so it wouldn't collide with the Port Sulphur High team bus. But now his confidence was shattered. What if he made a mistake and the players got hurt? His partner, Rodney Bartholomew, convinced him to come back for one more year. Little Wayne was a senior. And there was a good chance South Plaquemines would win the state championship.

Two days before the Northwest game, the driver of the other car had pleaded guilty to negligent homicide. The man's lawyer had apologized in the courtroom in Belle Chasse, and Big Wayne had responded, "It was a year's worth of sleepless nights."

The driver's guilty plea seemed to dissolve Wayne's insomnia. That night, he dozed off quickly and slept without interruption, no longer tormented by the face of a man he was about to kill because of someone else's negligence.

On the sideline tonight, Big Wayne shifted from foot to foot with nervous football energy. He was the keeper of the flame for the sport in Port Sulphur. He participated in the pregame prayer, wore a championship ring from Port Sulphur's 2002 season, barbecued at the concession stand for home games, and served as the de facto team historian.

Only once had Wayne ever encountered any real trouble while escorting a team. It had happened in 1992, he said, when Port Sulphur High traveled to play McCall High School in Tallulah in northeastern Louisiana. Both teams were highly ranked. And as the Bronchos drove for the final touchdown in a 42–40 victory, McCall fans bunched on the sideline and told the Port Sulphur coach, "If your boys score again, we're going to have some problems."

At the final whistle, Wayne said, the Port Sulphur players and about a dozen fans found themselves surrounded by angry McCall boosters. "I was scared to death," Wayne said. He unsnapped the holster on his .357 and told the crowd, "If I've got to pull this out, I'm shooting into the crowd and I'm not shooting the same person twice."

Fortunately, someone had called the local police, who gave Port Sulphur an escort to the Mississippi state line after the team bus was pelted with bottles and eggs. The team spent the night in Vicksburg, Mississippi, and from that point, Wayne said, "I knew all the parish teams needed a police escort."

There was no such hostility tonight, only a solemn Homecoming for Northwest, which fell behind 35–7 by halftime as Ridge threw a fifty-six-yard touchdown pass to Lyle down the left sideline. Still, Crutchfield was not happy. Northwest had scored when the Hurricanes snapped the ball over Ridge's head in the shotgun formation. This could prove disastrous in the play-offs, Crutchfield reminded his players. It was a mistake as unforgivable as talking during a pregame meal.

"Garbage," Crutchfield said. "We're not playing like a championship team. No matter how good or bad the other team is, you've got to dominate. I don't care if you're playing your sister. Whip her ass. Playing against your grandma and grandpa? Whip their ass."

He abhorred drugs, which had ravaged Port Sulphur before Katrina. Crutchfield had even given up alcohol for this season, intent on winning another championship. But he spoke of his craving for victory, this compulsion for supremacy, as if it were a chemical dependency.

"I'm addicted," he told his players, gesturing furiously, pacing, as if he were in a courtroom instead of a locker room. "It's like cocaine. I'm about to lose my mind. That's how bad I want it. All I need is for you to want it. It's not about winning. It's about dominating.

"I'm asking you to raise up your expectations. It's right there. All you have to do is reach down and get some balls. Don't think I'm bitchin'. I'm not going to lie to you. I'm addicted. When we're all together, there is no better team in 1A. But you know what can happen when we get in the play-offs? There will be one team we're better than, but on that night, they're going to give us hell. Imagine if we screw up like that. I don't want any more bad snaps."

His mood brightened as Lyle took the second-half kickoff, dipped and feinted, and ran to his left untouched for seventy-eight yards to the end zone. Lyle then returned a punt fifty-three yards for a touchdown. Quickly, he was becoming one of the state's most resourceful players.

Little Wayne Williamson and the rest of the Hurricanes' defense kept muscling Northwest into submission. After a sledgehammering tackle on a punt return, Big Wayne laughed and said, "We're coming at 'em like pit bulls on a fresh pack of pork chops."

Little Wayne lacked the speed and skill of many of his teammates, but he possessed a sturdiness that allowed him to endure criticism from Crutchfield that could be merciless. Once, the coach had told him, "Why don't you tell your father to get his gun and shoot you?" Little Wayne had always taken this verbal abuse without saying a word, and Crutchfield had come to admire his toughness.

In the spring of 2007, Little Wayne had finished sixth in the state wrestling tournament in the 171-pound class, a remarkable achievement for his first participation in the sport. He had seemed distracted after Katrina, his father said, but wrestling and football had given him a purposeful direction. Over the summer, Little Wayne had participated in an Olympic-sponsored camp at the Citadel in South Carolina, wrestling seventeen matches in a week, and had wrestled in a national tournament in Fargo, North Dakota.

"The kid was tenacious; he just wouldn't quit," said Roger Halphen, who was also the head wrestling coach at South Plaquemines. "He'll fight you to the death."

Wayne's cousin, Caileb Ancar, the Hurricanes' left tackle, served as the team's quiet authority at five foot eight, 260 pounds. He called out instructions during calisthenics and led the daily prayer. Otherwise, he seldom said anything. When he did speak, this natural reserve lent heft and urgency to his words.

Since Katrina, Caileb had been separated from his mother, who now lived in Dallas. They talked every day, but he missed her guidance. "I was an honor roll student," Caileb said. "Now, it's harder to concentrate; there's a lot more to think about after the storm." His mother wanted him to move to Texas, but he preferred to finish his career in lower Plaquemines, playing for Crutchfield. Caileb and his coach were opposites in temperament, one demonstrative and flamboyant, the other taciturn, but they provided each other with a counterweight and shared an indomitable desire to win a state championship. Caileb had been an all-league tackle as a freshman and a junior, and Crutchfield considered him the best lineman that he had coached.

"He's so consistent," Crutchfield said. "He seldom makes a mistake and he never takes a play off."

Caileb was also one of the only South Plaquemines linemen who hadn't been injured. Early in the third quarter against Northwest, Sal Cepriano was blindsided by a crackback block while playing defensive tackle. He threw up on the field and curled into a fetal position on the sideline, cradling his head, and moaning, "My stomach."

He would be taken to the emergency room and then to a specialist, who would diagnose the injury as a lacerated liver and a bruised spleen. With a comfortable lead and a patchwork line, the Hurricanes lost their concentration and gave up two late touchdowns. The 49–21 victory improved South Plaquemines to 2–1, but the mood in the locker room was somber. Crutchfield demanded dominance, and the game had not met his standard.

"I feel like we lost," he told his players, who dressed quickly and boarded the bus.

Big Wayne climbed into his cruiser for the long ride home.

"They better not make a sound," he said.

11

"LIKE CHASING A GHOST"

THE STORM NAME IN WAITING WAS JERRY, A COMEDIAN'S name. For the first time since Katrina and Rita, a tropical weather system had moved into the Gulf of Mexico. Circulation was disorganized. No real center had formed as the storm meandered. Such meteorological indecision might have brought public relief or disregard in the past, but not anymore. Now vacillation brought menace.

"It's wait and see," Stanley Gaudet said on Thursday, September 20, 2007. This week, the Hurricanes were scheduled to play in suburban New Orleans on Saturday afternoon. The school had an extra day of flexibility to decide whether to play or postpone. Gaudet advised his teachers at South Plaquemines to move equipment away from classroom doors and to shut off computers when they left for the day.

"Even if the storm is close and not big, they've got to evacuate those FEMA trailers," Gaudet said.

The 2006 hurricane season had come and gone quietly. But southeastern Louisiana was an exposed place, and the tentative recovery from Katrina was now being threatened by another storm. Melancholy, survivor bravado, and wariness swelled with the tides.

"People are apprehensive," Gaudet said. "They used to not worry too much about hurricanes. It's a different ball game nowadays."

Through the day, oil workers evacuated rigs in the Gulf. More than a quarter of the region's daily output was shut down. Oil reached a record, above eighty-four dollars a barrel, over the fears of interruptions by the storm. Kathleen Babineaux Blanco, the Louisiana governor whose reelection chances had been scuttled by an indecisive and defeatist appearance after Katrina, declared a state of emergency. The National Guard was placed on alert. New Orleans officials planned to open three public schools as shelters for the city's fifteen thousand residents living in FEMA trailers. Several coastal high schools switched their football games to Thursday night from Friday. All of southeastern Louisiana braced for a storm that had no name and no certain path.

"It's been like chasing a ghost for two or three days," Mike Hoss, the weeknight anchor at WWL-TV in New Orleans, said on the ten p.m. newscast.

IN 1870—SIXTY-SEVEN YEARS AFTER THE LOUISIANA PUR-chase—the landmass of southeastern Louisiana was as fat and curved as a lobster claw. Now Plaquemines Parish jutted into the Gulf as a reedy finger. Louisiana's coastline was disappearing at what scientists called an alarming rate from subsidence and erosion. Since the 1930s, an area approximately the size of Delaware had been lost. Katrina and Rita alone had scoured away two hundred square miles of marshland—equal to the area of Chicago.

Wetlands serve as a kind of speed bump to slow down hurricanes. For every 2.7 miles traveled over marshland, storm surge is reduced by a foot due to friction and cooling of the water, scientists said. For decades, though, Louisiana had been losing its natural shock absorption. The coastline was disappearing faster than it could be rebuilt.

In the Mississippi Delta, the land naturally compacted and sank at the rate of four feet per century, according to the LSU Hurricane Center. Until the 1930s, that sinking was balanced by sediment being rebuilt during annual flooding by the river. After the great flood of 1927, though, when a land area the size of New England was inundated and the river grew seventy miles wide at some points, the federal government began an urgent effort to reduce flooding and enhance navigation with levees. Sediment that once replenished the wetlands now flowed in a constricted path, like wet concrete down the trough of a cement mixer, dumping into the Gulf instead of nourishing the coastline.

Several thousand miles of channels also had been dug into the marshes for shipping and oil and gas exploration since the 1930s. Salt water intruded and killed trees and vegetation that sustained the wetlands. Also in the 1930s, ratlike rodents called nutria, introduced from Argentina, either escaped or were released into the marshes. They began feasting with the rapacious fervor of contestants at a Fourth of July hot-dog-eating contest.

Erosion kept accelerating as sea levels rose and waves scoured the shoreline. Once, a driver cresting the bridge in Empire, the highest point in lower Plaquemines, viewed Bay Adams and a vast stretch of marsh in which sportsmen could walk to hunt ducks. Now the view was open water. Groves of cypress trees had become ghost forests in Yellow Cotton Bay and Lake Hermitage. Oystermen piloted their boats over water that global-positioning devices still designated as firm green islands of land.

The severity of the problem was laid out in stark terms by coastal scientists in the March 4, 2007, edition of the *Times-Picayune* of New Orleans: Louisiana had ten years to act before erosion of the coastline became irreversible and New Orleans fell in danger of becoming beachfront property by midcentury. Some small coastal communities west of Plaquemines would have to be abandoned as they were submerged.

"If we aren't building land I can walk on inside of ten years, we'll be moving communities," one of the scientists, Kerry St. Pé, told the paper. "It's already the witching hour for a lot of these places. And a lot of other places are next."

St. Pé, who was fifty-seven, grew up in Port Sulphur. He was director of the Barataria–Terrebonne National Estuary Program at Nicholls State University in Thibodaux, Louisiana. The Barataria estuary stretched along the Mississippi's west bank, down the entire peninsula of Plaquemines Parish, from Belle Chasse in the north to Venice in the south.

Without an urgent rebuilding of wetlands, St. Pé said in an interview, "Katrina could be the straw that broke the camel's back in Plaquemines. No one will go back. The place won't be rebuilt. It'll be a mere shadow of what it once was."

The communities of Plaquemines Parish were protected by levees, but that presented an inadvertent consequence. No one could live in lower Plaquemines without these earthen walls to keep out the river and the Gulf. Yet the levees also served as a desiccant. Cut off from water, the land inside the levees had begun to dry out and sink, an inch a year around Port Sulphur, accelerating the natural subsidence. Roy Dokka, a geologist at LSU, had used Global Positioning System devices to map the elevation of the entire parish. One of the GPS devices sat on the ruined gym at Port Sulphur High. His results were disquieting. About half of interior Plaquemines Parish was now below sea level, while the marsh remained above sea level.

On Dokka's laptop computer, the area below sea level appeared in magenta. A series of black triangles showed the area of Highway 23 that was below sea level by as much as three to six feet. This included much of a twelve-mile stretch between

Buras and Boothville. Another storm like Katrina might cut lower Plaquemines into a series of islands, Dokka said. He recommended that no one live in the lower end of the parish. A "hardened city" could be built in Belle Chasse, or slightly south, that would be fortified against storms and would allow residents to quickly return after a hurricane. Perhaps a light-rail system could ferry workers to the lower end. But, in Dokka's estimation, south Plaquemines was only biding time until the next big hurricane. It was not a place to inhabit.

"When another storm comes in, it's going to take out everything," Dokka said. "It's two out and an 0–2 count in the ninth."

It might be prudent to buy a DVD of the movie *Jaws*, he said dryly.

"The mayor says, 'We've caught a large predator. The beach is open. The sun is shining. Come back in the water.' As it turned out, that predator wasn't the one," Dokka said. "There were more sharks in the water. It's a matter of time."

Such remarks evoked feelings of resignation and furor in lower Plaquemines. Residents understood that another storm could wipe out the parish. At the same time, they did not want to be told by outsiders where they could and couldn't put their trailers and modular homes.

"Those who say that haven't been here, to feel the breeze off the river or to hunt and fish," said Billy Nungesser, the stout, pompadoured, energetic president of Plaquemines Parish. "They say you shouldn't live in California because of the fires and the earthquakes. They say you shouldn't live in New York because of the terrorists. Or in tornado alley. You could make a claim against living anywhere. But home is home. I don't think anyone in America, scientists or politicians, should tell you where you can live. We're fighting a war in Iraq for freedom of the people. You look at that place on TV and you say, 'Why would people want to live there?' That's those people's homes."

The homes in lower Plaquemines were growing increasingly susceptible to the vagaries of the weather as the coastline kept disappearing. Continued erosion would have enormous consequences, both economic and gastronomic, according to coastal scientists. Southern Louisiana produced 20 percent of the nation's oil and a quarter of its natural gas. More than a quarter of the nation's foreign and domestic oil came ashore through the state. Southern Louisiana also contained five of the nation's fifteen largest ports, which transported 20 percent of the country's waterborne commerce. More than a quarter of the fish harvested by weight in the lower forty-eight states came from Louisiana's coastal waters, which also sustained 70 percent of the nation's migratory birds. Half of the nation's shrimp and a third of its oysters and blue crabs were hauled out of Louisiana's nets, dredges, and traps. Plaquemines, in particular, grew oysters the way Idaho grew potatoes.

Before Katrina, the *Times-Picayune* noted, efforts at coastal restoration had sunk—like the land itself—under the weight of two decades of indifferent public financing and competing private interests.

In 1994, for instance, Plaquemines oystermen joined a class-action suit over a freshwater diversion of the Mississippi, claiming that the state project, designed to replenish marshland, had adversely affected salinity levels and had silted over and smothered their oyster beds. In late 2000, the oystermen won a judgment worth more than one billion dollars. The case was overturned by the Louisiana Supreme Court in 2004, but it signaled the conflicting concerns of those who made their livings on the state's bounty of oil and seafood.

In 2002, Louisiana and the U.S. Army Corps of Engineers devised a $14 billion coastal-restoration plan, but President George W. Bush later agreed only to $1.9 billion in seed money. It took Katrina to bring real public urgency to the issue. In December 2006, President Bush signed federal legislation that opened 8.3 million acres in the eastern Gulf to oil and gas drilling. The Gulf states of Louisiana, Texas, Alabama, and Mississippi were granted 37.5 percent of the royalties from those leases. The money would be used for storm protection and coastal erosion and would eventually amount to $650 million a year, but not until 2017. Until then, Lousiana would receive between $20 million and $30 million annually, an amount that, according to the *Times-Picayune,* was "a pittance in the face of a problem that will require tens of billions of dollars to solve."

Experts said the state couldn't afford to wait another decade to begin serious efforts to reverse coastal erosion. A series of freshwater diversions of the Mississippi had been proposed in lower Plaquemines, but this continued to concern oystermen and shrimpers and scare some residents who feared that communities would be sacrificed to inundation. LSU agriculture experts had begun experimenting with marsh grasses that could tolerate brackish water and that would trap sediment, but grasses like smooth cordgrass had to be planted by hand, which made it difficult to plant in a wide area.

St. Pé advocated pumping sediment out of the Mississippi through large pipelines to rebuild four hundred square miles of wetlands over the next fifty years. Massive freshwater diversions of the river would take too long to replenish the coast and could severely disrupt the oyster and shrimp industries, he said.

"It took the Mississippi River six thousand years to build what we have," St. Pé said. "We don't have thousands of years now."

He had an ally in Nungesser, the parish president, who wanted to sell bonds on the future royalty earnings and begin pumping river sediment to rebuild wetlands and barrier islands, around the clock, by 2009. It was time, Nungesser said, for FEMA and the Corps of Engineers to bring restoration projects under one roof, under one manager, and to begin pumping sediment as quickly as possible. He feared that "overstudying" and "overengineering" were leading to bureaucratic sluggishness.

"Every year we don't start pumping that sand, we better hold our breath during hurricane season," Nungesser said. "It's not going to take another Katrina to cause a lot of damage."

FRIDAY, SEPTEMBER 21, WAS A BREEZY, CLOUDLESS MORN-ing at South Plaquemines High. Gaudet was convinced Saturday's game would go on as scheduled. "It never rains on a football field," he said. Still, a fragile normalcy was set on edge. The weather system in the Gulf was better organized and now had a name: Tropical Depression 10. A tropical storm warning was issued from the Florida panhandle to the mouth of the Mississippi River. Plaquemines Parish officials alerted the 2,500 residents still in FEMA trailers to make plans to move to safer ground if necessary.

It was always beautiful before a storm, said Michelle Tassin, administrative assistant to the Plaquemines Parish director of emergency operations. The emergency center was located in a double-wide trailer in Belle Chasse. Tassin pulled up a map of the Gulf and the Caribbean on her computer. The basin seemed ablaze with orange, like autumn foliage. She pointed to a system off Cancún.

"They're seeing some convection," Tassin said. If it got pulled into the Tropical Depression 10 in the northeastern Gulf, she said, "We could have some trouble."

Next door, at the parish government offices, which were built off the ground, the parish president, sheriff, and other officials gathered for a meeting. The mood was jovial, calm. A state of emergency would probably be declared after lunch, said Phil Truxillo, the parish emergency chief. If necessary, a shelter would be opened at an auditorium in Belle Chasse the next morning. Thirty or forty school buses were put on alert in case residents had to evacuate their FEMA trailers in high winds.

Nungesser was most concerned about a five-mile stretch of marsh levees on the west bank of the river. They were private levees, outside the federal system, and stood only three to six feet high. The ConocoPhillips refinery was located in this vulnerable area. If those levees were topped and Highway 23 was flooded, it might become impossible to evacuate the lower end of the parish.

Still, Nungesser remained upbeat.

"I think they'll play," he said of South Plaquemines.

"Maybe not," Truxillo said.

As the afternoon went on, the news kept getting better. Forecasters now thought the tropical system might make landfall far to the east in Florida or Alabama. Parish officials decided to delay any evacuation order.

At South Plaquemines High, Cyril Crutchfield was less worried about another storm than about his players' grades. Three of them in his government class were failing.

"If they're doing that in my class, what do you think they're doing in other classes?" he asked.

His main concern about the storm was this: Saturday afternoon's game was scheduled forty-five miles to the north, in the New Orleans suburb of Harvey. What if Plaquemines was evacuated after the team left for the game?

"We might not be able to get back in the parish," he said.

Mona Boutwell taught prekindergarten at South Plaquemines Elementary, located in the same complex of temporary buildings as the high school. When the lights went out during bad weather, which happened often, the kids got scared. Only two weeks earlier, she and her son, Dylan, a sophomore receiver, had moved into a trailer on their property in Buras.

"I never thought I'd enjoy washing and drying clothes so much," she said.

As for the storm in the Gulf, Mona said she would depend on her faith.

"What will be, will be," she said. And then: "I know there's not another Katrina."

Friday afternoon, football practice at South Plaquemines went on as usual. Players laughed and joked about how they played better in the rain. Still, some admitted concern about the storm. How much more could they be expected to endure? Katrina had wiped out what could have been a championship season at Port Sulphur High in 2005. Now, in 2007, there were high hopes again, this time for a state title at South Plaquemines High, but another storm loomed in the Gulf.

"It ruined my freshman year," Lyle Fitte said. "I don't want it to ruin my junior year."

Maverick Ancar had evacuated with his brother Jordan to Tennessee ahead of Katrina. "I don't want to go through that again," he said.

Elouise Bartholomew, the aunt of Ridge Turner, got a call at work from a neighbor. The weather might be getting bad. The neighbor had bread and sandwich meat and a generator. Elouise would stop for ice and juice. She still had nightmares about Katrina. She and Ridge lived in a double-wide between the highway and the river. When she heard ships blow their horns, she worried that they might punch through the levee. If it rained hard, she worried that Katrina was coming back. Even now, two years after the hurricane, she did not drive as far south as Buras. People told her how slow the recovery was, only thirteen miles away.

"I can't do it," she said.

Caileb Ancar's family reserved six hotel rooms in the New Orleans suburb of Gretna as a precaution. His grandfather worried about flying debris from airborne FEMA trailers. Caileb had another concern. If another big storm came, and people left, they might not come back.

Mike Barthelemy Jr. had the same fear. "People get scattered, we won't have a team," he said. "Football here is life."

It wouldn't be the worst thing in the world if the game was canceled, Crutchfield admitted privately. Three offensive linemen were injured. Seth Ancar, his best defensive player, might also be out.

"We're beat up," Crutchfield said. "I never thought I'd say that."

Friday evening, Crutchfield sat down to dinner with Mickey Sylve and Roger Halphen at a restaurant in Belle Chasse. Midway through a meal of shrimp and crabs, he said to his startled companions, "The game was canceled."

Eva Jones, the parish school superintendent, wanted all school buses available to assist in any evacuation, he said. So she called off the game.

Crutchfield had phoned Paul Lemaire, now the parish school-board president. Lemaire called Jones.

"You can't just cancel a game by yourself," Lemaire told the superintendent. "Both teams have to agree."

It might be raining, Jones said.

"As long as there's no lightning, that's part of the game," Lemaire said.

The game was uncanceled.

About an hour later, at seven on Friday night, the National Hurricane Center rescinded the tropical storm warning. Tropical Depression 10 had made landfall in western Florida. There was no more threat of strong winds or heavy rain in Louisiana.

SATURDAY MORNING DAWNED SUNNY AND HOT. FANS WOULD need umbrellas, but for the sun, not the rain. By seven a.m., clumps of players, a dozen in all, stood along Highway 23 in their matching black shorts and T-shirts and waited for Crutchfield to pick them up in his school bus.

By eight a.m., the entire team had gathered at South Plaque-mines High. Players walked a short distance through the fence that surrounded ruined Port Sulphur High, ignored the Keep Out signs, and grabbed their equipment from the makeshift weight room and locker room set up in the abandoned gym. Sal Cepriano had been advised by his doctor not to play this week because of his lacerated liver. Ridge Turner quickly talked him into it.

"Get your stuff," Ridge said. "We need you."

At nine thirty a.m., the Hurricanes began their forty-five-mile journey northward, with a stop for breakfast. This had to be the only team in the country to get a police escort to Shoney's. Players stood for a prayer in a separate dining room, everyone holding hands, then lined up for the buffet.

"Let's go, seniors," Crutchfield said.

"Did you say 'senior citizens'?" asked Romel Barthelemy, who drove one of the team buses.

He was a fishing buddy of Crutchfield's and the only one who could have gotten away with a joke. Every one else remained silent as players filled their plates with eggs, pancakes, sausage, and biscuits. Crutchfield walked around, his arms crossed. He told Mickey Sylve that her son Bradley was wearing earrings. A freshman cornerback, Bradley was sidelined today because of an eye infection.

"Remind Bradley to take off his earrings, even though he's not playing," Crutchfield told Mickey.

Jeffery Espadron, a 332-pound freshman nose tackle, went back for seconds.

"I'll tell you one thing," Crutchfield said to him. "You better move that fat fuckin' ass on the line of scrimmage."

Nobody else approached the buffet. Not after Sam McGinnis got smacked the week before.

"Can I tell 'em they can go back?" assistant coach Rod Parker asked Crutchfield. "They scared."

"It's okay," Crutchfield said.

As the players finished their meal and walked outside, Crutch-field paid the waitress.

"Y'all are very respectful," she said.

By noon, two hours before kickoff, South Plaquemines had ar-rived at Hoss Memtsas Stadium in Harvey. The temperature was in the high eighties, but it felt well over a hundred degrees on the artificial turf. The heat rose above the turf in waves. With no locker room available, players found a sliver of shade beneath a concrete overhang. Roger Halphen handed out bottles of Pedi-alyte to prevent cramping.

During warm-ups, Crutchfield told his team it would take plenty of points to defeat Helen Cox High, a Class 4A school. He urged his defensive players to tell him if they got tired. He would get them some rest. The Hurricanes were ranked fourth in the Class 1A sportswriters' poll and first in the strength-of-schedule rankings known as the power rating.

"Some teams are looking at South Plaquemines and they're not sure," Crutchfield said. "Beat Helen Cox and you'll get respect."

The Hurricanes dressed in white jerseys and white pants to de-flect the heat. On their first possession, Ridge Turner threw a slant pass to Cantrelle Riley for a twenty-seven-yard touchdown. Ridge had played at Helen Cox in 2005, after Katrina. It would be great fun to beat his old teammates. Late in the first quarter, he flipped a quick pass to Lyle Fitte and South Plaquemines jumped ahead 15–8.

Early in the second quarter, Ridge threw a sixty-six-yard pass to Cantrelle along the right sideline, then sneaked into the end zone from the one, putting the Hurricanes ahead 21–11. Two misting fans cooled players on the sideline, but the heat was al-ready influencing the game. Ridge unwrapped the tape around his right ankle and removed his right shoe and sock. The turf was burning his feet. He had a blister on his right big toe.

At halftime, the Hurricanes held a flimsy 21–19 lead. The players sat or lay beneath the stadium overhang. Ridge and other players removed their shoes. "It burns," defensive end Felix Barthelemy said.

Gaudet held up a pair of drinking cups. He couldn't get them apart. They had melted together.

"I don't know if we can hold up," he said.

Heavy clouds were approaching from the east.

"If we get that over us, maybe we'll be all right," Gaudet said.

Four minutes into the third quarter, Ridge threw another apparent touchdown pass to Cantrelle, this one from thirty-three yards. But Cantrelle had moved into the defender to make the catch. The referee threw a flag for offensive interference. No touchdown.

South Plaquemines could not get pressure on Helen Cox's quarterback, Darius Carey, who was making his first start. A thirty-two-yard touchdown pass gave the Cougars a 25–21 lead. A year ago, South Plaquemines might have collapsed at this point. This season, Ridge was much more poised, his team more buoyant. He threw a thirty-two-yard pass to Cantrelle, who snatched it away from two defenders and rolled into the end zone. The Hurricanes went back ahead, 27–25. A few raindrops had begun to fall.

"Hurricane weather, baby!" Lyle Fitte shouted, with ten minutes remaining.

Still, it was brutally hot. Playing both ways, at quarterback and cornerback, Ridge began cramping. His aunt, Elouise Bartholomew, came to the sideline and demanded that the coaches make a choice between offense and defense. After the season opener against Belle Chasse, Ridge had cramped so severely that he had to be placed in an ambulance, given intravenous fluids, and driven forty miles to a clinic in suburban New Orleans. The doctors told him that he risked a heart attack or a stroke, his aunt said. Now, she was scared. She wanted the coaches to choose—quarterback or cornerback. Otherwise, she would get the police to take Ridge off the field.

He waved his aunt off.

"It's my job," Ridge said.

With six and a half minutes remaining, Carey of Helen Cox threw a beautiful fade pass to the end zone. Ridge was beaten, and the Cougars took a 31–27 lead. Ridge got to his feet, dejected. On South Plaquemines' next series, he seemed exhausted. His lips quivered during a time-out.

"Suck it up," Parker, the assistant coach, said.

Running the option and counters, the Hurricanes reached Helen Cox's one-yard line and called a time-out with two minutes, thirty-two seconds remaining.

"This is going to determine how we end this season," Little Wayne Williamson said. "It's do or die. Ridge, we need you. Big-time players make big-time plays."

Ridge knelt uncertainly during the time-out, slumped backward, and had to be helped to his feet. Then he gathered himself and punched the ball into the end zone, giving the Hurricanes a 33–31 lead. But there was no stopping Carey, the Helen Cox quarterback. He would finish with 251 passing yards and 4 touchdowns. With one minute, sixteen seconds left, he threw a screen pass that was carried into the end zone from 19 yards. Helen Cox went back ahead, 39–33.

South Plaquemines had one final chance to win, but Ridge scrambled, took a hit and fumbled. At the final whistle, his former teammates from Helen Cox surrounded him in consolation. He had delivered 400 yards of total offense and 5 touchdowns—311 yards and 3 touchdowns passing, 89 yards and 2 touchdowns rushing. "You played a good game, boy," one of the Cox players said, but Ridge sat on the turf, unmoving, too tired and disconsolate to respond.

The Hurricanes removed their pads and walked toward their buses, somber, exhausted. Crutchfield sat alone, staring into the distance. As discouraging as the defeat was, South Plaquemines (2–2) had held its own against a much bigger school that was also headed toward the play-offs. The Hurricanes knew now that they could defeat any team in Class 1A. They would not expect to lose for the remainder of the season.

"Nobody can beat us," Lyle Fitte said, as he carried his helmet and shoulder pads. "We can only beat ourselves."

As South Plaquemines headed home, the sky was clear over New Orleans, but forecasters again went on alert. Another low-pressure system roiled in the Gulf.

12

"IF THERE WAS A TIME TO LIVE, IT'S NOW"

RIDGE TURNER DROPPED BACK TO PASS, PIVOTED, ROLLED to his right, and stumbled. "The turf, man," he said. "It's thick." The new field at Joe Yenni Stadium in the New Orleans suburb of Metairie was identical to the one that South Plaquemines had played on a week earlier. Yet this artificial surface felt more plush. Turner decided he would have to lift his feet higher as he ran. South Plaquemines' final nonleague game, against Class 4A East Jefferson High, was an hour away. Humidity was low in the early evening, and the temperature felt twenty degrees cooler than a week before, even if it was not. Ridge wore his helmet, silver pants, and a sleeveless Under Armour shirt. After a summer of weight lifting, he had added 15 pounds to his lean five-foot-ten-inch frame, filling out to 175 pounds. Delicately handsome, he had long eyelashes and kept his hair in braids, often beneath a do-rag or a stocking cap.

During warm-ups, Ridge was tutored by Corey Buie, perhaps the best football player to come out of lower Plaquemines Parish. At six foot three, 235 pounds, with agile bulkiness at quarterback, Buie had led Buras High to the Class 2A state championship in 1990 and second place in 1991. He could put the ball through the goalposts on kickoffs, and many believed he should have had an NFL career as a kicker. Such was his talent in high school that Buie was named to the all-league team ahead of Peyton Manning in 1991. It was said that after a 7–6 loss to Buras, during which Peyton threw four interceptions (two to Buie), Manning began to immerse himself in film study of his opponents.

"Corey was one of these big, heavy kids that was athletic," said Archie Manning, Peyton's father and a former long-suffering NFL quarterback with the New Orleans Saints. "Peyton didn't even make all-district his sophomore year because Corey was in the district. Corey was the man."

Buie was now recreation director of Plaquemines Parish. At thirty-five, he still threw a beautifully precise pass. Two weeks into the season, he joined South Plaquemines as an assistant coach, sitting in the press box during games, speaking to Cyril Crutchfield via a headset. His primary job was to groom Ridge, who had poise and a strong arm but needed polish. Sometimes, he did not grip the ball by the strings. Even when he did, Ridge sometimes kept his fingers too close together, as if shaking hands. This tended to make the ball wobble. Buie taught him to spread his fingers, placing his right index finger high on the ball to guide it, to square his shoulders, and to step toward his receiver when he threw a pass. With his junior season not yet at the midway point, Ridge had become one of the top quarterbacks in the state.

"When I got there, I thought he was better than a lot of people thought," Buie said. "He had the arm strength and speed and knowledge of reading defenses. He's a smart quarterback. He just needed to work on the little things. It's all about repetition. If he had another three inches in height, he'd have all the tools."

IT WAS EXTRAORDINARY THAT RIDGE PLAYED FOOTBALL AT all, much less at a high level. He had grown up in a troubled household in Port Sulphur as his mother, Roslyn Turner, slid into a dependence on crack cocaine. As young as four or five, Ridge said, he was left alone at night with his dog Sandy, and he learned to peel and fry shrimp to put something in his stomach.

In August 1991, when Ridge was fourteen months old, his mother was accused of jumping into a man's car outside a restaurant in Port Sulphur, putting a screwdriver to his side, and robbing him of thirty-five dollars late one night. In February 1992, Roslyn Turner pleaded guilty to a charge of theft under one hundred dollars and received a six-month suspended sentence. Five months later, court records indicated, she received a five-year suspended sentence for cocaine distribution.

When Ridge was eight, Roslyn was arrested on a second offense of cocaine distribution. Plaquemines Parish authorities accused her of selling crack to undercover agents. Court records indicated that her life had seemed to shrink into a desperate reliance on drugs. Roslyn said she began recreational use as a "way to fit in with the in-crowd," and later fell into a sense of desolation after the death of her longtime companion.

On the night of November 23, 1998, outside a bar in Empire, police said Roslyn sold two rocks of crack cocaine to undercover officers for forty dollars. Crack cocaine penalties tended to be stiffer than those for powder cocaine. Roslyn later pleaded guilty and was sentenced to twelve years in state prison at the Louisiana Correctional Institute for Women.

"I didn't do it," Roslyn said. "But what can I say? Nobody's going to listen to me."

On the verge of going into foster care, Ridge was rescued by his aunt, Elouise Bartholomew. An older sister of Roslyn's, Elouise worked as a deputy clerk at the Jefferson Parish Clerk of Court's office in suburban New Orleans. She gained temporary custody of Ridge, caring for him even though her own husband was ailing. "He would have been a ward of the state," Elouise said. "I couldn't see that."

With the assistance of Ridge's older brother, Raymond, and her own adult son, Ethan Barthelemy, Elouise helped shepherd Ridge into sports. She prodded him to improve his grades; took him fishing for drum and redfish in local canals; gave him an allowance for washing clothes, vacuuming, and cutting the grass; and kept him in the church at Greater Macedonia Baptist in Port Sulphur. Ridge became a spiritual dancer at Sunday services, and even now his aunt referred to church songs during games when she called out to him, "Get those shackles off your feet."

"His aunt is a saint; she saved Ridge," Big Wayne Williamson said. "There's no telling where he would be."

ON THE GAME'S FIRST PLAY, EAST JEFFERSON STUNNED South Plaquemines with a sixty-three-yard touchdown run. Immediately, Ridge put the Hurricanes up 8–6 with a forty-nine-yard scoring pass to Lyle Fitte and a two-point conversion. Still, South Plaquemines seemed out of sorts. Sal Cepriano had played with a lacerated liver a week ago, but his family forbade him to play against East Jefferson.

Jordan Ancar dressed in his uniform, but the broken bones in his left hand had yet to fully heal. His mother told him not to leave the sideline. This left the Hurricanes with an eighth-grader at guard and a ninth-grader at tackle. Ridge was pressed into duty as a deep snapper, and he bounced the ball on a punt. East Jefferson recovered for a touchdown. Another time, Ridge held the ball too long and was sacked.

"Ridge, what are you doing?" Cepriano yelled from the sideline.

Late in the first half, Crutchfield asked Marcelin Ancar if Jordan was ready to play. As a father, Marcelin did not want his son to play. As an assistant coach, he did. "Your mother is going to be mad at you, but I'm the one who's going to get his butt chewed out," Marcelin told Jordan.

As Jordan ran onto the field, Marcelin looked for his wife in the stands. Jeanitta Ancar was pointing at him: "Don't you put that boy in." After the game, she would stop Crutchfield and say, "We have to chat."

Ridge scored up the middle on an eight-yard run and added the two-point conversion on a counter to pull the Hurricanes within 25–24. But for the first time all season, South Plaquemines trailed at the half.

"We need to knock those dudes out," linebacker Seth Ancar told his teammates in the locker room. "We ain't worked hard all summer for nothing."

AT FIFTY-TWO, ELOUISE BARTHOLOMEW STILL HAD FEATURES as sharp as the creases she starched into a pair of jeans. She resembled Tina Turner, spoke with a casual eloquence, and did a funny impersonation of the ambling way that her nephew walked on the field. She had windbreakers and T-shirts and towels, even chocolate footballs, that bore Ridge's jersey number, 9. Yet she cried when she spoke of Ridge's boyhood and needed her friends around to support her.

When she took Ridge to visit his mother at the state women's prison in St. Gabriel, Louisiana, he would grow quiet and seem to push close to her in the car. "Promise me you're going to come back," Elouise remembered Ridge telling her. "Promise me you'll never leave me by myself." At seventeen, he still sat in her lap and said, "Hold me."

Ridge called his aunt "another mom." He said he did not mind talking about his mother—"It doesn't bother me"—but when he did, his voice trailed off. Ana Barthelemy, Elouise's daughter-in-law, said she had found on her computer a rap song, or something that Ridge had written, about being left alone.

"I wonder if he's really okay, or he's just being strong," Barthelemy said.

Roslyn Turner spent her time in prison resolutely, court records showed. She admitted to a fifteen-year addiction, underwent drug and alcohol counseling, attended religious services, and worked as a trustee at an LSU agricultural station located off prison grounds.

"I am very serious about salvaging my life," she wrote to Louisiana district judge William A. Roe.

In late March 2005, her twelve-year sentence reduced, Roslyn was released on probation. However, on April 7 of that year, Elouise said, her sister came to her house in Port Sulphur, demanding three hundred dollars. If Roslyn did not receive the money, she would take Ridge.

"You want to sell me your child?" Elouise said she asked her sister.

The next day, Elouise sought a temporary restraining order against Roslyn. In a court filing, Elouise wrote that her sister had cursed her, turned over a trash can, and wanted to fight.

"Ridge was crying in his sleep last night after all this happened," Elouise wrote.

He would agree to visit his mother but did not want to stay overnight with her. Elouise feared that Roslyn was using drugs again.

"He is a very good student," Elouise wrote of Ridge. "A good child. Heavily involved in the church, school, and sports. Please help us keep Ridge's life as it has been, moving in the right direction."

Shortly thereafter, Elouise said, she was granted full custody of Ridge, while his mother was given supervised visits. Roslyn Turner lived with her own mother and worked at a local greenhouse. Then, in late summer of 2005, Katrina struck. Again her life became untethered. "Katrina left me homeless and naked," Roslyn said.

Ridge and his aunt evacuated to Jacksonville, Florida, then took a circuitous path back to Louisiana. Elouise went to work as a security guard at an office building on Poydras Street in New Orleans. She lived in a suburban hotel, five women in a room, and downtown she saw things she never wanted to see again: a body in a car, people living under a bridge. The smell of the city was a stench of "rotten flesh and sour water and dead buzzards." New Orleans seemed to be a place of spoiled food and maggots. It took forever before Elouise could eat a hamburger again.

In the months after Katrina, Ridge lived with his cousin, Ethan Barthelemy, in suburban New Orleans and attended Helen Cox High. He saw his aunt mostly on weekends. She considered moving with him to Los Angeles, where she had a friend, but Ridge wanted to come home. He wanted to play for Crutchfield. Okay, she told him. They would return to Port Sulphur.

"I figured if I took him anywhere else, he might mess up," Elouise said. "That fast life ain't for nobody."

In his room at home, Ridge kept an old Port Sulphur High jersey and helmet, as much out of nostalgia now as regret. Katrina had been a complicated hurricane. It had destroyed his home but had provided a chance at unforeseen achievement. Before the storm, Ridge had been a cornerback. On offense, he was deep on the depth chart. "I never thought he'd be a quarterback," Caileb Ancar said. Now, Ridge carried a team's hopes for a state title largely on his shoulders. Apart from his Port Sulphur gear, his room was filled with football pictures, track medals from South Plaquemines, and so-called victory scarves in the Hurricanes' colors. On one of the scarves, he had written, "If there was a time to live, it's now."

When Ridge visited his mother, their meetings were awkward, Elouise said. Roslyn Turner said she remained in her son's life, sending him birthday and Christmas presents and money when she could. "He knows who I am," she said. She saw him play several games, but on August 17, 2007, two weeks before the season began, Roslyn said she was arrested for a parole violation for providing an unreliable address. She was sent back to jail. Halfway through the regular season, mother and son had not been in contact.

"If not for Elouise, Ridge would be living house to house," said Terese Ragas, a neighbor in Port Sulphur. "I know he loves his mother. In his heart, he probably says prison is the best place for her, instead of having to hear someone say she's gone. He might be praying that one day it will all change. That's the only thing he can do for her right now."

TRAILING 25–24, CRUTCHFIELD MADE A SIMPLE BUT EFFECtive adjustment at halftime. East Jefferson was overloading one side of the ball with linemen, then running to the weak side. South Plaquemines' aggressive pursuit had drawn the Hurricanes into a trap. The team's strength had become a weakness. Crutchfield countered by telling Seth Ancar, his best linebacker, to blitz to the weak side. By the time East Jefferson scored again, it was down 60–25.

Ridge led his team to thirty-six unanswered points. He ran with a sprinter's precision and fluidity, head perfectly still, his feet lightly touching the ground, his arms and legs pumping with great vertical efficiency. At these moments, he seemed as straight and slippery as a column of mercury. He was not the fastest player on the team—Bradley Sylve had won the league 100-meter title as an eighth-grader—but Ridge ran through defenders with an unhurried elegance. Twice, he scored on counters, faking to Lyle Fitte in one direction, shifting his hips like a slalom skier and running unhindered to the end zone.

When he threw the ball, Ridge stepped high onto his toes in such a manner that the coach of an upcoming opponent, Ridgewood Preparatory School, would take his quarterback aside and say, "Watch this, this is how it's supposed to be done." East Jefferson's cornerbacks were giving wide space to the Hurricanes' top receiver, Cantrelle Riley, so Ridge found him with short curls. And he sent Lyle deep, hitting him on a corner route for a seventeen-yard touchdown and again for a forty-nine-yard score.

"Ridge Turner is one of the best I've seen in a long time," said Norman Ryan, the coach of Ridgewood Prep. "Any team in the state would love him."

An inconsequential late touchdown by East Jefferson made the final score 60–33. Ridge had delivered a performance of such incandescence that he would be named state player of the week by a Web site called PelicanPreps.com—21 of 28 passes completed for 307 yards and 3 touchdowns, and 21 rushes for 182 yards and 4 touchdowns. He had also run for 4 two-point conversions and passed for 2 others. He now ranked second in Louisiana with 1,264 total passing yards, having completed 71 of 96 passes through five games for 10 touchdowns and 2 interceptions.

"He's just maturing," Crutchfield said. "He's coming into his own."

Weekly, Ridge spoke with Randall Mackey, who still had Bastrop High undefeated and ranked number 1 in Class 4A. They had lived on the same street in Port Sulphur—known as St. Joseph Lane or Flamingo Lane. Sometimes Ridge placed a piece of tape on his cleats with the initials "FLP," for "Flamingo Lane Posse." He and Randall had played football in the street, challenged each other at video games, ridden forty-five miles up the road to go to the movies. The quarterbacks talked of meeting at the Superdome in December and playing in state-championship games on the same day. But the South Plaquemines players joked that Randall was growing jealous of his former neighbor. He kept getting pulled from games in the second half as Bastrop built insurmountable leads, while Turner stayed on the field at South Plaquemines and rolled up numbers as if they were on a gasoline pump.

"Ridge is a better runner; he fits our scheme better," Crutchfield said. "He doesn't have the top receivers that Randall has. As a passer, Randall has better strength, accuracy, touch, but it's who fits our style better. That's Ridge. We need a runner at quarterback who can make the passes he has to make."

13

"LIKE THE STORM KEEPS HAPPENING OVER AND OVER"

AS CANTRELLE RILEY WALKED OFF THE FIELD FOLLOWING the rout of East Jefferson, having made a dozen receptions, Sal Cepriano smiled and began to needle him. "It's gonna snow tomorrow," Sal said. "Cantrelle didn't drop any passes."

Some of Cantrelle's teammates called him Crazy Legs. He had been born with legs so bowed they had been placed in metal braces. When he was three, his left tibia had been broken during surgery and reset. "He started running in a cast and hasn't stopped since," Lisa Riley, his mother, said. At eighteen, Cantrelle still had a bowlegged gait. He seemed to limp slightly and walk on the outside of his left foot, as if he had stepped on a sliver of broken glass. A receiver and cornerback, he was one of a handful of Hurricanes who played both offense and defense. Sometimes the coaches found him as maddening as he was versatile.

In the season opener against Belle Chasse, Cantrelle had caught a long pass to set up the Hurricanes' only touchdown. But he had dropped another pass in the end zone. In overtime, he had run the wrong route, slanting inside instead of breaking toward the corner of the end zone. The mistake led to an interception. A play later, Belle Chasse scored the winning touchdown.

"He can make you and break you in the same game," Roger Halphen said after the defeat.

As the season progressed, though, Cantrelle had become more sure-handed and reliable. After five games, he ranked second in the state, with 633 receiving yards. South Plaquemines had built a 3–2 record against much larger schools. The next five weeks would essentially serve as a rest and recuperation period for the play-offs.

The Hurricanes were entering league play in District 10 of Class 1A, against opponents of similar enrollment. The other five teams in the district were private schools located in the New Orleans suburb of Metairie. Those schools were situated within a few miles of each other and competed fiercely for students returning home after Katrina. None of the schools were strong in football this season. Some struggled to field enough players for a separate offense and defense at practice. South Plaquemines, meanwhile, had the skill to hold its own against much larger schools. League play should be a breeze.

Cyril Crutchfield would use this time to let his players get healed and rested. As long as the Hurricanes performed to expectations on Fridays, they would not practice in pads the rest of the week. Instead, they would concentrate on lifting weights, seeking to grow stronger and healthier for the postseason.

"Just think how fresh we'll be," Crutchfield said.

FOR THE FIRST TIME IN FIVE WEEKS, SOUTH PLAQUEMINES returned home to Port Sulphur, to play the Country Day Cajuns. An early-October storm had pushed over lower Plaquemines, bringing mosquitoes and the humid marsh smell of luxuriant rot. In late afternoon, the sun broke through, and the thin clouds seemed to be painted with a brush. As they did before each home game, two fans, Lorne Landry and Harold Sylve, cooked thirty pounds of food, stirring the pot with a paddle, feeding anyone who was hungry. Tonight's offering was "slap yo' sister" red beans, meaning the food was so good it made you want to slap your sister. Landry was known by everyone as Boo. His son, Lorne Barthelemy, an eighth-grade lineman on the varsity, was Little Boo. A former runner-up in the state wrestling tournament, Big Boo was a justice of the peace. During games, his deep voice cut through the night like the horn of a freighter in the fog. Surely, he was one of the parish's best cooks. He had learned from his grandfather, who made hog's head cheese and sent him outside on Saturdays as he prepared to make a gumbo, telling Boo, "Go kill me a couple yard chickens right quick."

Each year when it got cold, in December or January, Boo butchered a pig and made blood sausage.

"Killing a pig is more fun than a family reunion," he said.

IN THE TEAM TRAILER, CRUTCHFIELD PACED BACK AND forth, gesticulating, talking to himself. "I feel like Goldi-fuckin'-locks," he said. "Someone's been sittin' in my chair. Someone's been sleeping in my bed." His players gave him quizzical looks and laughed when he was out of sight. There was always a distance to Crutchfield on game days. A screen seemed to come over his face. He retreated into a private intensity before he coached a game, just as he had before he played a game. Sometimes he muttered confidentially. At other times, he lay on the floor of his office, where he kept his fishing poles and a folded flag from his father's memorial service. He kept the lights off and closed his eyes or stared ahead. On the field, he walked in a private reverie.

He gathered his players in the end zone. He would not tolerate penalties against Country Day. The Hurricanes should score a touchdown on each possession. The defense should allow no first downs.

"Intimidation, that's what it's all about," Crutchfield said. "Intimidation. Intimidation."

And he'd better not see any taunting, he told his players. "If you're going to celebrate, you might as well do a fuckin' flip; that's gonna be your last play on defense," Crutchfield said. "If you say something, you might as well 'cuss the motherfucker out. That'll be your last play on offense."

SEVEN TIMES, SOUTH PLAQUEMINES POSSESSED THE BALL in the first half against Country Day. Six times, the Hurricanes scored a touchdown. Cantrelle Riley caught a thirteen-yarder on a corner route. Then he took a short hook pass from Ridge Turner, pinballed off two tacklers along the sideline, and scored from twenty-eight yards. He was hit late in the end zone and came to the bench shaking his left hand. He poured water on it. "My fingers are numb," he said. He kept playing. Before halftime, Cantrelle outjumped a defender on an alley-oop pass for his third touchdown. The Hurricanes rushed ahead 39–0.

Cantrelle wore his hair in short dreadlocks. He was whippet-thin, but stronger this year with a regimen of weight lifting, better able to push his way past cornerbacks who tried to jam him on the line of scrimmage. He was a junior academically but a senior in football eligibility. When Cantrelle was in third grade, he was held back after missing a month of school when his grandfather died. He would turn nineteen before the 2008 season. To gain another year of eligibility, he would have to petition the state high school athletic association.

If this was to be his final season, he was making the most of it. Before Katrina, Cantrelle had played at Buras High with his brother, Christian. All that remained of their home were the steps and a basket of trophies that were stored on the family shrimp trawler. Cantrelle and Christian had evacuated to Dallas in 2005 and played football at Bryan Adams High. Cantrelle moved up from junior varsity to become a starting receiver. His brother became the starting quarterback. The players were bigger in Texas but seemingly not as fast as they were in Louisiana, Cantrelle thought. Early on, a dozen family members squeezed into an apartment in Dallas. It was so tiny, Cantrelle said, that the sofa had to be put in storage to make enough room for sleeping on air mattresses. Once, Cantrelle got on a city bus after football practice and ended up fifteen miles away in the northeastern suburb of Garland. He longed for Plaquemines Parish.

His brother remained in Texas. "I didn't want to go home and start all over again," Christian said. "You never knew what would happen the next hurricane season."

That mattered less to Cantrelle. By Thanksgiving of 2005, he had grown homesick. He rode thirteen hours on a Greyhound back to Plaquemines Parish, changing buses three times.

"He's not used to the city," Lisa Riley said.

Life in a FEMA trailer in Belle Chasse was hardly more spacious than in the Dallas apartment. Six or seven family members slept in bunk beds, on a sofa, and on a converted kitchen table. Formaldehyde had been used in the construction of the trailers, and Lisa Riley found herself with runny eyes, sinus problems, and headaches. Her mother got a FEMA trailer placed on family property in Buras in November 2006 but waited two months to get the electricity connected. Lisa requested a three-bedroom mobile home. She was given one, but it was located in Springfield, Louisiana, two hours from her job in Boothville, where she did custodial work on helicopters that transported workers to offshore oil rigs.

"They said, 'Take it or leave it,'" Lisa said. "They wouldn't put it where I lived. It's a flood zone."

She was now seeking twelve thousand dollars in financing to buy the mobile home and have it shipped to lower Plaquemines.

"It takes a toll on you," Lisa said. "It's like the storm keeps happening over and over."

She worked nights. If she wasn't off on a particular Friday during football season, she tried to see Cantrelle play during her dinner break. The consolidation of three schools into one had proved awkward for Cantrelle, given that he was from Buras and South Plaquemines High was situated in Port Sulphur.

"People were aggravating," Cantrelle said. "Like, 'This is Port Sulphur's school; y'all on our grounds.'"

He said he did not like Crutchfield at the beginning of the 2006 season. Too much cursing and yelling. Crutchfield made no secret that he believed Port Sulphur players were tougher than those from Buras and Boothville-Venice. Cantrelle felt the coach accepted mistakes more readily from Port Sulphur players and was quicker to yell at the others, while not appreciating their contributions to the team.

"They look at us like we can't get the job done as good as them, but really, they need us," Cantrelle said.

This season, thirty of the thirty-eight Hurricanes were from Port Sulphur. Cantrelle was the only player from Buras or Boothville-Venice playing a significant role. The team was also counting on Dylan Boutwell, another receiver from Buras, but he had missed the first half of the season with a hamstring and pelvic injury.

"He's a good coach, he knows the game," Cantrelle said of Crutchfield. "But all that Port Sulphur stuff aggravates me."

MIDWAY THROUGH THE THIRD QUARTER, SOUTH PLAQUE-mines trapped Country Day for a safety. Cantrelle retrieved the ensuing kickoff on the right sideline, cut inside, and ran 65 yards for his fourth touchdown, putting the Hurricanes up 47–0. The final score was 61–8. Ridge Turner completed 12 of 18 passes for

277 yards and 5 touchdowns, and rushed 14 times for 116 yards and 2 touchdowns. The Hurricanes were 4–2.

"Nobody can beat us, as long as we play our game," Crutchfield said.

There was other good news. Belle Chasse had lost for the first time this season.

"They say South Plaquemines will never beat them," Big Wayne Williamson said. "But I think we have a better chance of being on the sideline in the 'Dome in December than they do."

He was already planning to put his vacation on hold.

14

"NOTHINGNESS BUILDS BRIDGES TO NOWHERE"

IN THE VERNACULAR OF LOWER PLAQUEMINES PARISH, traveling to New Orleans was "going to town," suggesting a place that was more distant in custom and experience than mileage. As the South Plaquemines team buses ascended the steep, narrow Huey P. Long Bridge, Jeffery Espadron got on the floor and covered his head. A freshman nose tackle, he was the biggest player on the team at 332 pounds. He was also terrified of heights. He lived across the street from the Mississippi River in Happy Jack, just north of Port Sulphur. Still, it was one thing to see the river from atop a sixteen-foot levee and quite another thing to be perched 150 feet above the water on a roadway that seemed no wider than a school bus.

At the Jefferson Parish Playground in Metairie, the Hurricanes dressed in a recreation center for senior citizens. The room seemed to be a combination bingo parlor and dance hall, complete with a disco ball. Ridgewood Preparatory School had the misfortune of scheduling South Plaquemines for Homecoming, a game it had no chance of winning. It would be a bleak evening for all those girls in corsages. Cyril Crutchfield stood outside the dressing room and spoke with Paul Solis, who had coached football and taught at the former Boothville-Venice High School for three decades.

It was only mid-October, but Solis believed South Plaquemines was on its way to a state championship.

"I don't see anybody beating you," he said.

Crutchfield laughed.

"Man, I gotta quit talkin' to you."

Predictions of a championship were premature, Crutchfield believed. South Plaquemines was playing in a weak district. Crutchfield worried that his team's knife-edge sharpness might grow dull before the play-offs.

"I don't know how my kids are going to handle it after being basically off for five weeks," he said.

THE STADIUM LIGHTS WERE DIM AND SET LOW TO THE ground; the visor on Lyle Fitte's helmet seemed to interfere with his ability to see the ball as South Plaquemines took an early 6–0 lead. "He needs to take that damn visor off," assistant coach August Ragas said. Lyle was a likely selection to the all-state team. The Hurricanes could not win a championship without him. At the same time, Crutchfield had to strike a balance between what was best for Lyle and what was best for the team. Lyle was determined to get a college scholarship. To attract the attention of recruiters to such a small school, he had to put up big numbers. Yet the roster was full of star players. Ridge Turner was one of the state's leading passers, Cantrelle Riley one of its top receivers. A week earlier, apparently unsatisfied with his carries and receptions, Lyle had seemed to sulk on the sideline.

"He's selfish, not a team player," Crutchfield said before tonight's game.

Seven minutes into the first quarter, though, Crutchfield was more solicitous. "What's wrong?" he asked Lyle. "Don't press too hard. Just relax. Let the game come to you."

A two-yard touchdown pass to Lyle put the Hurricanes up 12–0. Then he lined up in the slot on the right hash mark and caught a fifty-one-yard touchdown pass. South Plaquemines was ahead 20–6 early in the second quarter, when Roxanna Cepriano appeared behind the Hurricanes' bench. She was worried about her son, Sal.

"He's supposed to be padded," Roxanna said to the coaches. "He can't play like that. Make sure he puts on those rib protectors."

After Sal had suffered the lacerated liver and bruised spleen, specialists had advised him not to play for three or four weeks. He did sit out the East Jefferson game, but this was his senior season at left guard. No matter what, he was playing.

"Sal, come here," Crutchfield said.

At six foot, 190 pounds, of Italian and Filipino heritage, Sal was darkly handsome, funny, respectful. But no football player wanted to see his mother on the field in the middle of a game.

"Oh my God!" Sal shouted.

He meant to wear the plastic and foam rib protectors under his jersey, he told his mother. But he had forgotten.

"Mom, I know what I'm doing!" Sal said. "I'm not stupid!"

Roxanna Cepriano gave in.

"You know, Crutchfield," she said, "if I pull him out, he'll never speak to me again. This is his life."

FROM THE TIME HE WAS A YOUNG BOY, SAL SAT IN FRONT OF the television, watching live football games or playing video games. Sports were his distraction and escape. His parents' relationship, by all accounts, had been tempestuous. The children described fraught moments of sofas placed against pounding doors, of frightened escapes out of bedroom windows.

On January 6, 2002, after a night of drinking and arguing between Sal's parents, the Ceprianos' house was set afire in Port Sulphur. Salvador Cepriano Sr., Sal's father, was charged with aggravated arson. He denied setting the house on fire and later pleaded guilty to simple criminal damage to property, court records showed. He spent a brief period in jail and was ordered to pay restitution of five thousand dollars to the homeowner and to attend a substance-abuse program, according to family members and court records.

A commercial fisherman, age forty-four, Salvador Cepriano Sr. was known to his friends as T-Man. Over two decades, he had numerous conflicts with law enforcement, court records indicated, and had faced charges for such various maritime transgressions as trawling out of season, operating a vessel without a license, and illegal taking of oysters. He had pleaded guilty to simple burglary of a business, theft over five hundred dollars, receiving stolen items, and simple criminal damage to property.

Sal Sr. said in court papers that he had cordial relationships with his children. Sal Jr. said he seldom spoke to his father, and when he did, their conversations were strained.

"I think I'm scared of him," Sal said.

His relationship with his mother was also complicated with love and regret.

After the house fire, Roxanna Cepriano said, "I kind of gave up on being a parent."

At the time, five of her seven children were still living at home. Full of fear and stress, Roxanna said, she entered a wild period when she was "always out partying, coming in at all hours of the night." Sometimes she did not come home, her eldest daughter, Jenna Lupis, said. Then a senior in high school, Jenna said it was left to her to make sure her younger siblings were clothed and fed and sent to school.

"I never had a childhood," Jenna, now twenty-three, said. "I always had to be the mother."

Their home burned, their security charred, Sal and his mother said the family began to drift into a life of overdue utility bills and unpaid rent, of evictions, of desperate shuttling from house to hotel to apartment. Football became a kind of security blanket.

"When I didn't have anything, it was here for me," Sal said. "When things were going bad at home, I came to football and everything was better."

BY HALFTIME AGAINST RIDGEWOOD, RIDGE TURNER HAD thrown five touchdown passes and South Plaquemines led 39–6. Late in the second quarter, Cantrelle Riley caught a slip screen, dashed free over the middle, and ran for an eighty-three-yard touchdown. Then Cantrelle ran a streak route down the right sideline and caught a sixty-six-yard scoring pass. But Crutchfield was not happy. In recent weeks, the Hurricanes had begun to commit loutish penalties—personal fouls, blocking opponents in the back far away from the ball, hitting after the whistle had blown.

Six years earlier, Port Sulphur High had lost by one point in the 2001 state-championship game after having three touchdowns nullified by penalties. Crutchfield still remembered each play the way golfers remembered missed putts. He gathered the Hurricanes in the bingo parlor of a dressing room and said, "If you think penalties won't stop you from winning a state championship, that's a goddamn lie."

A reputation was a fickle thing, Crutchfield said. Once it was lost, it was difficult to recover. People were beginning to say that the Hurricanes lacked discipline. It could repulse the referees, college recruiters, voters who chose all-district and all-state teams. "If you're not going to discipline yourself now, you're not going to discipline yourself in life," Crutchfield said. "You won't have a whistle to tell you to stop, and you'll end up in the fuckin' penitentiary."

He wanted his team to be ravenous, but not reckless.

"We should be building character," Crutchfield said. "That's sad. It shows how selfish we are. It's not going to hurt against a team like Ridgewood, but it will come back to haunt us in the second, third, fourth round of the play-offs. Real teams dominate with character. You whip their ass and knock their lights out, and when the whistle blows you help them up. Some of you too big for that. You gotta whip their ass and talk shit. Well, what have y'all done? We ain't done shit. You selfish. You think you the biggest and baddest ones out there, but you're not. In the second half, I want some fuckin' licks. When the ref blows the whistle, go back to the huddle. You got it backwards. You play with a nasty attitude when the ball is snapped, not after the whistle blows."

Before the second half began, assistant coach Rod Parker told Crutchfield that Randall Mackey and Bastrop High were up 28–0 on another state power, Evangel Christian of Shreveport.

"What is Belle Chasse doing?" Crutchfield asked.

It was not playing until tomorrow, Parker said.

Too bad, Crutchfield said. "I want them to get their asses whipped Friday and Saturday."

ON THE FIRST PLAY OF THE THIRD QUARTER, SAL CEPRIANO and Caileb Ancar pulled from the left side of the line, herding around right end. Ridge Turner followed them on a quarterback counter. He cut across the field, darting back and forth like a polygraph needle, and sprinted seventy-one yards to the end zone. After South Plaquemines kicked the extra point, the referee threw a flag. Sal had committed a personal foul. Late hit.

"The ref said, 'That's enough,'" Crutchfield told him. "Let it go."

Sal said something, but Crutchfield cut him off.

"He kicked it," Crutchfield said. "It went through. Let it go."

In 2004, when Sal was a confused freshman at Port Sulphur High, Crutchfield brought him home one night, cooked him a meal of pork chops, and spoon-fed him the Bronchos' offense. Sal became a starter at center, but he struggled late in the season and Crutchfield benched him. Just as the play-offs started, Sal quit. The team reached the state quarterfinals, but he did not attend the games. After the fire in 2002, Sal had lost his home, his sense of purpose. Aimlessness set in.

"What did I have to look forward to?" he asked.

He was angry. He did not care about his grades. Really, he did not care about anything but football. He talked rudely to his teachers. And if he brought home an F on his report card, so what? His mother didn't punish him. At one point, he was sent to an alternative school for misbehaving kids.

"I was horrible," Sal said. "I felt like, for a few years, I lost something."

If he had a regret back then, it was quitting the football team in 2004. He couldn't wait to get back on the field in 2005. Then Katrina struck. His mother did not have a car, so Sal and his younger siblings piled in with his older sister Jenna and evacuated to Texas City, Texas, southeast of Houston. Hurricane Rita arrived a few weeks later and pushed them in a panic north to Dallas, nine hours bumper to bumper without air conditioning.

The family returned to Texas City, but Sal said he felt too depressed and dislocated to play football. His sister inquired about Sal's moving to Bastrop with Randall Mackey and the others from Port Sulphur. Jenna said she was told there was no more room at the apartment where those players were staying. Sal remained in Texas for a couple of months, while Jenna returned to Louisiana. One day, she got a call from him. He was tired of eating food from shelters. He didn't know anybody. His relationship with his mother was tense. He missed football. Money was scarce. (Shortly thereafter, Jenna said, their mother would have to get running water from a hose next door.)

"He couldn't take it anymore," Jenna said.

Hurricane Katrina made landfall near Buras, Louisiana, with such force that it knocked down the water tower. (Plaquemines Parish Government)

Coffins popped out of the ground and floated away in Port Sulphur. (Cheryl Gerber)

The Hurricanes practice in 2006 on a borrowed field thirty miles from school.
(Cheryl Gerber)

Fourteen months after the storm, a Homecoming game is played in lower Plaquemines
Parish; guard Dwayne Ancar is named Homecoming king. (Cheryl Gerber)

Coach Cyril Crutchfield addresses his players after they have traveled a half hour to practice in a school bus. (Cheryl Gerber)

The Hurricanes have no locker room, so they dress for practice in 2006 under a moss-draped oak tree. (Lee Celano)

Coach Cyril Crutchfield is hoisted on the shoulders of fans as the Hurricanes win their first-ever playoff game in 2006. (Michael Stravato)

Coach Crutchfield is congratulated after the playoff victory by Keven Smith (10) and Jordan Ancar (64). (Michael Stravato)

Guard Sal Cepriano (53) and teammates raise their helmets during the national anthem before a 2007 game against Helen Cox High. (Cheryl Gerber)

Dylan Boutwell (1) catches a touchdown pass during the title game. (Barry Spears)

Cantrelle Riley (6) catches a long pass during the 2007 state championship game. (Barry Spears)

South Plaquemines High School

HURRICANES 2007

James Whigham PHOTOGRAPHY STUDIO

The Hurricanes pose for a team picture before Homecoming in 2007. Homecoming king Jordan Ancar stands in the middle in a white suit and crown. (James Whigham)

Ridge Turner reaches across the goal line for a touchdown in the championship game.
(Barry Spears)

Lyle Fitte catches a
touchdown pass as
Coach Cyril Crutchfield
and Principal Stanley Gaudet
celebrate on the sideline.
(Barry Spears)

Ridge Turner receives the most valuable player award after South Plaquemines wins the 2007 Class 1A state title. (Barry Spears)

Randall Mackey receives the MVP plaque after Bastrop wins the 2007 Class 4A championship. (Barry Spears)

So Sal came home. Jenna became his guardian and he entered Belle Chasse High. His sister drove him to school each
day, gave him a place to stay, food to eat, money to spend.
"Without her, I don't know what would have happened to me,"
Sal said.

Around New Year's of 2006, he ran into Crutchfield at Balestra's
supermarket in Belle Chasse. They shook hands.

"There's my boy," Crutchfield said.

When South Plaquemines High opened in the summer of 2006,
Sal followed Crutchfield back to the lower end of the parish. He had
missed one football season and was not about to miss another. His
sister and her husband relocated to Port Sulphur, and Sal lived with
them and their two young children in a travel trailer. The place was
cramped, but Jenna kept photographs of Sal in the bedroom and
even got a purple bedspread—Port Sulphur High's color—for his
bunk bed.

When Sal needed someone to talk to, he knew he could go to
her or to Crutchfield. "Everyone needs that person," Sal said.
Crutchfield had given him confidence, had heated his aggressiveness on the field from a simmer to a boil. Sal loved the way
Crutchfield accepted nothing but winning. The way he once
rubbed the bleeding knee of Little Wayne Williamson and then
licked his finger, saying, "You bleed for me, I'll bleed for you." The
way he said things like "Excuses are monuments to nothingness,
and nothingness builds bridges to nowhere."

Crutchfield appreciated Sal's tenacity and found in him a similar
obsession with football. Of South Plaquemines' half-dozen seniors,
Crutchfield said, "It means the most to Sal."

Sometimes, it meant so much to him that he risked his health.
He had played against doctors' orders after lacerating his liver.
Jenna screamed at him after the Helen Cox game, saying, "You
don't want to risk your life for one game."

"This *is* my life," Sal told her. "This is all I've got."

So his mother backed off when he forgot his rib protectors in the Ridgewood game. Sal and the other starting linemen, then their replacements, kept pulling right and left as the second half played out, swinging like a pendulum from one side to the other, and Ridge Turner kept following them on the counter. He ran to the end zone twice more, from seventeen and sixty-seven yards, and the Hurricanes improved to 5–2 with a 58–6 victory.

After the game, as he always did, Sal sought out his girlfriend, Stephanie Barthelemy. She was a cheerleader; president of the student council; a softball, volleyball, and basketball player; the first A-plus student-athlete at South Plaquemines. At graduation, she hoped to be named valedictorian or salutatorian. "Val or Sal," she called it.

They had started dating shortly after South Plaquemines opened. Some teachers disapproved, warning Stephanie that Sal was "too dumb" for her. He had tried talking to her in class once in 2004, when they were freshmen, but she had brushed him off, saying, "You're too bad." Now Sal had changed. He didn't seem disrespectful to his teachers. He appeared to genuinely care about his grades. Stephanie cared about him and ignored her teachers' concerns. Yet she also gave Sal an ultimatum: If he wanted to be with her, he had to work as hard in the classroom as he did on the field.

"I didn't want him sitting around like those others who played football and went to college, and a few months later, you see them on the street and they're on crack," Stephanie said.

It was funny what Katrina had done, Sal thought. It had uprooted him, destroyed the few things that he owned. But it had also washed away the futility of his life. School mattered to him now. And others seemed to care about him, offering structure and discipline in a way that his parents had not. People looked after him, told him what he could and couldn't do. *If only this had happened earlier,* Sal told himself. After the hurricane, he studied sometimes with Little Wayne Williamson. Big Wayne made them hit the books before they turned on the television. "I wish you could adopt me," Sal told him.

There were others in his support system. In recent days, after his sister's husband broke his leg on a shrimp boat, Sal had moved to Buras to live with his godparents. He had his own room in their mobile home, his own space. For the first time in years, he could stretch out.

"I guess I've overcome a lot," Sal said. "A lot of people would have given up and given themselves to the street. I bettered myself."

And now the Hurricanes were among the favorites to win a state championship. Still, Sal had his doubts. His self-assurance seemed to lag. He didn't set his goals high, so he wouldn't be too disappointed if he failed to achieve them. "I don't look forward to the best things," he said. Maybe his luck would change with football. Crutchfield insisted on nothing less than a state title. And Stephanie kept exhorting him.

"You always expect the worst," she told Sal. "Go for the positive."

WIN OR LOSE, FOOTBALL SEASON WOULD END BY EARLY December. Sal dreaded the thought of it. Even if he won a state championship, he would probably never play another game. Then where would he be? He thought he was too small to get a football scholarship. Perhaps he would go to a community college and become an electrician. No, his sister Jenna insisted: Go to a four-year school. Get your degree

She had a child at nineteen and another at twenty-two. College was out of the question for her. Sal's father had finished the seventh grade, his mother the sixth. Jenna wanted him to be the first in the family to finish high school and earn a college diploma.

"Sal, you've got to be better than me," she told him.

It was Jenna, petite and cheerful, who held the family together. She was trying to start a cleaning business with her mother, Roxanna, who still lived in a FEMA trailer park in the community of Diamond. When her own daughter became a mother, Roxanna said, she finally learned to become one, too.

"If it wasn't for her, I don't know how I'd survive," Roxanna, who kept her brunette hair long at age forty-six, said of Jenna. "She's my backbone."

She could kick herself in the ass, Roxanna said, for some of the things—irresponsible things—she did before Jenna had her first child in 2003, a year after the family's house burned.

"So much happened to me, I didn't know how to be a parent," Roxanna said. In her forties, she said, she had finally grown up. "Nobody else can take care of them," she said of her children. "That's your responsibility."

Still, it was difficult raising the three teenagers who still lived with her in a FEMA trailer, one of them sleeping on the sofa, all of them limited to fifteen minutes in the bathroom as they got ready for school. Phillip was sixteen, Ryan fourteen, and Olivia thirteen. The trailer park in Diamond had streets named after ballplayers: Berra, Ford, Gehrig, DiMaggio. But it was a numbing place, all gravel and withered hope and stress over gunshots, drugs, fights, stabbings. What kind of home was it when the guards were chasing someone and you had to yell at your kids to hit the floor? People were on edge. Small disagreements escalated into big explosions. It was difficult to tell how people would react. Roxanna said she had been called names "lower than a dog." *The hurricane had taken more than people's homes*, she thought. It had also destroyed their sense of perspective.

At one time, the traffic came in and out all night. Drugs. The noise felt as if she were living on Bourbon Street. Now the park was quieter. Half of the original 450 trailers had been moved out. Still, the place was infested with ants, roaches, and mice. Her eyes watered, and Ryan had a constant cough. She wondered if it was due to the formaldehyde used in construction. The trailers were also flimsy, not built to withstand high winds, but there was no shelter in the park to house residents against threatening weather. The previous spring, during a tornado alert, Roxanna had stayed awake around the clock, moving everything from under her bed in case her children needed a place to hide.

"I'm scared to death in here," she said. "I thank God I have this, but I want out of here."

"When are we leaving?" the kids kept asking. "When are we getting our own place?" FEMA planned to close all its trailer parks in Plaquemines Parish by May 2008. Roxanna was not sure where she would go. She wanted a place with a yard, where her kids could play with friends. FEMA planned to sell the trailers to residents, but Roxanne did not know where she would put hers. She did some cleaning, and some paperwork for a friend who owned an excavation company, but she relied on food stamps to make ends meet. She did not know if she could afford to pay rent or to buy a plot of land. And she still did not have a car.

Jenna had no idea what her mother would do. Her own plans were also unsettled, though she and her husband and their two kids planned to move west to Thibodaux, Louisiana. As for Sal, he knew he wanted to get out of Plaquemines Parish as quickly as he could.

"I hate the water," he said.

Commercial fishing could be a difficult way to make a living. His father averaged nineteen thousand dollars a year, according to court records. There always seemed to be something wrong with the boat, Sal said. Or his father went into the bays and caught little or nothing. If Sal stayed around, he knew he, too, would end up on a boat. It was the last thing he wanted.

"There's nothing for me here," he said.

He missed his brothers and sister, living away from them. He saw them at school each day, but he was not around after school to discipline them, keep them in line. His mother seemed more responsible now. Sure, he loved her. She was the one who encouraged him to play football. When he joined Bantam League football as a kid, she stayed up late making posters and then ran up and down the sidelines cheering him on. Now, she was his biggest fan. She attended his games, sat with him at the hospital when he lacerated his liver.

"She got it together," he said. Still, he seemed conflicted about her.

"I feel she never did enough," Sal said. "It was like we were on our own. I only wish I had someone to tell me, 'Do this, do that.'"

He did not like being with his father. Their relationship had been frayed.

"I told myself, I'll never in my life be like them," he said of his parents.

He refused to stay in Plaquemines Parish. He was not a waterman.

"I'm staying on the land," Sal said. "I'm leaving."

15

A COACH SUSPENDED, A PLAYER HURT

THERE WAS PLENTY OF WATER AROUND SOUTH PLAQUE-mines High School, but none of it was located in a pool. Kids in lower Plaquemines learned how to swim in canals and bayous and in the river. Before Katrina, one of the players even went to school by boat. So it was with some amusement that the Hurricanes dressed in the natatorium at St. Martin's Episcopal School in Metairie. How dainty it seemed, other people swimming in bathing caps against a clock, when they had learned to swim with alligators.

"If we had a swim team, we'd win nationals," quarterbacks' coach Corey Buie said. "Put an oyster sack on those kids' backs, they'd still win."

The light mood was tempered by the absence of Roger Halphen III, the football line coach and head wrestling coach at South Plaquemines. He had been suspended after an altercation with a wrestler at practice. Neither Roger nor school officials would discuss the details because it was a personnel matter. Witnesses said one of the wrestlers had cursed Roger and tossed a letter with names of potential donors, along with money for a team fund-raiser, into a trash can. Roger had chased the kid and tried to prevent him from leaving the wrestling room. The incident was caught on videotape. Roger's arm went up, and what happened next—whether he struck the kid or they inadvertently collided while losing their balance against a wrestling mat—depended on interpretations of the video.

In any case, Roger would be suspended without pay for the rest of the school year. He would be accused of initiating physical contact with the wrestler and would be told he could no longer coach in Plaquemines Parish. The suspension could not have come at a more inopportune time. Roger had nearly nineteen years of teaching on his resume. At twenty years, he would be eligible to collect a pension. And the Hurricanes were on their way toward a possible state championship. Now his season was done. In a spark of temper, a career seemed to have been incinerated.

Little Wayne Williamson, the school's top wrestler, had attempted to intervene. He believed both Roger and the other wrestler should have used more restraint. Still, he thought Roger had meant only to grab the kid. The wrestler had not been hurt, Little Wayne said. Yet Roger knew it looked bad on tape. He was six foot four, more than three hundred pounds, a former lineman at Mississippi State in the 1980s. The wrestler had been a hundred pounds lighter. His head had snapped back.

"I feel like an axe murderer," Roger said. "Eighteen years gone in one second."

He felt even worse for his wrestlers and football players. Who would coach them? It had been increasingly difficult to find or keep certified teachers and coaches in lower Plaquemines, even before Katrina. He and Cyril Crutchfield were the only two faculty football coaches. Now the Hurricanes would have to play the rest of the season without their line coach.

"I feel terrible," Roger said. "I feel like I let them down."

How could it have come to this? The Halphens were a prominent coaching family in Buras. The family patriarch, Roger Halphen Jr., had played on Buras's six-man state-championship football team in 1956. For a time, he had held the state record in the discus. Later, as a recreation director in Plaquemines in the 1970s, he bought sporting equipment in New Orleans, spending his own money as many coaches did, and handing out balls and bats to kids in Port Sulphur, Buras, and Boothville-Venice. He also helped to integrate Dixie Youth Baseball at a time when the segregationist Perez family still ran the parish like a fiefdom.

"He wasn't necessarily a civil rights activist walking on the streets, but he felt like those kids needed to be playing," Roger III said.

His father had literally given his life to kids in the parish. In 1983, while trying to help calm a melee in a Bantam League football game between thirteen- and fourteen-year-old players from Port Sulphur and Belle Chasse, Roger Halphen Jr. suffered a heart attack. He was found slumped over the wheel of his car near Port Sulphur High School, his foot on the brake, the car in drive. After the brawl ended, he apparently attempted to drive himself to a hospital near the school. He was forty-nine. Buras honored him with a recreation field in his name.

Charles Allen, Roger III's half brother, had played on Buras High's 1966 state-championship team. He had served as defensive coordinator on the Buras teams, with Corey Buie at quarterback, that won the state championship in 1990 and finished second in 1991. Charles was now a guidance counselor at Boothville-Venice Elementary School.

Roger III twice won the state heavyweight wrestling championship at Buras High, from which he graduated in 1981. A degenerative disk in his back sabotaged his football career at Mississippi State. For years, he drifted away from sports. He had not intended on returning to Plaquemines when he got his degree in communications in 1985. But his father had died, and his plans changed. He shrimped and fished oysters, then returned to school, taking another degree in education and a master's in administration and supervision.

"I figured if I got certified, I'd probably have job security the rest of my life," Roger said. "They'd never be able to take that away."

He taught and coached at the middle school in Buras for fifteen years before Katrina struck, helping out at times with the varsity for no pay. It was a comfortable bachelor's life. Outside school, Roger owned a bar in Buras called the Rex Club and had a video poker business. That was all wiped out by the hurricane, along with his house and rental property. Still, he had returned to the parish, teaching P.E. at South Plaquemines, serving as head coach of the wrestling team and the line coach for the football team.

"You feel like these are your kids," Roger said. "It felt like the right thing to do. There's not many coaches down here to begin with."

Even before the temporary buildings were up at the new school in 2006, Roger and Crutchfield had been out there with the kids, trying to meld three football teams into one. He picked up ice each day at a shrimp dock so the players could have drinking water at practice, spent his own money on Pedialyte so the players would not cramp during games. As the inaugural South Plaquemines wrestling season started in the fall of 2006, Roger did not bother getting cable or satellite television hooked up to his FEMA trailer. Instead, he watched wrestling videos, learning the latest techniques without distraction. In the summer of 2007, he spent several thousand dollars of his own money transporting players to a wrestling camp at the Citadel in South Carolina. And now, in a split-second confrontation, his coaching career and his teaching career had come undone.

"I feel like my past has been wiped out," Roger said.

BY NOW, RIDGE TURNER WAS THE STATE'S MOST PROLIFIC quarterback. Through seven games, he had thrown for 1,863 yards and 21 touchdowns against only 3 interceptions, while rushing for 979 yards and 12 touchdowns. Ridge was becoming one of the most efficient passers in the history of high school football, having completed 98 of 137 (71.5 percent) of his passes. Cantrelle Riley, his favorite receiver, also ranked first in Louisiana, with 43 receptions for 880 yards.

Against St. Martin's, Cyril Crutchfield wanted to run the ball. Counter right, counter left. During warm-ups, he noticed that tonight's referee was the same official who had moved the ball as South Plaquemines threatened at the goal line in the final seconds of regulation against Belle Chasse.

"I'll never forget that my whole life," Crutchfield said now as he walked among his players.

St. Martin's took the opening kickoff and ran a fake punt after its first drive stalled. Given a reprieve, the Saints exploited the Hurricanes' one weakness—pass coverage—and took a 7–0 lead. The advantage was as surprising as it was short-lived.

Lyle Fitte ran a counter right, once then twice, following Sal Cepriano into the end zone. Then he ran another counter right on the extra point, and South Plaquemines took the lead, 8–7. Ridge then put his hand on tackle Jordan Ancar's back, followed him on a counter left, tightroped the sideline, and ran sixty yards to make it 16–7.

"No mercy," Crutchfield said. "Let's finish this off."

Quickly, the Hurricanes did, with another counter, then touchdown passes by Ridge of three, twenty-three, and thirteen yards. Dr. Jorge Martinez, whose son, Jacob, played guard for St. Martin's, walked the sideline, assisting the chain crew. The night before, he said, he had told his son to protect himself for baseball season.

"You know, y'all are going to get killed," Dr. Martinez had told his son. He said he was impressed by the resilience of the players from lower Plaquemines.

"They got wiped out in a hurricane; this is what they have left, pride in their football team," Martinez said. "They want to beat the crap out of you."

With nearly eight minutes remaining in the first half, South Plaquemines sprinted ahead 46–14. Then the season took a chilling turn when Cantrelle Riley twisted his knee on a kickoff return and fell awkwardly. He had banged his right knee repeatedly in previous games, receiving medical attention but always getting up to play again. This time, the injury seemed serious.

At halftime, with South Plaquemines ahead 68–14, Cantrelle was examined by an orthopedic surgeon. He sat on the ground, and the top of his right leg seemed to move independently from the bottom of the leg. Luis Espinoza, the orthopedist, told Cantrelle that he had torn the medial collateral ligament (MCL), which prevents the knee from collapsing toward the body. There also seemed to be some laxity in the anterior cruciate ligament and the posterior cruciate ligament, which together keep the knee from moving too far forward or backward.

The good news, Dr. Espinoza said, was that most MCL injuries healed without surgery. The bad news was, Riley might be out for a month or more.

Crutchfield walked over.

"How long does it take to heal?" he asked.

"Four to six weeks," the doctor said.

"Oh, Lord."

Cantrelle got up and limped away down the sideline, refusing to believe what he had heard.

Dr. Espinoza explained that Cantrelle needed a hinged brace to stabilize the knee, an X-ray, and a magnetic resonance imaging test. If Cantrelle did not take proper care of the knee, the doctor said, he risked further stretching of the ligaments simply by getting in and out of a car.

"That's a bad injury," Dr. Espinoza said. "It heals very predictably, but you have to protect it."

Lisa Riley, Cantrelle's mother, listened to the doctor, then told Cantrelle they should leave the stadium. They could get to a hospital tonight or in the morning. Cantrelle refused, so his mother took his helmet and shoulder pads with her. This would keep him from trying to get back in the game.

"I think he's lying," Cantrelle said of the orthopedist, upset, still in disbelief. "I'm going to my own doctor."

The final score was 74–21. Later, Guy Farber, the St. Martin's coach, shook Crutchfield's hand and said, "Thanks for calling off the dogs."

Farber was certain the Hurricanes would win the Class 1A championship. One of the St. Martin's players had said that Caileb Ancar, the Hurricanes' left tackle, was the best lineman he had ever faced.

"I'm gonna come watch y'all in the 'Dome," Farber told Crutchfield.

Belle Chasse had lost again. Crutchfield smiled. Later, he hoped aloud that Cantrelle's injury was not as bad as the doctor said.

"That would put us in a bind."

16

"I'D RATHER THEM DO ANYTHING BUT THIS."

IT WAS HOMECOMING WEEK. TWO GAMES REMAINED IN THE regular season, but already Cyril Crutchfield was thinking ahead to the play-offs.

The news about Cantrelle Riley was encouraging. He had gotten a second medical opinion and was told the medial collateral ligament in his right knee was strained, not torn. He bought a knee brace at a sporting goods store.

"Are we the best team? Yes," Crutchfield told his players at practice on a gray day. "Does the best team always win? No. There's one game in the play-offs when adversity is going to hit. You've got to be mentally tough."

He would make sure his team kept its composure. The goal was not to get to the Superdome. The goal was to win a state championship. No other verdict was acceptable.

"I am the district judge, I am the appellate judge, and I am the goddamned Supreme Court," Crutchfield said.

He could not wait until the Hurricanes practiced in the 'Dome a day before the title game, the huge arena empty as players lined up for the team picture.

"I promise you, it will blow your mind," Crutchfield said.

He had taken Port Sulphur to the 'Dome in 2001 and 2002. Last year, he had gone again, but as a spectator, not a coach, to watch Randall Mackey win a championship for Bastrop.

"I felt out of place," he said.

This year he planned to be back on the sideline.

"I can't wait," Crutchfield said. "I ain't gonna lie to you."

TRUSTIES FROM THE PARISH PRISON SET UP METAL TRAFFIC barricades along Highway 23 leading into Port Sulphur. It was a cloudless day, perfect for a Homecoming parade. By noon, Big Wayne Williamson had fired up the sheriff department's portable grill at the stadium concession stand. He wore a blue 'Canes sweatshirt and talked about the recovery from Katrina.

"This is a fairy tale," Big Wayne said, looking over the football field. "We're winning. It's bringing the communities together. It's been a quiet hurricane season. People are coming back. It all starts here, on the football field."

The ambiguity of recovery was evident along the highway through Port Sulphur. Beige-colored trailers had begun to fill the lanes that ran to the river and the marsh. "Did you see, so and so's back?" people asked each other at the dollar store and the doughnut shop. Signs announced the coming of the Mississippi River Bank and the Greater Macedonia Baptist Church and the availability of live bait. There were less-welcoming signs, too. A forbidding notice offset the picket-fence normalcy at one trailer: "Warning: Armed Guard on Duty."

A few houses perked up under the restorative effects of table saws and paint brushes. Others staggered, punch-drunk, or kneeled submissively like circus animals to the trainer's whip. The fire station still had a wall missing. Driveways led to empty slabs. Moldy jerseys were still strewn about the floor in the ruined locker room at Port Sulphur High. Plays from an exhibition game played two days before the storm were still written on a greaseboard. Lower Plaquemines felt emaciated with its skeletal churches and gaunt, wasted buildings. Signs that once bore the names of restaurants and boat dealerships and convenience stores were now just empty rectangular frames.

For some along the parade route, Homecoming meant a continued rebirth. Others found a more complicated reality. Willie Mae and Finley St. Ann had driven two hours from Picayune, Mississippi. Their granddaughter was a maid on the Homecoming court. Buras had been their home before the storm. Willie Mae said she felt good to see familiar faces but depressed to see the halting recovery. She wanted to come back for good, but her husband needed dialysis for his kidneys several times a week. There was no treatment facility available in lower Plaquemines.

"My situation is, we're stuck," Willie Mae said. "That's sad. This is where we were born and raised. Katrina killed us all. When I come back, I don't want to leave, but you've got to go where you can live. I like Mississippi, but it's just not home."

Willie Encalade had a grandson on the team, linebacker Trey Stewart. She sat on the tailgate of pickup truck, holding an umbrella against the sun. She had lived through Betsy, Camille, and Katrina and was not about to move from Plaquemines Parish.

"Whatever the good Lord has in store for you, no matter where you are, you gonna get it," she said. "I ain't gonna move 'til the good Lord takes me. At least you get a warning for a hurricane. A tornado, an earthquake, you don't get nothin'."

CRUTCHFIELD HAD FORBIDDEN THE HURRICANES FROM AT-
tending the parade. He wanted their minds on the game. An excep-
tion was made for right tackle Jordan Ancar, who was voted the
Homecoming king. He wore a white suit and a velvet crown and
rode in a Corvette convertible driven by his father. There were forty-
three floats and cars in the parade along Highway 23. The Homecoming king and the Homecoming maids and the cheerleaders
tossed beads and candy and plastic footballs. The parade's grand mar-
shals were the Fremin brothers, who owned the only supermarket in
lower Plaquemines. They tossed slips of paper to make grocery lists.

In his pregame speech, Crutchfield gave a valedictory to his six
seniors: Caileb Ancar, Jordan Ancar, Sal Cepriano, Little Wayne
Williamson, Cantrelle Riley, Shane Dinette.

He cared about all of them, Crutchfield said, but he had special
feelings for the kids who had been with him at Port Sulphur High
before the hurricane. The number of those players was rapidly
dwindling.

"Caileb, in 2004 I said you were going to be the best lineman I
ever had.

"Sal, you quit and came back.

"Jordan was a big fuckin' pussy. Now you've grown into a man.

"Wayne, I cussed his ass out pre-, during, and post-Katrina. I
respect him a lot. Others would have quit."

If not for the hurricane, Crutchfield said, Port Sulphur might be
playing for a third consecutive state championship.

"That bitch ass Katrina," Crutchfield said. "Now it's time to start
a new legacy. Ten years from now, when we come back for our reunion, you can say, 'I was the first one to win a state championship
at South Plaquemines.' It's something I want to do. It's something
we need to do. Malcolm X said it: by any means necessary."

He had begun to get headaches in anticipation. He was nervous,
anxious. Sometimes he felt chest pains.

"I can't let it go what that bitch Katrina took from us," Crutchfield said. "For us, and the other survivors, we gotta get this one. The storm taught us we are not promised tomorrow. Play like this is your last one. Let's finish it out as state champs. Look how far we've come in two years. Let's not get complacent."

Then he told his players about a conversation with Nick Saban, the current Alabama coach and former LSU coach.

"He said something I'll never forget," Crutchfield said. "'You don't always get what you want, but you always get what you deserve.'"

If any team deserved a state championship, he said, it was this one. For the six seniors, this would be their last Homecoming. In a few weeks, their careers would end. "If you love football, there's no worse feeling in the world," Crutchfield said.

The only thing to do was postpone that moment as long as possible, until the Hurricanes had won a title.

"High school ball, that's the best there is," Crutchfield said.

Who knew what would happen next season, he told his assembled team. Another hurricane might come and take everything away. But as long as there was football at South Plaquemines, he would be there. He guaranteed it.

"You boys are gonna have kids and they're gonna come home with a cracked eye and say, 'Coach fucked me up.' And you're gonna say, 'Don't worry, he fucked me up, too. He crazy.'"

BEFORE KICKOFF, UNDER A PERFECT SKY THAT MELTED FROM silvery blue to orange and pink at sunset, Megan Barthelemy was named Homecoming queen. She was a star player on the basketball team and a statistician for the football team. It was the start of a grand night for the Barthelemy family. Her brother Felix, a defensive end, scooped up two fumbles for touchdowns in a 54–0 victory over Crescent City Baptist. Ridge Turner completed 13 of 18 passes for 243 yards and 2 touchdowns. Lyle Fitte ran for 137 yards and 2 touchdowns and caught 6 passes for 179 yards and a third touchdown on an eighty-nine-yard screen pass.

Good news came from elsewhere, too. Belle Chasse had lost its fourth straight game. Its players and coaches were arguing on the sideline, according to word that got back to South Plaquemines.

"I like it," Crutchfield said.

Meanwhile, South Plaquemines was 7–2 and had secured a play-off berth as no worse than cochampion of District 10, Class 1A. The postseason would start in two weeks.

"It's serious now," Crutchfield said.

WEARING THE FIRST SUIT HE HAD BOUGHT SINCE KATRINA, Phan Plork escorted his daughter, Jenny Taing, onto the field for the introduction of the Homecoming court. Jenny wore a floppy hat, a dark suit, heels, and a silver corsage. In her junior year, she was an A student and a cheerleader who participated in volleyball, basketball, softball, and track. She was also a member of the student council. Jenny was fascinated by football and had encouraged her younger brother, Jesse Phan, a freshman, to join the team. He was the only boy among five children. There was little else to do in the fall, and Jenny thought Jesse might learn a few things about cooperation and belonging as part of a team. He played linebacker and saw most of his action on special teams.

"I didn't know I was tough enough to be able to play, but I rode it out," Jesse said.

His father attended games when he could, but Phan Plork had little time for sports in the fall. He was a shrimper, and the white shrimp season ran from August until December. Several days after Homecoming, Phan and his wife Tal set out from the Buras Boat Harbor at dusk aboard their thirty-five-foot skimmer, the *Five Star.* They had come to Plaquemines Parish a decade earlier, joining the three dozen families from Cambodia who trawled the bays of Plaquemines Parish. Like the others, Phan and Tal were survivors of the genocidal regime of the Khmer Rouge, which killed 1.7 million Cambodians between 1975 and 1979.

On this night, Phan, who was forty, had climbed out of his suit and into more familiar and comfortable jeans, a white T-shirt, and a camo cap. He wore a thin goatee and had a dragon tattooed on his right arm. He set out for Bay Pomme d'Or in his shallow-draft boat, then lowered his skimmer nets into the five-foot depth. The nets, sixteen feet wide and twenty-eight feet long, were attached to aluminum frames and unfolded like wings on either side of the boat. A pair of "tickle chains" dragged along the bottom to coax the shrimp out of the mud. A pelican skimmed across the water.

Phan had bought the fiberglass hull for fourteen thousand dollars in 2002 and had put another hundred thousand dollars into the trawler. He installed a 375-horsepower Caterpillar engine and built the deck, the cabin, a freshwater shower, and a refrigerated hold that would carry nine thousand pounds of shrimp. He had been offered a job building trawlers, but he preferred to be his own boss as a fisherman, staying on the water by himself for five to seven days at a time, working until sunrise, falling asleep until early afternoon, then starting again.

"When I'm out for a week, I get homesick," Phan said. "When I'm home too long, I want to be out here. I guess that means I'm a fisherman."

He especially loved the lively action of white shrimp, which announced their presence by jumping acrobatically out of the water. Brown shrimp, caught from mid-May to early July, were more indolent. Like crawfish, they preferred to remain in the mud. Extra weight had to be added to the nets to scoop them from the bottom.

Katrina damaged or destroyed 85 percent of the commercial fishing fleet in Plaquemines Parish, according to the LSU Agricultural Center. By 2006, only about two hundred of the parish's

1,300 shrimpers had returned to local waters. Many had lost their boats, had no insurance, struggled to get loans, and were swamped by the high cost of ice and diesel fuel. Even now, two years after the storm, one trawler still sat abandoned in the marsh outside the Empire Marina.

At the Buras Boat Harbor, sections of the cement docks remained collapsed into the water. Electricity and fresh water were scarce. But Phan and other shrimpers who returned to Plaquemines quickly after the storm found that Katrina's pounding havoc above the water had stirred a bountiful, nutrient-rich turbulence beneath it.

The first push of Phan's nets in the fall of 2005 snapped a belt on his hydraulic winch. The second push strained the teeth on the sprocket. In one night, he caught 8,500 pounds of shrimp. In those plentiful days, he paid off a twenty-five-thousand-dollar loan on his boat.

"I've never seen so many shrimp in my life," Phan said. "And I don't think I'll see that kind of shrimp again."

Certainly not this white shrimp season, which would end in a few weeks. Shrimp, like sunbathers, preferred warm weather. Colder temperatures inhibited growth. As the tides lowered and temperatures dropped, the shrimp headed for deeper water and warmer, more constant temperatures.

After fifteen minutes tonight, Phan reeled in the tail pouch from his nets and unloaded the catch onto a rear table. This was a test to see what the night might have to offer. It was not encouraging. The two pounds of shrimp were small, mostly 80–100s, meaning there were eighty to one hundred of them per pound.

"It's not good," Phan said. "You can't make a profit with this."

OVER THE PAST FIVE OR SIX YEARS, SHRIMPING HAD EXISTED in the harrowing balance between the high price of ice and diesel fuel and the low price of seafood. Louisiana produced more than 40 percent of the nation's domestic shrimp, but the vast majority of shrimp in the United States—about 90 percent—was imported from countries in Asia and South America, industry officials said. Tariffs had not slowed the imports. Prices at local docks were about half of what they had been six years earlier, shrimpers said.

Jumbo shrimp that once brought three or four dollars a pound were now going for about $1.80. Tiny shrimp that once brought ninety cents or a dollar a pound now sold for forty-five or fifty cents. The night before, Phan said, he had caught just enough shrimp to pay for his diesel, which was $2.70 a gallon and rising. He had quit drinking and smoking years earlier to save money. Still, the family relied monthly on food stamps to make ends meet.

"In real money, these people are trading shrimp for diesel and ice, and getting a loaf of bread and lunch meat and going back out, hoping things will get better," Rusty Gaudé, a fisheries agent in Plaquemines Parish for the LSU Agricultural Center, said in 2006.

A year later, he said, "It's even worse."

"They're eating their own catch, so they're well fed, but as far as disposable income, it's bleak," Gaudé said. "The condition of the boats is deteriorating. There's no cash to put into refurbishing. Half of them are not sure how long they're going to be at it."

In the seafood heyday of the mid–1980s, the Louisiana Department of Wildlife and Fisheries issued forty-four thousand shrimping licenses. Now that number had dwindled to fifteen thousand. Of that number, about ten thousand were commercial and recreational shrimpers. Some believed the actual figure may have shrunk again by half. If prices were cratering, at least the shrimp had been generally plentiful since Katrina, said Acy Cooper, vice president of the Louisiana Shrimp Association. The 2006 haul of white shrimp had set a state record.

"We're making it because we're catching a few shrimp," Cooper said. "If there are no fuel subsidies, or we have a bad season, we're on the brink of not making it. It would be devastating."

IT WAS WARM AND CALM ON THIS FALL EVENING. THE SUN did not seem to set as much as melt into an orange yolk on the horizon. Perhaps things would pick up after dark. Holding a coffee mug, Phan headed west into Bayou Auguste, past PVC pipes that marked oyster leases. A dolphin leapt off the starboard side. There were only about ten Cambodian boats out tonight. Earlier in the season, there would have been twenty or thirty. Vietnamese shrimpers preferred to work deeper waters, while the Cambodians preferred inland bays, Phan said.

"The Vietnamese are very brave in the water," Phan said. Then he laughed. "Cambodians like to work near the house. Most have to take seasick pills, let me put it that way."

He did a second test of the tail pouch.

"Not bad," Phan said. "I wish they were bigger."

His wife Tal radioed their children at home. "Do your homework," she told them. The shrimp were too small. She and their father would be home soon. By now, the catch had reached fifty pounds. Tal stood in her red sweater, sweeping the shrimp into a tank full of briny solution and scooping out the trash fish like pogies and croakers.

"This is not good," Tal said. "This is why I tell my kids, 'Go to school, get your education, don't be a fisherman.' You never see your family. It's a hard way to make a living. The kids need stuff. Sometimes, it's hard for us."

Phan spoke on the radio to a handful of Cambodian boats in nearby English Bay. Everyone complained that there weren't enough shrimp. If he were alone, Phan might venture farther out and catch a thousand pounds, but his wife got motion sickness in deeper, choppier water. Tonight, he would call it quits early.

"I wouldn't work all night for this kind of shrimp," Phan said.

Still, the disappointment was relative. A downturn in the shrimp industry seemed a meager setback compared to the savagery of the Khmer Rouge.

"If you can get through Pol Pot, you can get through anything," Tal said.

Phan was eight when the Pol Pot regime came to power and began its brutal killing and forced labor. His father, a soldier, was shot by the Khmer Rouge. He was separated from his mother, forced to build levees for rice fields and to chop weeds and mix them with chemicals as a kind of fertilizer. Repeatedly, he disobeyed the rules of the agricultural commune. He stole away to look for his mother or tried to hide a fish to eat or called his friends by their names instead of "friend" or "comrade." When he was caught, for punishment he was forced to stand in a circle of kids who yanked on his ear so severely that it became infected. Other times, Phan was forced to haul water in heavy buckets so that the camp leader could take a bath. Rations were meager. Two of his younger brothers died of disease, one from chicken pox, another from eating dirt and coal and pencil lead.

Tal believed that her father had been an undercover policeman in Phnom Penh, the Cambodian capital. He wore formal clothes, carried two guns, and spoke English and French. He had sent one of his sons to study in Paris before the arrival of the Khmer Rouge and urged the rest of his family to leave the country. He was later imprisoned, confined in a cage in solitude, where he died. Tal said her mother had a rope tied around her neck and was dragged to her death by horses. Her sister witnessed the killing, Tal said, and was driven mad with grief, wandering into the forest alone, refusing to eat. Presumably, her brother was alive, perhaps still in

Paris, Tal said, but she did not know how to look for him. She was young at the time and could not now remember his name.

After her father's death, Tal survived a near drowning in a flood. She was later befriended and essentially adopted at a labor camp by a fisherman named Taing Young and his wife. (Tal would later give her daughter Jenny the last name of Taing in gratitude.) Sometimes, Taing hid fish for Tal so that she might have something to eat other than scant portions of rice. "She looked like one of those Ethiopian girls you see on TV," Taing said.

When the Vietnamese invaded Cambodia in 1979 and deposed the Khmer Rouge, Tal and her adoptive parents escaped toward the sprawling refugee camp in Thailand called Khao I Dang. A Vietnamese soldier advised them they could find bread crusts in the thatch-and-bamboo camp. They traveled under cover of darkness for several days, eating dried fruit and rice. A year later, Phan also made it to Thailand, having reunited with his mother and an older brother. An uncle, he said, shot several Vietnamese soldiers as the family made it across the border. He had never been back to Cambodia.

"There are only nightmares," Tal said.

Eventually both Phan and Tal immigrated to the United States, where they met in 1987 while picking mushrooms outside Philadelphia. A decade later, while they were picking onions and cucumbers in Stockton, California, they made contact with Taing Young and his wife. The couple was living in Plaquemines Parish. Phan and Tal moved to Louisiana to join them.

Phan began working as a deckhand, then bought his own boat. The American, Cambodian, and Vietnamese shrimpers mostly kept to themselves. There had been conflicts on the water, even gunshots, in his decade in the parish, Phan said. When other shrimpers confronted him over a particular fishing spot, he said, he moved on, even if he had arrived first. It was not worth it to argue.

The family bought a used trailer, and Phan was remodeling the kitchen, bathroom, and living room when Katrina struck. His was one of the last boats to make it into the Empire Marina, about thirty-six hours before the storm hit. The family truck was broken down, so they borrowed a Chevy Lumina from Paul Lemaire, the school-board member and a longtime youth coach. The family drove to Orange, Texas, six of them piled into the tiny car with only five hundred dollars to spend. By mid-October 2005, Phan returned to Buras. At first, he could not find his boat. He feared he might have to pick up and move yet again.

"During Pol Pot, there had been so much moving and running," Phan said. "We couldn't establish anywhere for a long time. It seemed like my life, my house, is on the road. Every place we come by is just another view."

Just as Phan was about to accept insurance money for the *Five Star,* a wildlife agent located the skimmer. It had floated near the river levee, several hundred yards out of Empire Marina. Tangled in electrical wire, it had somehow avoided going into the Mississippi. Only a small hole had been punctured in the hull. Before Thanksgiving of 2005, Phan was back on the water, catching more shrimp than he had ever caught.

The 2007 white shrimp season had not been nearly so encouraging. Phan had let the insurance lapse on his boat. He could get coverage for only seventy thousand dollars, about half what the *Five Star* was worth. And, he and fellow shrimpers said, insurers were declining to provide coverage for hurricane damage, unless the boat was a total loss. "So you take a chance," Phan said.

After a couple of hours on this autumn night, he had caught about a hundred pounds of white shrimp. Perhaps it would bring in fifty-five or sixty dollars at the dock, for a hollow profit of thirty dollars. Tal separated the shrimp by size and Phan dumped them into the refrigerated hold. Then they headed home. He would go out again tomorrow. Perhaps his luck would change by

Thanksgiving. Phan hoped to shrimp at least until his children graduated from high school. Then he might look for another job, perhaps piloting a river vessel. A decade ago, shrimpers did everything they could to get their children to continue in the business. Now it was different.

"I'd rather them do anything but this," he said.

17

BLOODY MARY

ON HALLOWEEN, A HANDFUL OF PLAYERS GATHERED IN A school bathroom to summon the ghost of Bloody Mary. According to the urban legend, Bloody Mary had been disfigured in a car crash, had been a medieval queen who bathed in the blood of virgins, or had killed her own baby. The players wrote her name on a mirror in lipstick, flicked the lights three times, flushed the toilet three times, and called "Bloody Mary" nine times. At this point, a shadow was supposed to appear. Unless the conjurers ducked to the ground, Bloody Mary would kill them or scratch their eyes out. Sal Cepriano wasn't waiting around to find out. He took off running. So did Ridge Turner.

"I was so scared, my hand fogged up the whole mirror," Jeffery Espadron admitted.

There were other ghosts to summon after dark, and the players seemed distracted at practice. Cyril Crutchfield was upset by the inattentiveness. The final game of the regular season was in two days, and the play-offs were around the corner. All this hard work could be futile if his players didn't concentrate. Asked what his plans were for trick-or-treating, Crutchfield glumly climbed into his bus to drive players home and said, "Find a gun and blow my fuckin' head off."

AFTER PRACTICE, ESPADRON'S RIGHT KNEE HURT. THE FRESH-man nose tackle had caught his leg in the sand while fishing, wrenching his knee upon falling in the marsh near his home in Happy Jack. A visit to the doctor would have to wait, though. Before heading out on Halloween night, there was time to hunt rabbits in a thicket of pecan trees, Johnson grass, and blackberry bushes behind his house. Dressed in a T-shirt and basketball shorts, his glorious, mossy Afro subdued in a ponytail, Jeffery grabbed his crack-barrel twelve gauge. He put a handful of number 3-½ shells in a sock and walked along a ditch bank, looking for swamp rabbits that were coming out to feed at dusk.

"I wouldn't want to be anywhere else," he said.

His father, Jeffery Sr., had been a star running back on Port Sulphur's 1979 state-championship team. He wore number 32 and people called him "the Juice." Of all the men who stood in the stands each week, saying that they had been the best to play the game, Jeffery Espadron Sr. could make a legitimate claim, said Paul Lemaire, a former teammate at Port Sulphur.

Jeffery Sr. now worked as a handyman for the school district. Jeffery's mom, Denise, was a nurse. The family lost everything twice in 2005, first when Katrina hit, then when Rita struck. The Espadrons relocated to El Dorado, Arkansas, seeking higher ground and lower risk, signing papers on a house with a corner lot. Before they could move in, they changed their minds. The family was still living in a hotel when a man approached Jeffery Jr. and offered to sell him drugs. There were rumors about a crystal meth lab in the area, and Jeffery got so afraid, he wouldn't even go to the hotel lobby. What if he got shot and could never play football again? It was something he never had to worry about in Plaquemines Parish, so the family moved home. The only advantage to living in Arkansas, Jeffery Sr. said, was the low cost of dentures.

Denise Espadron put her faith in God that another hurricane like Katrina would not strike for fifty years. "I'll be dead and rotten," she said. "Let my casket pop open. I'll be in my glory. They can put me right there, under the oak tree."

The family returned to its property in Happy Jack and the ten acres it had bought for a dollar per acre from the Catholic Church. Denise would have preferred to keep her kids in school in Belle Chasse, but Jeffery wanted to return to lower Plaquemines to play for Crutchfield. So the family came home, where Jeffery could walk a block, climb the levee, and go fishing in the marsh. Before Katrina, he and his father went coonin' for oysters, feeling for them as raccoons did in shallow waters and tossing them into a boat. It was nearing Thanksgiving, and his father collected empty gallon jars, filling them with shucked oysters that sold for up to fifty dollars a jar around the holidays.

Jeffery Jr. had shot his first rabbit from a car. If he killed any today, his grandmother would smother them in wild onions.

"I see one!" he said, leaning nimbly from side to side, walking on his tiptoes. Then he took off running, strikingly fast for his size, hitching up his shorts as he sprinted along the ditch bank. He raised his shotgun but didn't fire.

"They don't go far," he said, hissing in frustration, hoping the swamp rabbit might circle back into view. Then he aimed his gun again, and the blast shattered the evening quiet. If he had hit a rabbit, though, he couldn't tell. Perhaps it had zigzagged into the tall grass, but if it had, Jeffery was not chasing after it.

"Water moccasins," he said.

He cracked open the shotgun and used a stick to push the spent shell out of the barrel. Then he realized he had dropped the sock containing his other shells. Quickly, he found the shells and noticed a series of rabbit tunnels in the grass.

"They run crawlin' like a cat do," Jeffery said.

He kept walking slowly, carefully, trying to spot the round, dark eye of a rabbit that would betray its camouflage. Then there was a flash of movement at the edge of the thicket. "I saw something jump," Jeffery said, firing at a target thirty yards ahead, to his left.

"I know I had him on aim," he said.

Again, he must have missed.

"Where that thing went?"

He walked to the canal at the back of the family property and pointed to a bridge. The previous summer, he had spotted a six-and-a-half-foot alligator under the bridge, with a noose or something caught around its neck. He hit the gator over the head with a pipe, a friend cleaned the animal, and the Espadrons fried the tail for dinner.

"Fishy tasting but very good," Jeffery said.

It was getting too dark to hunt now, so he began heading home. There would be plenty of other days to stalk rabbits in the brambly woods.

"When the snakes go away, I'll go get 'em," he said.

Anyway, he had other plans for tonight. He was meeting up with his freshman teammates to search for the ghost of Tee Jack. According to the folklore of Plaquemines Parish, Tee Jack had been a murderer who was killed by a train. Some swore he was real, or real enough. Jeffery Espadron Sr. said that when he was younger, he and his friends had built a symbolic grave for Tee Jack at a nearby Catholic Church. If you called his name three times, "Tee Jack, Tee Jack, Tee Jack, come out your grave tonight," he was supposed to appear with a lantern and a gun.

Plaquemines Parish, reflecting its French, Indian, African, and Caribbean influences, was as historically rich with folk beliefs as it was with oil: Ghosts that marched over the levees as phantom evacuees the night before Katrina struck; dancing lights, or *feux follets*, that flitted about cemeteries, balls of flaming marsh gas taken to be spirits of unchristened babies or apparitions of felonious adults that could be silenced by the blade of a knife stuck into a tree; home remedies that included spider webs to help clot blood and sassafras filé to cure an infected tooth; remedy-men and remedy-women who placed a rattlesnake vertebra around the neck of a baby to soothe its teething. Many of these beliefs were now held only by the elderly, or discontinued entirely. Just this season, though, the grandmother of freshman cornerback Bradley Sylve had applied drops of holy water in his eyes in an attempt to help cure an infection that kept him out of several games.

Most ominously, the elderly told stories of *loups-garous*, or werewolves, shape-shifters that transformed from humans into animals of many kinds, including cats and dogs, causing suspicion and malevolence. In his 1944 book *Deep Delta Country*, Harnett T. Kane told a classic tale:

Madame A. wondered when her husband stayed away for a week or more in the marsh, but like an obedient housewife she raised no questions. Occasionally, she noticed a curiously spotted tomcat slinking around the levee. It peered and peered at the house, as if it wanted to make sure that it missed nothing. Madame A. grew annoyed, and tossed a bit of mud at it. The cat slipped away. The next day it was back, and she threw a stick. Crying, it moved off. The third morning, truly angry when it made its appearance, she advanced with a kitchen knife. It snarled; she tossed the knife, and it cut deeply into the left hind leg. The cat vanished at once. In an hour or so, Monsieur A. came from the marsh, limping, his left foot heavily bandaged. "I drop my axe on it," he said and avoided her eye. "Oui," she nodded, and went back to her housework. That cat didn't come back anymore, let me tell you!

On this Halloween night, a dozen freshmen and eighth-grade players from South Plaquemines gathered along the river road in Diamond, just beyond the FEMA trailer park. On the lookout for Tee Jack, they laughed easily as they walked along the lighted two-lane blacktop that ran along the river levee. Then, coming to a gate that said, "Keep Out," they grew quiet, timid. Down the long, dark gravel road was a cemetery. Halfway down, the wind was supposed to stop blowing in a place of dead calm. Beyond that, a ghost reportedly moved among the gravestones. The players linked arms and walked slowly. Beau Fitte, the best among them on the field at defensive end, carried a flashlight. They were not as bold tonight as they were when shielded by helmets and shoulder pads on Fridays.

"I'm scared," someone called out.

"I'm not going all the way."

"I'll wait for y'all by the road."

Then an angry voice called, "Hey," not the vaporous shout of a ghost but the mortal irritation of the landowner. The players scattered, some finding cover in the grass, others sprinting toward the river road and escaping along the levee. The landowner explained that someone had overturned gravestones on a previous Halloween, so he was keeping a close eye on the property. Later, as the players reassembled, they laughed again in that relieved way of settled fear.

"I nearly ran out of my shoe," Jeffery Espadron said.

Given his size eighteen feet, he had only one good pair.

"I wouldn't have been able to go to school."

THE NEXT DAY, UPSET WITH THE CAVALIER PRACTICE ON Halloween, Crutchfield put his players in pads for the first time in five weeks. They tackled vigorously, linemen against linemen, backs against backs. Several times Jeffery Espadron went down and did not get up.

"Get up off your ass," assistant coach August Ragas told him. "Don't be a big fuckin' baby."

There was more brutish name calling and yelling by the coaches and his teammates:

"You Abominable Snowman, you shouldn't let people push you around."

"Let me have that weight, I could do some damage."

Jeffery did not say a word. He was not loafing or being a coward. His knee was hurting again. It seemed to grow numb and burn at the same time. But he wanted to play the next day, so he ignored both the pain and the insults.

He was only fifteen, and he still lacked explosiveness. If a lineman pushed him one direction, he did not yet have the forcefulness to shove his way back into position. But he was huge and mobile and took up enormous space in the middle of the defense. Against Ridgewood, he had collected four tackles and sacked the quarterback twice.

"I like him," Crutchfield said. "He's fast."

Increasingly, high school players were growing to the size of NFL linemen, recent studies and anecdotal evidence showed. Doctors had begun to express concern about the health risks of being overweight and obese. High blood pressure and high cholesterol ran in the Espadron family. Jeffery Sr. had just lost thirty pounds on a more selective diet. Denise Espadron said she tried to avoid serving white rice, white bread, potatoes, and sugary drinks. But sometimes it was a chore just to keep a son like Jeffery fed.

"We love our Popeye's down here," she said. As for fried seafood, "I think it's a curse on people in Plaquemines Parish."

After practice, Jeffery and his younger brother, Jacob, headed back into the marsh in Happy Jack, fishing off the levee bank. Whatever they caught would be eaten at a Sunday fish fry. The refuse of Katrina was still evident in the marsh—the railing of a deck, somebody's front steps, a picnic table. Dressed in shorts and a T-shirt, Jeffery quickly had his shoes off. His size-eighteen feet squished into the mud as he fished for redfish at the Tennessee Pipeline Canal. The first one he ever caught was still in the freezer, waiting to be mounted.

THE FINAL REGULAR SEASON GAME, AGAINST ECOLE CLAS-sique, marked the day that Crutchfield and Micquella Sylve finally moved to a spacious trailer on the South Plaquemines campus from their cramped FEMA trailer behind Belle Chasse High School. They were now engaged. This school year, Mickey drove a school bus and served as a substitute teacher. Previously, in their FEMA trailer, Crutchfield had said he could put one foot in the shower and the other in the living room.

The final game began with some doubt, not as to the eventual winner but as to whether it would be played in full. Ecole Classique, like many other private schools in New Orleans, was still struggling to boost its enrollment after Katrina. Injuries had further reduced the Spartans' roster to fifteen available players. The team was winless this season, except by forfeit. Ecole's top quarterback had suffered a dislocated elbow, and his backup was out with a rib injury.

If South Plaquemines thought the game would be a waste of time, Ecole was willing to forfeit. Even if the game was played, Ecole might have to halt the contest if its third-string quarterback suffered an injury. The Hurricanes wanted to play. They needed a final tune-up for the play-offs. If South Plaquemines scored sixty-four points, it would average fifty for the season. It would have to temper its aggressiveness, though. On the sideline, Crutchfield told his players bluntly, "Be physical, but if you hurt the quarterback, it's over."

The job of emergency quarterback for Ecole Classique fell to a blithe senior named Zack Ham. After serving as a backup quarterback for much of his career, Ham had gained fifteen pounds to become a center. The number on his helmet was 50, while the number on tonight's jersey was 3. He had jogged a mile or two after each practice during the week, trying to drop a little weight from his 190-pound frame.

"I didn't really eat, so I could get into my jersey," he said.

Late in the first quarter, he threw a pass and later came to the bench to confirm that it had been completed.

"One for two, sweet," Ham said. "Maybe my name will be in the paper. A center's name is not usually in the paper."

Crutchfield had assigned a more arduous obligation to the Hurricanes. They had to make a first down or score on every play, or they would have to punt. This would keep the game from getting embarrassingly out of hand in the opening minutes. On South Plaquemines' first play, a curl pass to Lyle Fitte gained four yards. On the second play, the Hurricanes punted. The crowd groaned in disbelief.

"Come on, get serious," Paul Lemaire shouted.

On the next possession, Lyle returned a punt forty-three yards, then sprinted into the end zone from the seven to put South Plaquemines up 7–0. A thirty-seven-yard touchdown pass from Ridge Turner to tight end Seth Ancar, and another thirty-seven-yarder, to Cantrelle Riley, made it 21–0 in the first quarter. Early in the second quarter, Jeffery Espadron went down again. The area just below his right knee felt numb. Otherwise, it felt as if he were kneeling on a rock.

A doctor examined Jeffery and said the injury did not appear serious. Eventually, it would be diagnosed as a bruised nerve, and Jeffery would be prescribed a week's rest. If he had to miss a few days of fishing, that was a small price to pay.

"I ain't worried about fish," he said as he limped toward the locker room at halftime. "I'm worried about gettin' better for the play-offs."

By halftime, the Hurricanes were up 42–0. South Plaquemines would eventually win 55–0. Zack Ham made it through the game for Ecole Classique without throwing a touchdown pass, but also without getting hurt. The South Plaquemines players had shown great sportsmanship, he said.

"We heard stories that they were rough and mean, but every time I got sacked, there were three hands reaching in to pick me up," Ham said. "They were tapping me on the helmet, saying, 'Good job.' I hope they win state."

In five league games, the Hurricanes had outscored their opponents by a collective 302–35. Ridge had finished the regular season as Louisiana's leading passer with 2,658 yards (on 157 of 212 attempts) and 31 touchdowns versus 8 interceptions. Cantrelle was the state's leading receiver, with 57 receptions for 1,098 yards. Lyle was the state's second-leading receiver, with 50 receptions for 1,095 yards. Both Ridge and Lyle had also rushed for more than 1,000 yards.

South Plaquemines had delivered one of the greatest offensive performances in Louisiana's history, but something was eating at Crutchfield. Lyle again appeared to be pouting on the sideline. The early punts and substitutions had tempered his statistics against Ecole Classique. How would he ever attract recruiters unless he accumulated spectacular numbers? Crutchfield sympathized, but not to the point of tolerating Fitte's sulking and failing to offer encouragement to his teammates.

"That's a selfish SOB," Crutchfield said to August Ragas.

The coaches believed Lyle's father was complaining to him that he was getting too few carries, too few yards, even though he had rushed for 1,416 yards and 15 touchdowns during the regular season.

"Run or pass, we go to Lyle," Marcelin Ancar said. "The kid's in every play. What more do you want?"

Crutchfield was also irritated with the crowd for questioning his play calling. Fans thought nothing of screaming at him in the middle of a game, offering their advice on any particular play or formation. They were not happy with punting on second down. Couldn't they see he didn't want to humiliate Ecole Classique? If only there was a track around the field, Crutchfield said. That would back the crowd up.

"They think it's the community's team," Crutchfield said. "It's my team."

Assistant coach Rod Parker laughed. All this complaining would be forgotten by next Friday and the first play-off game.

"They gonna love you," Parker said. "Each week they gonna love you more and more. As long as we win."

Crutchfield was sure South Plaquemines had the best team in Class 1A.

"We've just got to prove we're the best five more times," he said.

18

CONTROLLED RAGE

MARCELIN ANCAR SHOOK HIS SONS JORDAN AND MAVERICK awake. It was one o'clock in the morning on November 9. The first play-off game was eighteen hours away. South Plaquemines (8–2) was seeded third among thirty-two teams in the Class 1A bracket. Its first opponent was thirtieth-seeded Mangham High (4–6) of northeastern Louisiana. Marcelin couldn't sleep. He awakened his sons and said, "Let's talk football." They stared at him groggily. "Get up," he said. "Y'all don't feel this?" For forty-five minutes the boys talked as their father unwound. Twenty-three years earlier, Marcelin's own high school career had ended prematurely in the play-offs. That defeat stuck with him, and he did not want his sons to feel the same disappointment.

"You never forget," he said. "It's like when you burn yourself the first time with a match. It's always going to burn when you put it on you."

By three forty-five a.m., Lorne "Boo" Landry was up, too. His stomach was tight. Who could sleep the night before the first play-off game? A whole season was on the line. By early afternoon, Boo and his friend Harold Sylve would start cooking cases of "slap yo' mother-in-law" fried chicken for the home fans, but that was hours away. So he began ironing clothes, first the work

225

clothes for his wife, then the school clothes for their son, Little Boo, an eighth-grade lineman. By the time Boo had worked off his nervous energy, he had ironed Little Boo's clothes for an entire week.

When the clock struck five, three hours before the start of school, Ridge Turner was wide awake. He got up and took a shower. Denise Espadron, the mother of Jeffery Espadron, had tossed and turned through the night. She had been having a recurring nightmare: She arrived at the South Plaquemines stadium only to be told that the game was six or seven hours away in Mangham. Frantically, she tried to reach the game, driving on back roads with no hope of arriving on time, screaming, "No, no" in her dreams.

"This is when we find out what we're made of—whether we're hype or real," Big Wayne Williamson said in midafternoon as he barbecued at the concession stand. "I'm not ready to cry yet. I'll be ready to cry on December eighth, when we win it all."

It was cool, overcast. The wind was out of the west, which brought armies of gnats out of the marshes. They were as fierce as they were tiny, swarming into eyes and noses, biting scalps. On warm autumn days, players constantly slapped at their arms and legs at practice. If someone had a can of bug spray, it was slathered on between plays like tanning lotion. If you played basketball outdoors, assistant coach Rod Parker liked to say, your face was soon covered by a mask of insects. Tonight, a truck equipped with a chemical spray circled the stadium, then drove down the field, from goal post to goal post, trying to subdue the pests.

Roger Halphen could not bring himself to attend the game. He did not want to sit in the stands and have to explain his suspension to everyone who asked.

"I don't know if I could be more depressed," he said. "I thought this was the one chance I would have to win a state championship. I feel sick."

Mangham arrived after a bus trip of seven and a half hours. In New Orleans, traffic was backed up by an eighteen-wheeler whose axle fell off and whose contents spilled onto Interstate 10, covering the road with feathers for Mardi Gras costumes. The trip through lower Plaquemines had been illuminating for Mangham's coach, Bo Meeks. At thirty-one, thin with a shaved head, he was in his first season as a head coach. Previously, Meeks had been the offensive coordinator at Bastrop High, tutoring Randall Mackey. The trip to Port Sulphur had taken Mangham's bus past the street on which Randall had lived, St. Joseph Lane, before Katrina swamped it.

"It really hits home," Meeks said of Port Sulphur. "Nothing but slabs."

This week, Meeks had been set up as a straw man for South Plaquemines. He was a bogeyman, the coach who would not let Randall return to his hometown. This was not true, but it hardly mattered in Port Sulphur.

"It's personal," Marcelin Ancar said.

Let's see how Meeks could do without a quarterback of Randall's caliber, Crutchfield told his players.

"It's payback time," he said.

He did not want to lose this game, Crutchfield said during warm-ups. Not only because of the perceived injustice of Randall's departure, but because the potential of a great season would be snuffed by a defeat.

"Football is the game of life," Crutchfield told his players. "If they call and tell me my mother passed, I'll cry because I love her. If we lose this game, I'll cry because I love the game."

There seemed to be little chance of South Plaquemines losing. Not only did Mangham not have Randall Mackey at quarterback, but its own starter had suffered a fractured wrist the previous week. The replacement was a sophomore from the junior varsity.

Mangham's spread offense had another vulnerability, discovered by Crutchfield during one of his late-night film sessions. The

Dragons tipped off their plays. If the running back lined up even with the quarterback in the shotgun formation, he never got the ball. Instead, Mangham ran a speed sweep to the receiver in motion or threw a pass. If the running back lined up behind the quarterback, he got the ball on an option play or a cut-back run to the opposite side.

As the game opened, though, Mangham's passing overcame its predictability. The Hurricanes were susceptible in pass coverage, and a fifty-nine-yard throw beat Cantrelle Riley at cornerback, setting up a short touchdown run. Fifty-five seconds into the first quarter, South Plaquemines trailed 6–0. This is what had both scared and intrigued Crutchfield. How would his team respond in the play-offs if it fell behind? Would it counterpunch? Would it stumble into the ropes and surrender?

The answer was immediate and startling.

"This is when true players step up," Marcelin Ancar had told Lyle Fitte before the game. "This is when scouts are looking at you, when all-state teams are made. This is when you need to be part of the team and stop being selfish."

Lyle took the ensuing kickoff at his twenty-yard line as Mangham tried to pinch him along the sideline. Dressed in a dark blue jersey and pants, he began to cut across the field to his left. He ran in cleats wrapped with blue tape and "GOD" written along his ankles. A towel swung from his left hip like a wind sock. Nimbly setting his blockers in place, Fitte ran with subtle shifts of his head and shoulders and hips, as if trying to balance himself on a swaying bridge. He kept moving left and Cantrelle redeemed himself with a springing block and within a few yards Fitte entered a hollow space, a tunnel. Everything roared around him, tacklers in white jerseys and purple helmets in pursuit, all of them running past, threatening but never touching him, pinwheeling off blockers and suddenly behind him, their angles miscalculated. Lyle was alone now, protected like a surfer inside a curl.

The Mangham kicker rushed ahead as Lyle crossed his own forty-yard line, carrying the ball in his left hand, his face invisible behind a visor. Lyle planted his left leg and sidestepped with an evasive pirouette, turning his back to the other players and keeping his balance as the kicker reached desperately, head down, unable to change direction, his head and shoulders too far ahead of his feet, grabbing at the air and stumbling to the ground in a helicoptering fall. Lyle spun neatly and nodded as if his head were an accelerator and picked up speed down the sideline to the end zone.

Two and a half minutes later, Lyle muscled into the end zone again from the five-yard line. Then linebacker Trey Stewart reached in with his right hand and stripped the ball from a Mangham back, juggling the ball as it came free, trapping it between his legs and scooping it into his hands before it hit the ground and running twenty-four yards for a touchdown. Stewart was the strongest and most athletic of the Hurricanes, lithe at six foot two inches, 215 pounds, and he spoke in great rapid bursts, as if his tongue were trying to keep up with his legs. A season ago, with no weight-lifting equipment available, he had lost twenty-five pounds. Sometimes he also seemed to lose his determination, playing with a perplexing indifference. He had missed one game this season with headaches, another with pinkeye. But he could be voracious, and Crutchfield considered Stewart indispensable to winning the state championship.

"You play like that and we can order our rings," he would tell Stewart later.

The game had changed now, and South Plaquemines' linebackers knew the Mangham plays before they could be run. The Hurricanes rushed six defenders on each play, slanting furiously from the outside while linebacker Seth Ancar hatcheted through the middle. Mangham's young quarterback grew besieged by the pressure. Cantrelle intercepted a screen pass, then Ridge rose high on his toes and threw a soft, easy spiral to Ancar, a tight end on offense, for a twenty-two-yard touchdown. The first quarter was not halfway done, and already the Hurricanes had drawn ahead 28–6.

Cantrelle intercepted another pass, then Lyle ran an option play around left end. He was fast and patient at the same time, catching the ball slightly over his head, sprinting wide past a tackle and a linebacker, and feinting inside as Jordan Ancar sealed off a defender. This jab inward left a Mangham safety with his feet flat and his hips twisted futilely and Lyle ran sixty-five yards to the end zone without having been touched, nothing chasing him closely but the towel that flapped from his waist.

Stewart intercepted a slant pass and ran fifty-seven yards for his second touchdown. After the Hurricanes recovered a fumble, Ridge kept the ball on a quarterback counter and scored from seventeen yards to put South Plaquemines ahead 48–6. Lyle's father, Darrel Parker, sat in the stands. He said he understood that football was a team sport, but believed that Crutchfield could have kept Lyle in the games longer, to build a more enticing résumé for recruiters.

"If an injury is going to happen, it's going to happen," Parker said.

As his father spoke, Lyle took a pitch around left end, following Sal Cepriano for a four-yard touchdown. Again, no one laid a hand on him. Eight seconds later, Sal, now at defensive tackle, pounced on a fumble and returned it eighteen yards to the end zone. With five seconds still remaining in the first quarter, South Plaquemines had taken an astonishing 60–6 lead.

Ten days earlier, Smith Center High School in Kansas had scored seventy-two points in one period. The only other American high school team to outscore South Plaquemines in a quarter, with sixty-six points, was Prescott High of Arizona in 1925.

"Scary," Marcelin Ancar said.

By halftime, the Hurricanes led 72–6. After a scoreless second half, Meeks, the Mangham coach, expressed some irritation that South Plaquemines had attempted an onside kick with an overwhelming lead. Otherwise, he spoke in awed tones of the Hurricanes.

South Plaquemines could probably hold its own against Bastrop, the Class 4A favorite, Meeks said. Bastrop would wear the Hurricanes down, but it would be a competitive game.

"Randall's as good a pure passer as I've seen," Meeks said. "He's got a great release and he's as cool as can be in the pocket. Turner's a great athlete, but his release is a little unorthodox."

He did not mean this as a slight, only a comparison, Meeks said. "There's nobody in the state better than this team in 1A. If there is, I don't want to play 'em. They're fast, mean. It's controlled rage."

Cantrelle had intercepted four passes—catching more balls thrown by Mangham's quarterback than by his own. South Plaquemines had forced eight turnovers, scoring on three of them. Lyle Fitte had been unstoppable on the field and magnanimous on the sideline, shaking the hands of his teammates, patting them on the shoulder pads. This is what his coaches had wanted to see, Lyle recognizing those who blocked for him and encouraging those who sat on the bench while he received much of the glory.

"If I took you out, I took you out for a reason, to let them young boys play," Crutchfield said the next morning during a film review of the game. "When I was in college, I didn't want to come out either. When the coach took me out, he never knew how I felt. I don't want to see no more poutin'."

FOLLOWING THE ROUT OF MANGHAM, KEVEN SMITH showed up in the trailer as the Hurricanes changed out of their uniforms. He stepped among the helmets and shoulder pads and cleats tossed on the floor and said, "I don't remember that last year, a defense like that."

He was now attending Delgado Community College in suburban New Orleans, studying to be a nurse. He had received a scholarship upon graduating from South Plaquemines the previous spring. Even though Keven was out of high school, he had continued to see most of the Hurricanes' games, watching from the sidelines or the stands, his own footballs dreams shelved by a lack of height and the responsibilities of fatherhood.

"I wish I had another year," he said.

He kept in touch with his football buddies from Boothville-Venice who had played on the first team at South Plaquemines. The 2007 Hurricanes seemed different, Keven said. He would not concede that they were more talented, but they appeared to play more as a team than a collection of individuals.

"Last year, everyone was from different schools, everybody had been all-stars where they were," he said. "When we stepped on the field, you couldn't tell us what to do."

He was living in Uptown New Orleans now. Keven was nineteen, and his girlfriend, Whitney Allen, was seventeen. Keven, Whitney, and Keven Jr., who was ten months old, lived with Whitney's mother. Ten people occupied five bedrooms, spread over two floors, and shared one and a half bathrooms. It was crowded, but Whitney's family was welcoming and the rent was free. Keven's father had bought him a Mazda 626, 1998 model, and had installed a new transmission. At some point, Keven planned to get a razor and slice off the old bumper stickers, like the one that said, "I Love GRITS (Girls Raised in the South)."

Most mornings, Keven crossed the twin-span bridge over the Mississippi, took classes at Delgado from eight to eleven, then returned to his apartment. Math was his favorite subject, but he struggled with the unity of his paragraphs in English composition, and the tenets of Freudian psychology seemed like a foreign language. He would have to take both courses again in the spring semester.

For psychology, he would buy a digital tape recorder and replay each lecture to fill out his notes.

He had graduated from South Plaquemines with a 2.9 grade-point average, but post-Katrina, education had become a kind of scavenger hunt. He had attended four high schools in his final three years. In algebra II in Lafayette, Louisiana, he repeated the study of fractions that he had already learned in Boothville. One school used a textbook for chemistry, and another relied on formulas on a blackboard. Each move required some alteration, catching a bus where he had once walked, adjusting to new teachers and new expectations, always starting over, hardly anything continuous from beginning to end.

"I'm prepared, but I feel if I could have taken more classes in high school, like advanced math, I'd be more prepared," Keven said.

It was a funny thing about Plaquemines Parish, he said.

"We've got the athletes, but we never have the grades," Keven said. "There's not enough dedication to school. I think it's the parents' fault. They should have you inside. A lot of kids want to run around, play that football. It's up to the parents to set you down, make you learn the times tables, write your name twenty times. Good grades get you into college, not just sports."

Keven and Whitney wanted to put Keven Jr. in day care, but after Katrina the cost for nurseries had skyrocketed, up to $250 or $300 a week. That was beyond their means, so Keven watched his son when he came home from class while Whitney started her shift at McDonald's, working the cash register.

At night, the three of them found solitude in their small bedroom, which had a crib and toys next to the bed, a television and entertainment center along the far wall, and a chest of drawers along the other. Behind the bed, duct tape had been crisscrossed around a used air conditioner to seal the room against the noise and the warm, humid air from the outside. Sometimes Whitney's brothers came in to play video football. Or Whitney and Keven played alone with the baby, teaching him shapes and colors and his ABCs.

Keven Jr. was walking and getting into everything, trying to unplug the television, gnawing on video-game joysticks, playing with Elmo and SpongeBob SquarePants.

"It is hard, tiring," Whitney said of motherhood. "I still love him. If I had waited a few more years, it would have been better."

Their Uptown neighborhood, with shotgun houses huddled shoulder to shoulder like linemen, was seventy miles and cultural light years from Boothville. In Plaquemines, the land was open and school was a five-minute walk and Keven knew everybody. In New Orleans, he felt cramped, hemmed in, not scared exactly but careful to avoid any situations where he might become scared. He turned on the news and saw the stories that confirmed New Orleans as a murder capital. His apartment was set back off the street, and one of Whitney's brothers was a member of the Guardian Angels, so his own block felt safe enough, but there was trouble a few streets over in either direction. He had heard gunshots, and one person had been killed nearby. There were fights, screaming, yelling. That was enough to keep Keven Jr. indoors unless they were down in Boothville.

"I'd rather be in the country, chillin'," Keven said one night at dusk, sitting in his bedroom. "I'd be outside, playing basketball. He'd be outside with me. Not here."

Whitney, who was tall and quiet, grew up in the Calliope Projects in the Central City section of New Orleans. She had never heard of Boothville before she met Keven in Lafayette after the hurricane. She liked the silence, the peacefulness of rural Plaquemines. It was the first time she had ever ridden in a boat. The previous summer, Keven had worked at Boothville-Venice Elementary School. He planned to work there again in the summer of 2008. Once he got his nursing license, he might open a day-care center down the road. Whitney had other ideas. She wanted to move to Lafayette. It seemed to be a place of possibility. She planned to get her GED and go on to college at some point.

Since Keven was a freshman in high school, he had three long-range goals: to become a lawyer, a professional football player, or a nurse. A year out of high school, he had expected to be attending a four-year college on a football scholarship. He had sent a highlight tape to Auburn and Ole Miss, and they had replied cordially, but both schools told him he was too short at five foot six. In moments of private honesty, he had known even before Katrina that football might be a pipe dream. He had asthma as a kid, and he grew wide instead of tall. Even now he breathed loudly and spoke as if his sinuses were blocked.

"Somewhere in there, I got fat," he said. "I knew I probably wasn't going to make it in football. But I tried."

Law school seemed beyond his reach at the moment—expensive, interminable—and so he would concentrate on becoming a nurse, a job in high demand. He liked working with people. It would take him two years to become a licensed practical nurse. Then he planned to work and take night classes for another year and a half until he became a registered nurse.

Fatherhood was complicated, he said. Sometimes it came so naturally, it felt like something he had been doing every minute of his life. Labor had been difficult; when Little Keven was born, he was so tired he couldn't even cry. Now, when his son ran toward him, arms out, smiling and trusting, Keven said, "I guess I must feel the way my father did when I first ran to him."

Sometimes, though, he wished Little Keven had his own room, especially when he cried at night. "Sometimes you want to kill him," Keven joked, "but you roll with the punches."

Keven had no more time for himself, but he liked it that way. He was on a schedule, and it kept him focused on the things that mattered most urgently: getting his degree, finding a job, buying his own home.

"Little Keven made me want to finish school, made me want to go to college," Keven said. "I love my mom and dad to death, but sometimes we only had enough money to put food on the table and pay the bills. Not enough for things like PlayStation. I want him to have what he wants."

He and Whitney had their disagreements, Keven said, but in the end they knew they loved each other. A week after the Mangham game, Keven got on his knees, proposed to Whitney, and gave her an engagement ring in an apartment full of family members. They planned to get married when he finished school.

"Hardest thing I ever did," Keven said of the proposal. "Harder than cutting the umbilical cord. I was shaking so much then, I thought I was going to cut the nurse's hand."

19

"HOW 'BOUT THEM COWBOYS!"

CYRIL CRUTCHFIELD PULLED UP BEHIND THE SOUTH PLAQUE-
mines stadium in his school bus, blowing his horn and screaming
over the latest victory by Dallas, his favorite NFL team.

It was a Sunday night, always a practice night during the play-
offs. The next opponent was nineteenth-seeded Northlake Christian
School, located in Crutchfield's hometown of Covington.

Before practice, the Hurricanes were to lift weights in the ruined
gym next door at Port Sulphur High. Weights and benches and
towers of medicine balls had been set up on the misshapen floor of
the basketball court. The building had no electricity, and when
Ridge Turner yelled, "Possum!" frightened players scattered from a
side entrance in the dark.

It was only a prank, and soon the players walked carefully back
into the gym, using the light from their cell phones to step around
the obstacle course of weight equipment. Crutchfield had set up a
pair of generators near the front entrance and looped a string of
eleven lightbulbs overhead to provide some dim illumination
during the workouts.

"They chased a raccoon out of here once," Sal Cepriano said.

The generators sputtered to life, the bulbs produced wan light,
and a smell of gasoline filled the gym. Not much had changed in

the two-plus years since Katrina's storm surge pushed water above the rims on the backboards. One rim was missing, the other lacked a net. Thick pads of insulation hung from the ceiling above midcourt. Windows were broken out, the front doors were gone, the clock was permanently stopped at one forty-three. Katrina's water line was visible on the velvet curtains along the stage. Bits of marsh grass remained stuck to an oil painting of a rearing Broncho, the Port Sulphur mascot, ten feet above the floor. Tattered championship banners drooped from the roof. In classrooms and hallways that connected to the wrecked gym, walls were moldy and peeling.

Crutchfield had set up a row of lockers under one of the backboards. He swept the floor himself, but dust and trash accumulated quickly, and the snack food that players ate attracted rodents. A temporary gym, along with a separate locker room and weight-lifting facility, had been promised to South Plaquemines by the school board, but these had fallen months behind schedule.

Several weeks earlier, the school board had been embarrassed when Ed Daniels, a New Orleans sportscaster who did a Friday-night show on high school football, visited the gym and said on the air, "I was very disturbed by what I saw."

Daniels offered equal airtime to any Plaquemines school-board official who wanted to explain the situation. Stanley Gaudet wrote a letter to Daniels, explaining that bureaucratic red tape had delayed the new gym and weight room. While the football field had been refurbished, and new uniforms and equipment had been secured, the first priority for Plaquemines schools was education.

"We, like the parents of our students, are at the mercy of FEMA," Gaudet wrote.

Crutchfield received a reprimand from Eva Jones, the Plaquemines school-board superintendent, who believed the gym should have been kept cleaner. But the matter soon died, and the players kept lifting weights in the abandoned building. They believed it was a key to their dominant season. On this Sunday night before the Northlake Christian game, the generator faltered, and the lights flickered, went dark, and came back on. The players never stopped their bench presses, squats, and power cleans, and the gym filled with sounds of clanging metal and the heavy thumping of weights being dropped on mats. Felix Barthelemy set an unplugged treadmill on an incline, providing his own power as he jogged for several minutes.

"I don't think there's no other team doing this," Cantrelle Riley said, sitting in his locker. "Not any that we're playing. What you gonna say? They're not going to do anything about it. You just deal with what you got."

AFTER AN HOUR OF LIFTING WEIGHTS, THE HURRICANES SAT in Crutchfield's classroom to watch video of Northlake Christian. He told his players not to forget about their studies, reminding them that college recruiters would begin calling and if their grades weren't sufficient, "Forget about it." He also reminded them that last year's team had also reached the second round of the play-offs. This was no time to be satisfied.

"We haven't done nothin'," Crutchfield said, wearing a long-sleeved T-shirt, a pencil behind his ear. "I don't see anybody having birthday cake when it's not their birthday. Our goal is to win a state championship."

Northlake Christian could be troublesome, because it used multiple formations. It was clear from the video, though, that the Wolverines were vulnerable to defensive pressure. Their quarterback was short and might have trouble seeing downfield.

"Y'all bring that pressure, he'll throw interceptions," Crutchfield said.

He began to speak more generously of his own star running back, Lyle Fitte, who had made a splendid kickoff return for a touchdown against Mangham and had no longer seemed so self-centered on the sideline.

"I know he loves himself, but you made a hell of a cut," Crutchfield told Lyle. "You stepped your game up."

And: "Maybe I was drunk or something, and you know I don't give praise too often, but that sumbitch made a cut."

As he spoke to the team, Crutchfield appeared to be tired. He was fueling himself with candy, staying up late watching video, getting up early to look at more film before heading out on his bus route. He was still getting headaches and the occasional chest pain. His incessant drive toward a title was taking a toll. As the team went onto the field to practice under the lights, Crutchfield said, "I hope I don't catch a stroke by the time we get to the Superdome."

THE NEXT DAY AT PRACTICE, CRUTCHFIELD TOLD LYLE, "Come on, Clark Kent. You not Superman yet, but you went in the phone booth. Now you got to put your cape on."

As his receivers ran pass routes, Crutchfield called out to them in the teasing, casually taunting way of athletes and coaches, a sign that he was confident and believed his team would win on Friday.

"Boy, you run like you gay," he said to Andrew Barthelemy, a seventh-grader. "You run a route like that, they gonna take advantage of you in the penitentiary."

And to himself: "Man, Northlake Christian in trouble. At birth those white kids couldn't block our kids."

ON GAME DAY, THE HURRICANES TRAVELED THROUGH NEW Orleans, then skirted the shores of Lake Pontchartrain to reach the play-off site at Southeastern Louisiana University in Hammond. On the bus ride, an assured Crutchfield began writing plays on a notepad, already anticipating next week's quarterfinal round.

In his pregame speech, he told his defense, "They want to say how fast we are. Let's be heat-seeking missiles."

On the game's third play, Felix Barthelemy tipped a pass, but it bounced off his shoulder pads into the hands of a Northlake Christian player who ran fifty-eight yards for a touchdown. For the second week in a row, South Plaquemines had fallen behind 6–0 in the first fifty-five seconds. This seemed only to inflame the Hurricanes.

Lyle Fitte ran untouched into the end zone on a counter from two yards, then from twelve. Sal Cepriano rushed from defensive tackle and hurried the Northlake quarterback; Ridge Turner intercepted the pass, carrying it thirty-six yards for a touchdown. Lyle's younger brother, Beau Fitte, a freshman defensive end, intercepted a second pass and returned it twenty-eight yards to the end zone, such an enormous display of hustle and athleticism that Crutchfield began referring to him as "Beau-zilla."

"Rock-a-bye baby, put 'em to sleep," Crutchfield said on the sideline.

The first period was not yet done, and already South Plaquemines led 32–6.

"Let's run it up!" Lyle said.

"Leave no doubt!" Marcelin Ancar screamed.

Lyle caught a screen pass and dipped through the middle for a thirty-yard touchdown. He ran to the sideline and yelled at his linemen, "I love you boys."

The second-half kickoff came to Lyle at his own twenty-three-yard line. He ran into a knot of Northlake players, but they had clumped too tightly in the middle, like kindergartners playing soccer. Lyle came to a near stop, slid behind a pair of blockers, then lanced upfield. A tackler slid off him near the fifty-yard line and he darted left and ran seventy-seven yards for his fourth touchdown. Late in the third quarter, Lyle took a shovel pass and spun into the end zone, and South Plaquemines went ahead 59–14, which became the final score.

"I think you're looking at the 1A state champions," the public address announcer said.

Perhaps, but Crutchfield gave his players the same admonishment he had given them weeks earlier: "Katrina taught us a tough lesson. You can't take anything for granted. Tomorrow, nothing. You've got to take each game as it comes."

Lyle and Ridge would be named the week's top area performers by the *Times-Picayune* of New Orleans. Ridge had thrown for three touchdowns and scored a fourth on an interception. Lyle had scored five times, twice rushing, twice receiving, and once on the kickoff return.

"Lyle's on a mission," Crutchfield said.

Escorting the team home, Rodney Bartholomew Sr. wanted to avoid driving through New Orleans.

"No," Big Wayne Williamson said. "Pass by the 'Dome."

THERE HAD BEEN ONE MOMENT OF CONCERN FOR SOUTH Plaquemines as Jordan Ancar suffered a concussion in the second half.

"Who am I?" Marcelin Ancar asked him.

Jordan shrugged his shoulders.

"That's your dad," Jamie McQuarter, the South Plaquemines athletic director, said.

"You're my dad?"

Marcelin laughed. "That's what your momma said."

Taylor Ancar, Jordan's sister and a team statistician, went to tell her mother what had happened.

"Is it his hand?" Jeanitta Ancar asked.

No, Taylor said. Jordan's mended hand was fine. It was his head.

Jeanitta came across the field.

"What's the matter?" she asked Jordan.

"Nothing."

"What happened?"

"Nothing."

"What's my name?"

"I don't know."

"What you mean you don't know?"

She asked McQuarter to get some help.

"My boy don't know who I am."

Jeanitta accompanied Jordan on the team bus home. Before the Hurricanes arrived back in Port Sulphur, his memory began to return.

The next morning at practice, Crutchfield joked with Jordan: "Hi, I'm the coach. This is the South Plaquemines football team. This is the year 2012 and we wear our cleats on our head."

THE COACH HAD A MORE SERIOUS CONVERSATION WITH Lisa Riley about her son. Cantrelle had intercepted three passes against Northlake Christian. He now had seven interceptions in two play-off games. Still, he had stood alone on the sideline, annoyed. He was the number 1 receiver in the state, but he felt he was not sufficiently part of the offense during the play-offs. He seemed glum after the dominant victory, remaining on the fringes of the postgame huddle as the elated Hurricanes recited the team prayer.

Sal Cepriano had tried to talk to him during the game, but Cantrelle brushed him off.

"He thinks coach hates him," Sal said.

Cantrelle was one of a handful of Hurricanes who started on both offense and defense. Crutchfield had placed much trust in him, but Cantrelle was still convinced that the coach favored the players from Port Sulphur and was quicker to criticize those from Buras and Boothville-Venice. Cantrell was from Buras, and in recent weeks he had grown to believe that his contributions were not fully appreciated.

"I feel unwanted," he said. If the players from Buras and Boothville-Venice left the team, he said, it would be weakened. "I don't think they would go too far."

Thirty of the thirty-eight Hurricanes players, and most of their fans, were from Port Sulphur. When Paul Lemaire told Cantrelle, "You're with us now, you don't have to worry about losing," it was meant as a joke. When Boo Landry cooked pregame meals for the players and said of Cantrelle, "He's from Buras, he's not used to that," he was only kidding.

But Cantrelle had chafed at these comments, taking them to be slights. He was a sensitive kid. His home had been destroyed, his high school had been wrecked, and his hometown of Buras had shown little signs of recovery. During the previous summer, Cantrelle had felt that Crutchfield unfairly blamed him for pranks that some players had pulled at training camp. And now, in Cantrelle's mind, Crutchfield and the Port Sulphur fans seemed to be dismissive of the players from Buras and Boothville-Venice. As the play-offs started, he considered quitting the team.

"They're not throwing me the ball," Cantrelle told his brother, Christian, a former star at Buras High who was now an electrical engineering student at the University of North Texas.

"Don't worry, they can't stop you on defense," Christian told Cantrelle. "What would you rather do? Catch two touchdowns or make three interceptions to change the game?"

His brother's words had not placated Cantrelle. Both he and his mother were growing irritated with what they perceived as the favoritism of those from Port Sulphur.

"Those people are weak-minded," Lisa Riley said. "Anybody can go out and play football. Hitting the books is more important."

The morning after the victory over Northlake Christian, Crutchfield explained to the Rileys that he wanted Cantrelle to turn his head back toward the ball when he was covering a receiver. He said Cantrelle had become a more disciplined player and that he liked him, considered him an important part of the team. He criticized all the players, Crutchfield said, many of them more harshly than Cantrelle, especially those from Port Sulphur. It was nothing personal, but he wasn't going to change his methods.

"If you mess up, I'm going to get on you," Crutchfield said.

Later, Lisa Riley said she was glad things were now out in the open.

"It's not Port Sulphur anymore," she said. "It's not Buras and Boothville-Venice. They're supposed to be one."

AFTER THE MORNING PRACTICE, THE PLAYERS HAD THE REST of Saturday off. Cantrelle went fishing with Dylan Boutwell, a fellow starting receiver and his best friend on the team. Cantrelle, a senior, was black and wore his hair in dreadlocks. Dylan, a sophomore, was white and wore a crew cut. More and more, Cantrelle had been spending nights at Dylan's house. Lisa Riley worked the late-night shift at her custodial job, and Cantrelle did not want to stay alone in the family trailer.

Mona Boutwell was happy to have Cantrelle stay over. Her other football-playing son, Devin, was now a freshman defensive tackle at Southeastern Louisiana University. It was just she and Dylan living in their trailer in Buras. Her husband Donnie spent much of his time in Belle Chasse, running his oil-field trucking business.

When friends saw Mona with Cantrelle, they sometimes joked, "That's your son?"

"My good son," she told them. Cantrelle playfully admonished Dylan not to sass his mother. And he even carried Mona's purse for her in the mornings when they left for school, where Mona taught prekindergarten at South Plaquemines Elementary.

Once, Buras had been the middle-class hub of lower Plaquemines. There were two supermarkets, a YMCA, and a game room where kids could shoot pool. At the local stores, Devin and Dylan could sign a ticket and say, "My mother will pay for it." In a town of 3,358 residents, a person's word could be as valuable a currency as money. Then Katrina came and shoved the Boutwell's cypress-timbered home a football field's length, slamming it into another house. A collection of teapots survived the vagary of the storm with only a missing lid, but just about everything else in the home and the town was destroyed. A year after the storm, sand still sat in the family's mailbox.

Two-plus years later, Buras was empty and ghostly at night, with few streetlights working. The fire station had no walls; curtains swayed through broken windows in the library. No school was open. Sixteen coffins remained unidentified in their concrete vaults at the Our Lady of Good Harbor cemetery. A sign next to the coffins, laid side by side like piano keys, gave a phone number in case anyone knew the names of the deceased. On the storefront sign at Barrios Drugs, letters were missing as if in some destructive game of *Wheel of Fortune*. Frantic messages remained spray-painted on the store's brick wall, now with a faded urgency: "Do Not Bulldoze," and "Helen call me, Sang Vo."

The school board had voted to build a new school that would house South Plaquemines High in Buras, but the building was not expected to be finished for several years. Some civic leaders clung with desperate nostalgia to the memory of the destroyed town, wanting to paint the new water tower green and gold, the colors of Buras High. The old tower, which collapsed during Katrina, had been painted blue and white and was seen around the world as an iconic symbol of the hurricane's destruction. Blue and white also approximated the colors of South Plaquemines High. Mona Boutwell believed a green and gold water tower would perpetuate divisiveness, undermining the sense of unity that a consolidated school and football team were supposed to bring to lower Plaquemines.

"The kids have let go, but the adults have not," said Mona's sister, Sue Cook, the guidance counselor at South Plaquemines High.

On Mona Boutwell's desolate street, there had been eight homes before the hurricane. Now there were only two trailers, hers and one across the street. She and her husband had built a new home in Ponchatoula, northwest of New Orleans. Buras was her hometown, but it did not make financial or geographic sense to her to rebuild there. Before Katrina, she was paying $1,400 a year in homeowner's insurance and $700 in flood insurance. Now, she figured, she would have to pay at least $12,000 in homeowner's alone. And she might have to build her house eleven feet or higher off the ground to qualify for federal flood insurance.

"Another Katrina comes, it doesn't matter how high you are," Mona said. Even if a storm as strong as Katrina didn't hit, the Plaquemines coastline was eroding, leaving the parish like a boxer with his gloves down, with little to blunt the next punch.

"If they don't do anything about coastal restoration, we're history," Mona said.

She felt frustrated, too, about what she believed to be the inequity of recovery money offered by the state. She received $108,000 in insurance money after Katrina, leaving her $31,000 in the clear after paying off a $77,000 mortgage. Because the insurance payment covered the full prestorm appraisal of her home, however, she did not quality for the state's Road Home program, which offered grants up to $150,000 to homeowners. Yet she knew of others who had paid no insurance and received 70 percent of the value of their houses from Road Home. This did not seem fair to her.

"You get penalized for paying insurance," Mona said.

Sometimes she looked at the destroyed high school in Buras and broke into tears. Life had been so convenient and comfortable. Now Mona lived apart from her husband much of the time. This put a strain on their marriage. Inevitably, she and Donnie had developed their own separate routines, and when he came to Buras and wanted to watch TV with her and she wanted to go into her room to read her Bible, Dylan told his father, "This is not your house; it's Mom and I's house." The parents had made huge sacrifices for their sons' football careers. Often Mona asked herself if she was doing the right thing. A week earlier, a car full of kids had followed Devin, Cantrelle, and Sal home from a Sunday-night practice, asking if they had marijuana. A thrown can of beer led to a confrontation, threats, a head-butt, punches, a shotgun fired in warning.

"If I had a girl, I don't know if I'd be down here," Mona said.

Mona and Cyril Crutchfield were both opinionated and forceful. They did not always get along. A year earlier, Mona felt that Crutchfield did not care enough about her son Devin after he tore up his knee. She argued with him one day, and Crutchfield told her to get out of his classroom. At the time, the Boutwells lived next door to Crutchfield at a trailer camp near South Plaquemines High. Dylan briefly quit the team, tossing his equipment into Crutchfield's yard. After sitting out a game, he reconsidered.

"I couldn't leave my team," Dylan said.

This year, he had Crutchfield for free enterprise and American government classes. He liked the way Crutchfield cracked jokes and did not try to muffle his students' opinions.

"He makes it fun," Dylan said.

A kind of cease-fire had also been declared between Mona and Crutchfield. She said she appreciated his dedication. "I bet college coaches don't put in the time he puts in," she said.

Immediately after Katrina, Dylan had enrolled in school in Ponchatoula. While Devin assimilated quickly into football, Dylan felt overwhelmed as an eighth-grader. He was introverted, not the kind to go out and make a lot of friends. "It was too big for me," he said. Mona homeschooled him until the schools in Belle Chasse opened in October 2005. Even then, Dylan felt out of place.

"I don't think they wanted us there, because we were from down the road," he said. "I was coming home, no matter what."

He much preferred to be in lower Plaquemines, where the schools were smaller and he could fish and hunt rabbits and ducks and the occasional wild hog. The 2007 football season had been somewhat frustrating, though. Dylan missed the first six games with a hamstring injury that resulted in a ligament or tendon pulling away from the bone and leaving his pelvis with tiny fractures. Dylan was not even sure how he had gotten hurt, but he was back in the lineup and had caught five touchdown passes midway through the play-offs.

"I wish I had more white boys," Crutchfield sometimes told him. "They do what they supposed to do."

Devin Boutwell had seen more of his younger brother this season than he had expected. Just as he made the starting lineup at defensive tackle at Southeastern Louisiana, Devin developed a sore throat and nausea. He grew so tired that he began skipping class to sleep so that he would have enough energy for football practice. Then he got hit in the spleen during a game and began spitting up blood. Finally, he went to a doctor and was diagnosed with mononucleosis. He was forced to sit out the last half of the season, which inadvertently gave him more time to watch Dylan play at South Plaquemines. Devin attended the games and spoke regularly to Dylan and Cantrelle by phone. The night of the game against Northlake Christian, which had been played at Southeastern, Devin greeted the players and showed them to the locker room. He had even helped Crutchfield to develop weight-lifting workouts for the Hurricanes.

"He's got that swagger," Devin said of Crutchfield. "He makes kids believe in themselves. Once you think you can't be beat, you're not going to."

When Dylan asked him if he missed not being part of what appeared to be a championship season, Devin said no.

"I got what I want," he said.

On this Saturday afternoon, Devin had remained in Hammond to watch Southeastern play, so Dylan and Cantrelle hitched a fishing boat to a four-wheeler, rode across the highway, and climbed over the levee into the marsh. It was a warm, breezy day. The gnats were out. Dolphins jumped from the water and ducks flew overhead, but the tide was low and the fish bit reluctantly. All Dylan and Cantrelle had to show for the trip was a lone redfish, but it didn't seem to matter. Cantrelle was relaxed, smiling again. His differences with Crutchfield seemed to have drifted out with the tide.

"Everything's cool," Cantrelle said.

His mother came to pick him up in late afternoon and brought him a hamburger.

"It's all in the open now," Lisa Riley said. "Cantrelle holds things inside. You gotta let 'em know what you're feeling. You can't bottle it up. It'll wear you down."

THAT NIGHT, CRUTCHFIELD, A FEW SOUTH PLAQUEMINES fans, and many of its players drove up to suburban New Orleans to watch Belle Chasse play Archbishop Shaw in a second-round playoff game in Class 4A. Shaw was undefeated, headed for a rematch with Bastrop in the state-championship game. Boo Landry, one of South Plaquemines' most vocal fans, said he hoped Belle Chasse won.

"I don't want them at our game next week," Landry said. "They'll be saying, 'Yeah, y'all still in the play-offs, but we beat y'all.' Let 'em come see us in the 'Dome."

The Hurricanes sat on the Belle Chasse side of the field. A number of the Fighting Cardinals were their friends and former teammates. But there was little encouraging to see. Shaw won 34–6. Crutchfield left long before it was over.

The next day, as South Plaquemines began to prepare for its quarterfinal game, Crutchfield lamented the fact that two of his former players—cornerback Emmette Sylve and running back Avery Riley—had ended their careers in Belle Chasse. They had missed out on a chance to win a championship. Bob Becnel, the Belle Chasse coach, had given them false hopes, telling them they could receive scholarships if they stayed up the road, Crutchfield said.

"They'd rather that white man lie to them," Crutchfield said. "I hope they're happy."

(Such remarks aggravated Becnel. "It irritates me when I hear that we used those kids from Port Sulphur, Buras, and Boothville," Becnel said. "We did nothing but try to help those kids.")

Crutchfield also had word about Randall Mackey. His Bastrop team was still undefeated, but Randall's name seemed to be tumbling on recruiting lists. He was a great football player but, by all accounts, a weak student. It seemed increasingly likely that he would not be eligible to play major-college football right out of high school.

Crutchfield had spoken with Randall's mother.

"She says the teachers are not working for him," Crutchfield said during a night practice. He was not buying it, not completely. "You do all your work and turn in your assignments, they gonna give you an F because they don't like you? Come on. If he got four Fs here, they'd be blaming it on me. You're not going to hear a word up there. That coach is just using him."

20

LIFE ON THE HALF SHELL

A HORN BELLOWED AS THE POINTE A LA HACHE FERRY began its first run of the morning. A gauzy fog covered the river levees, and the late November dawn cast a blue metallic sheen on the Mississippi. Burn-off from a natural gas well flared on the east bank. Mike Barthelemy Sr. drove his van onto the ferry and parked behind a friend named Curt Dufrene. It was six o'clock. Some people ate cereal for breakfast. Dufrene preferred bivalves.

"Want an oyster?" he asked Barthelemy, reaching into a sack in the bed of his pickup. Dufrene was an oil-field worker. Only a couple of years ago, he had been a commercial fisherman.

"Sold my boat a week before Katrina," he said. "I'm a lucky man."

With a short knife and an expert twist of his wrist, as if starting a car, Dufrene opened an oyster and served it on the half shell to Barthelemy. He slurped it down.

"They salty?" another friend, Mike Alexis, asked.

"Ooh," Barthelemy said.

Plaquemines Parish was Louisiana's top producer of oysters. Dufrene opened another shell of iridescent purple and brown nacre, plump with meat.

"The perfect oyster," Alexis said.

Cock oysters, they were called, though there was no certainty whether they were male or female. The night before, Dufrene had shucked three dozen for his wife.

"Here you go," he told her. "That might be your Christmas present."

It was a great day to be an oyster fisherman, Alexis said. The wind was calm. The temperature was moderate. The tide was not too low. It would be easy to maneuver a boat over the reefs.

"Too bad I got out of it," he said.

Alexis operated a tugboat now, and this morning, he was making a run down to Venice, near the mouth of the Mississippi. On Fridays, he paid for the spaghetti and chicken cooked for tailgaters at the South Plaquemines games. As the ferry reached the east bank, Barthelemy and Alexis headed for Beshel's Marina, past the parish courthouse that had burned in 2002, past a rural landscape that Katrina had left empty and defeated.

His friend had left the business, but Mike Barthelemy was still oystering. He figured he might get four more years out of it, maybe five. By then, his three children would be out of high school. His son, Mike Jr., a freshman linebacker, had sacked the Northlake Christian quarterback twice and had hurried several passes, one of which was returned for a touchdown in the 59–14 play-off victory. It was an emergent moment in a difficult season. Little Mike had dislocated his kneecap during a baseball slide the previous spring. The injury lingered into football, and when he twisted his knee awkwardly or took a hard blow, sometimes the patella still floated loose, not unlike an oyster in a half shell. Strengthened by weight lifting, the knee remained sturdy during the play-offs, and at one disruptive moment against Northlake Christian, Little Mike had hopped in celebration. It was only a tiny gesture, nothing planned or ostentatious, but even restrained jubilation was a departure from his usual taciturn demeanor.

"First time he's ever shown emotion," Mike Sr. said.

Big Mike was forty-three, with a broad chest and thick arms that came from a lifetime of strain and leverage, the lifting of one-hundred-pound sacks of oysters and the maneuvering of heavy dredges. His hands were huge and rough, leathery. His wife liked it when he scratched her back, but not when he stroked her face.

It was two days before Thanksgiving. The holidays were prime season for oyster dressing and oysters in seafood gumbo. If you didn't sell oysters in November and December, Big Mike said, forget about the rest of the year.

"It's going to be crawling after Christmas," he said.

This had not been a good November for him. He needed to sell at least three hundred sacks a month to make an adequate living. A delayed opening to the season in 2007 had kept the public oyster grounds closed until November 12, eight days earlier. It was getting late in the month, and he had sold only 240 sacks. It might have been his worst November ever. Diesel was rising toward three dollars a gallon. And oyster prices were sluggish.

"That's the ruination of my business," Big Mike said, pointing across to other squat, shallow-draft oyster boats in the marina. "Mexicans."

It was a generic term of derision for the Spanish-speaking deck-hands from Mexico, Honduras, El Salvador, and elsewhere in Central and South America. Increasingly since Katrina, Hispanic oystermen had been working Louisiana waters on Texas-based boats. This was mainly due to wet weather in Texas that reduced the salinity levels needed for optimal oyster reproduction. Typically, there were about 130 local oyster boats working Plaquemines Parish and about 10 boats from out of state. Now there were 40 or 50 boats from Texas and Mississippi. Local oystermen resented them as outsiders who encroached on their home fishing grounds, working for cheap, glutting the market, driving up resentment, and driving down prices. Shrimpers in Plaquemines had felt similarly aggrieved with the arrival of Vietnamese shrimpers in the late 1970s.

There was some irony to this local bitterness. It had been foreigners—Croatians—who built the oyster industry in Plaquemines in the 1800s, performing the exhausting labor of harvesting mollusks with tongs that resembled a pair of long-handled garden rakes.

History aside, it seemed unfair to Big Mike and others that Texas oystermen could work Louisiana waters by simply purchasing a nonresident harvesting license for four hundred dollars, while Texas had put a moratorium on issuing new permits. Moreover, with the holiday season arriving, Mike said, oysters were selling for sixteen dollars a sack in Texas, compared to eighteen dollars in Louisiana. Several days had passed since he had an order from his dealer, who was buying cheaper product from out of state. It was said that boats from Texas also enticed dealers by putting extra oysters in a sack—like adding a thirteenth doughnut to a box.

Big Mike and his colleagues were attempting to convince the Louisiana Department of Wildlife and Fisheries to limit the number of sacks caught per day and to restrict oyster fishing to five days a week. Their effort would be denied as an unfair restraint of trade. Competition may have been great for the consumer, but for Big Mike, "Mexicans" and "Texans" were interchangeable names for a Category 5 fiscal hurricane.

"That free-trade crap, they're killing us," he said.

Katrina had destroyed about 70 percent of Plaquemines' public oyster grounds east of the Mississippi River, smothering the bivalves with silt and suffocating them under rotted vegetation. But by 2006, the industry had made a comeback, in price if not in quantity. Oysters sold for twenty to twenty-four dollars a sack. For the first time, statewide dockside sales topped thirty-six million dollars—nearly fifteen million dollars in Plaquemines alone.

Oystermen in general did not suffer the same economic vagaries as shrimpers did. They did not have to contend with vast amounts of imported meat. They could take oysters from public waters and seed private leases, which were available from the state for two dollars per year per acre. And they were organized politically.

"Before Katrina, I had it made," Big Mike said.

He had eighty-six acres of private leases to work when the public grounds were closed from April through August. He had bought a five-thousand-dollar all-terrain vehicle for Little Mike and a pitching machine to help the softball careers of his daughters, Stephanie and Alexis. He could afford the best furniture, big-screen TVs. After the storm, insurance covered the mortgage on his home, but there was nothing left over for luxury. His oyster lugger, the *St. Anthony*, a forty-seven-footer with an open front deck and a rear cabin, was operable but weather-beaten. The family's mobile home was not fully furnished. The Barthelemys made do without a sofa and dining-room table and slept on air mattresses as they awaited their rebuilding grant from the state. The offer had been downsized from an expected seventy thousand dollars to thirty thousand and, finally, to sixteen thousand, he said.

Katrina had pushed the *St. Anthony* out of the marina in Empire and onto the marsh levee more than a mile away. For nearly a year and a half, Big Mike was not able to fish. He came back to Plaquemines two months after the storm and slept with seven other men in a bunkhouse made from a cargo container, working as an electrician, helping rewire the lower end. His boat remained stranded for six months until he could pay eighteen thousand dollars to get it off the levee. By the time Mike had patched four holes in the cypress hull and repaired the windows and door in the cabin and rebuilt the motor, another year had passed. He finally got back in the water in January 2007, having missed the oyster renaissance of 2006.

"I'm back to square one, trying to hold on," Big Mike said.

In a good year, he could make one hundred thousand dollars. Now, he said, "If I make sixty thousand, I'll be lucky." Expenses, especially diesel fuel, would eat into any profits the way predatory drumfish crunched through oyster reefs. "Everything is so expensive and oysters are so cheap."

In American Bay, Big Mike poked in the shallow water with a cane pole, feeling for a reef. Oysters grew in jagged clumps, attached to other shells or to mussels or beds of limestone and crushed concrete. He tossed a triangular dredge into the water, and it scraped along the bottom, its metal teeth scooping oysters into an iron mesh bag. Once aboard, the shells were dropped onto a culling table. Wearing heavy rubber gloves and using small hatchets, Mike and a deckhand chopped quickly and precisely at the clusters, as if carving a mollusk sculpture. They separated the oysters that would end up in restaurants in New Orleans and elsewhere on the Gulf Coast and the West Coast, scraping everything under the legal limit of three inches back into the water. The saved oysters were tossed onto the deck, shoveled into baskets, and loaded into burlap sacks as the fronts of the men's shirts and jeans became spattered with mud. On it went like this, as Big Mike moved limberly along the front of his boat. He filled one burlap sack after the next, working with muscle and finesse, keeping his lugger circling the reef and raising and lowering the dredge and slicing with his hatchet, every movement assured and purposeful as if he were dancing some maritime two-step.

Big Mike had been a commercial fisherman since he graduated from high school in 1982. Five or six years later, he bought the *St. Anthony.* It was forty-three years old now, as old as he was. The front of the cabin was adorned, like mud flaps on an eighteen-wheeler, with stick-ons of exotic women in silhouette. Mike had worked as a sheriff's deputy, but he had always preferred fishing, especially on a clear, warm day like today, everything peaceful, working for himself, nobody on his back. If he got out of fishing, he wanted to remain on the water, maybe piloting a tug or driving a crew boat. Oystering was long, hard work—sometimes he slept on the boat four days a week and left the marina at four in the morning—but he could take time off when he wanted. He did not miss a football game. There seemed to be a certainty and reliability with football that there no longer was with oystering.

Big Mike's father had been a fisherman, and his grandfather before that. His early years were spent in the marshes on Grand Bayou. His grandparents and parents spoke French and trapped muskrat and mink and otter and nutria and drew water from a cistern. He was amazed at the strength in his grandmother's arms from paddling a pirogue to the general store on Foster Canal. After Hurricane Betsy in 1965, the family moved to adjacent St. Bernard Parish. Mike's great-grandfather had defanged a rattlesnake and kept it as a pet. He wrapped it around his chest and kept it inside his shirt when he went dancing. Sometimes it popped its head out, and he patted it back inside his collar. Occasionally it slept in the bed. At least that was the story told by Nicholas, Mike's father.

"I'm a young man raised in an old life," Mike said.

It was not the life for his three kids, he hoped. He had gone to trade school; they would finish college. His wife, Wanda, was studying to be a teacher. The kids were expected to follow her lead. Mike pushed them, insisting that they play sports and excel in the classroom. He stood with them as they lifted weights and told them to hoist a few more pounds, to raise the bar a few more times. He admonished them when they brought home Bs on their report cards. He was not mad, but he knew they could do better. They usually did. Stephanie Barthelemy was president of the student council and one of the top students at South Plaquemines. The girlfriend of Sal Cepriano, she was named academic all-state in volleyball. Mike could not see his kids going on welfare. He did not want his daughters dependent on men. He wanted Little Mike to have something in life beyond tying a boat up and going into the bayou to work.

"I don't think Little Mike is going to come here," Big Mike said. "I'm going to do everything I can to make sure he doesn't. It's too hard. Those young kids are not that strong."

Big Mike knew that some people believed he pushed his kids too hard. He wondered whether Little Mike was playing football for his father or himself. Last year, Stephanie sometimes threw up before basketball games, knowing that her father would be in the crowd and wanting to please him, said her English teacher, Colleen Carroll.

"My dad said you've got to get your education; it's the main thing you need in life," Little Mike said. "Since I was little, he demanded that I get straight As. He said it's tough in the real world."

At the same time, Little Mike said, "I'm not looking forward to college. I'm tired of school. I've got to keep making straight As. It's hard."

When his kids resisted, Big Mike kept pushing.

"I want them to see the big picture," he said. "They're not used to wearing old clothes or shoes with holes in the bottom. They don't know what it's like to go hungry. They don't know what it's like working after school, scraping a meat counter, packing coolers with ice. One day they'll understand why I was so hard on them."

Stephanie said she understood.

"He doesn't want us to live the same life he did," she said. "He had to wake up early in the morning, embarrassed that his friends would see him get water to take a bath. His dad blew their money. He and his brothers were separated. He lived house to house. He wants us to have it better. He's a good parent."

His daughter embellished his early struggles, Big Mike said. "I don't know where she got that from." Still, it had been a hard life. And he wanted an easier one for his kids. He had a big fan in Cyril Crutchfield.

"Those kids are going to be better prepared for college than any other kids," Crutchfield said.

BIG MIKE CONSIDERED HIMSELF A BLUNT REALIST, LIKE Crutchfield. If the coach ever left South Plaquemines while Little Mike was in high school, the Barthelemys would follow him. "The man don't lie," Big Mike said. "He calls an apple an apple, not an orange or a banana."

One of the biggest lies, Mike said out on the water, was coastal restoration. Who were they kidding? He stood on the front of his boat and pointed ahead to Pelican Point, where oystermen once tucked in by the dozens at night. Now, it was a speck of an island. He pointed to wooden pilings sticking out in the water, an abandoned dock.

"See that boat dredging over there," he said, pointing to an oyster boat to his left. "That was all land."

He could point in any direction and recall similar disappearances. Or glance at his GPS device, which repeatedly showed shapes of land that were now open water. As the wetlands eroded and salt water continued to intrude, scientists said, excessive salinity levels could threaten the oyster industry by allowing an invasion of parasites and predatory snails. Oyster reefs also could move closer to shore, putting them at greater risk of contact with human waste. Already demand suffered from rare, but highly publicized, reports of death from eating oysters. The fatalities were caused by a bacteria prevalent especially in the summer months. Each sack that Mike filled carried a tag that warned that there was a risk associated with eating raw oysters for people with liver, stomach, or immune disorders. The Food and Drug Administration was pressuring oystermen to get their catch refrigerated as quickly as possible—six hours after harvest during the summer months. According to state wildlife officials, this put an onerous constraint on boats in Plaquemines Parish, which sometimes required trips of several hours just to travel to and from the reefs.

"It's too late," Big Mike said of replenishing the Louisiana wetlands. "Nothing they can do. All this talk about restoring the coast is a bunch of crap. Who they lying to?"

With no order from his dealer today, Mike headed home after filling eighteen sacks. "That's it," he said to his deckhand in late morning, slicing his hand across his neck. Today's catch was for Mike's own Thanksgiving weekend and for friends who might need a sack or two for their holiday meals. An agent with the state wildlife and fisheries department pulled alongside the *St. Anthony,* and bought three sacks. Mike charged him only forty dollars—well below market value—and handed the money to his deckhand.

"Everybody owes you a thank you," Mike said.

Back at the dock in Pointe a la Hache, he sold a sack for ten dollars to a man who worked for the district attorney's office.

"Never know when I might need him," Mike said.

He told the man that business had been slow.

"I can't believe y'all ain't had no oysters before Thanksgiving," the man replied.

About four in the afternoon, the sky going gray with a front approaching, the dealer who usually bought Big Mike's oysters arrived at the dock, dressed in an LSU cap and T-shirt. For the first time in days, the man had an order for Mike for the next morning. The order was for eighteen dollars a sack, but Mike refused, on principle. Where had the guy been? This was supposed to be the busiest time of the year. Anyway, the day before Thanksgiving was a day to spend with family. Plus, he couldn't make it all the way to Belle Chasse before the bank closed. How would he pay his deckhand before the holiday?

"They trying to play a game now," Mike said.

His father met him at the dock and said, "They make you wait and try to lower the price."

What would the dealer offer next? Sixteen dollars? Fourteen? Mike couldn't make a living on that.

After he moored the *St. Anthony* in its slip, Mike and other oystermen gathered around the dealer's pickup truck. The men leaned their arms on the bed of the truck as if sitting at a bar. They talked for a long time, and Mike's voice got loud. He shouted that Louisiana didn't have the balls to keep out boats from Texas. He had worked these waters most of his life, and this is what it had come to?

"You mean to tell me we can't make a week's work?" Mike asked the man in the LSU cap.

He was considering moving his boat to a marina in Hopedale in St. Bernard Parish. Word was, sack prices were higher there.

"I ain't got no choice," Big Mike said. "This is the worst November I ever had."

ON THANKSGIVING MORNING, THE HURRICANES MET FOR A brief practice. The players split into pairs for a passing contest, stepping back five yards after each completion until only one pair had not dropped the ball. Crutchfield had done this every year that his Port Sulphur High team had remained in the play-offs. Now he brought the ritual to South Plaquemines. The players laughed and teased as they dived for passes or threw awkward wobbles in the wind. Everyone toed the five-yard stripes when they heaved the ball, as if they had tossed a javelin in the Olympics and were trying to avoid a disqualifying foul. After an hour or so, they were loose and perspiring lightly, and Crutchfield sent them home for turkey and gumbo and sweet-potato pie and an afternoon of football on television.

"Two years ago, I didn't want to think about this," Crutchfield said, referring to the absent season caused by Katrina. "Now, we've got a lot to be thankful for."

Ridge Turner, of course, had an advantage in any passing contest. Another of the stronger arms among the Hurricanes belonged to Jeremy Sylve, a fifteen-year-old freshman who was the starting right guard. He was six foot one and weighed 225 pounds, none of it unnecessary. His country strength was evident in the way he threw a football without winding up, and cast his fishing rod with a casual backhanded flick, and carried his camouflaged twelve-gauge like a tennis racket.

"Hey, Jeremy," Boo Landry called out on the field, one of several fathers who had come to be with their sons on Thanksgiving morning. "You catch the ball like you catchin' a sack of oysters."

The wind came out of the northeast, pushing low, dark clouds as the temperature dropped into the fifties. After practice, Jeremy phoned his father, Paul, who met him on the bank of Foster Canal along Grand Bayou. Even in the seclusion of Plaquemines Parish, Grand Bayou was considered a remote place, three-quarters of a mile down a gravel road from Highway 23, the homes accessible only by boat and lying outside the levee system that protected the Port Sulphur area from the marshes and Barataria Bay.

Running water and telephone service had become available only within the last fifteen years. Before that, families collected water in cisterns or had it brought in by tugboat. The first phone had been a community pay phone. Even the gravel road along Foster Canal had been built only two decades earlier. Until then, residents had parked their cars on the levee nearly a mile away and flashed their lights, signaling so that they could be picked up by boat.

Before the hurricane, Grand Bayou had been home to about two dozen families who claimed Attakapa Indian and French and

Spanish ancestry. Their forebearers had lived in the area for two to three centuries, shrimping, crabbing, oystering, and trapping. Paul Sylve had been born fifty-three years earlier aboard a shrimp trawler named *Prosperity,* ostensibly because his mother had been on the way to the hospital, but more likely because she had felt more at home on the water. The previous April, she had died. After the funeral service, her casket was placed on an oyster boat and carried across the water to Grand Bayou cemetery.

There were no roads in Grand Bayou itself, no need for cars. Boats provided transportation for shrimping and neighborly visits and even for school. In the mornings before Katrina, Paul Sylve drove a yellow school boat from dock to dock, collecting a dozen or more kids, transporting them a short distance to the road at Foster Canal, where they caught a bus for classes in Port Sulphur. Jeremy had begun to drive the school boat, too, by the time he was twelve, even though steering was difficult—"It only turned one way and it wasn't right." When school-board officials objected, he told them, "No matter who you get to drive that boat, they ain't gonna be better than me."

If the school boat was not waiting when the bus dropped him off from school, Jeremy sometimes left his backpack on the bank, swam thirty yards or so across Foster Canal, walked a quarter mile to his home, got a boat, and came back for his books. Denise Espadron, the mother of Jeffery Espadron, recalled going to a bar some years earlier with her sister and a woman from Grand Bayou. When the evening was done, they dropped the friend off at Foster Canal.

"How you gettin' home?" Denise asked.

"Girl, I'm swimmin'," the woman answered and dived into the water.

"Swam like a dolphin," Denise Espadron said. "It was a way of life. You couldn't mess with 'em in the water."

As Louisiana's coastline eroded and land subsided over the preceding seven decades, Grand Bayou had become increasingly vulnerable to seasonal flooding and storm surge from hurricanes. According to disaster scientists from LSU, Hurricanes Isidore and Lili flooded homes with as much as three feet of water in 2002. A year later, waves whipped up by Tropical Storm Bill kept water in some homes for twenty-four hours. Paul Sylve had brought in boatloads of dirt to sustain a bulkhead on his property.

During Katrina, the Sylve home, with its five bedrooms and a porch facing the bayou, was apparently hit by a tornado. The roof and part of the back of the house were sheared away, leaving the inside exposed to rain and the strafing of Hurricane Rita three weeks later. Mold flowered on the walls, and the home became unrepairable. It had been torn down and piled next to the family wharf, to be taken away by a barge. A new home would be rebuilt with the help of the Mennonite Disaster Service. The date was uncertain. There was a bureaucratic maze to navigate, permits, soil samples, the paper requirements of delay. In the meantime, Paul Sylve had constructed a shed on seven-foot pilings to store a generator and other supplies. For Thanksgiving, he would haul a picnic table up the steps. The wind and cold came through unfinished walls beneath the eaves, and the ground was visible through holes and spaces between the floorboards, but the family was determined to get back home, if only for a meal. The Sylves were outdoor people, and it was too claustrophobic to spend Thanksgiving inside a FEMA trailer in Belle Chasse.

"What a glorious day," Paul said.

He was a Pentecostal preacher and a sign on his dock said "Hotel Hallelujah." He worked as a groundskeeper for the school district now that Katrina had taken him off the water. He wore jeans and sneakers. His skin was bronze, and he had friendly eyes that seemed brown one moment, green the next.

"I've longed to see this day, with the enthusiasm a child has for his mother," he said. "This is our home."

At the end of the gravel road, Paul and Jeremy stood for a few minutes near the tiny enclosure where bayou kids had waited for the bus after stepping off the school boat. Katrina's surge had set a barge atop the boat, crushing it.

"You killed that rabbit I cleaned today?" Paul asked his son.

"Paul Jr. run over with it a truck," Jeremy said of his older brother. He was paler than his father, with high cheekbones, resembling his mother, Carolyn, a Cherokee who had grown up in the Lower Ninth Ward in New Orleans.

The Sylves' fishing boat, a thirty-foot Lafitte skiff, remained moored in the canal. It had gotten hung up on pilings on the family dock during the hurricane. The deck had been ripped off. A smaller aluminum boat had sunk, too, along with its outboard motor, but Paul salvaged them. The engine cover was missing, and the key switch had corroded, but he hot-wired the motor on Thanksgiving and headed into the bayou.

Paul had completed eighth grade at the Grand Bayou school. The "red" school, they called it in the segregated parish. At the time, Plaquemines did not provide further education for French-and-Indian kids who lived on the bayou, but even if it had, Paul was ready for a life of fishing and trapping.

"I had too much salt water in my head," he said.

He learned how to cure the skins of mink, muskrat, otter, and nutria, nailing them to boards, and how to take a 'coon skin and stretch the hide on sticks as if he were making a kite. And he taught what he knew to his sons. Jeremy had learned to swim in the bayou by age three. He started driving a boat when he was four, picking up crab traps and running nutria traps with his father and uncle. By six, he began to take his cousins out to catch redfish, speckled trout, drum, and sheepshead. At nine, finally strong enough to open the snares, he began setting traps by himself. At twelve, he hunted ducks in a pond behind the house as his father watched from the back porch.

Once, when Jeremy was eleven or twelve, he hooked a forty-two-inch redfish, and the fish and the tide dragged him up the bayou, so he jumped in the boat of a passing stranger until he could reel the catch in. He was a sturdy swimmer, and even in winter, he would jump in the water to retrieve greenhead ducks he had killed. Sometimes, fishermen paid him to swim under their trawlers and untangle their propellers from ropes and nets. It was an easy way to make twenty bucks.

"If I could shoot my gun every day, I would," Jeremy said. "I like it, me."

Before Katrina, Thanksgiving would have included marsh hen, gumbo, oyster dressing, duck, rabbit, and sweet dough the size of a basketball, boiled in a pillowcase or a sack, then sliced and eaten with sweet gravy. This year, the family had planned to eat the redfish and speckled trout that Jeremy had caught the day before, but his father arrived in the yard this morning to find a cooler overturned. He held up a plastic bag with only a pair of fillets left inside.

"We won't have no fish today," Paul said. "A raccoon got in my ice chest."

It didn't matter. There was still a ham and sausage to boil, using a propane burner. And a neighbor, Ruby Ancar, arrived with small containers of turkey, ham, tomatoes, corn, pecan pie, and even a piece of her daughter's wedding cake. She hugged Carolyn Sylve and they both screamed, "We home! We home!"

Too bad they didn't catch that 'coon, Ruby said.

"It would have been dessert."

Ruby also brought a battery-powered CD player, and she put on Cajun Christmas songs. Her home had been rebuilt by the Mennonites, but she was still waiting for the electricity to be hooked up. Entergy, the local energy company, wanted returning bayou residents to pay a seventy-dollar monthly surcharge for ten years, she said. Residents had long complained of dismissive treatment by utility companies. When Katrina hit, many families did not have septic systems.

"We've gone through greater hurricanes than Katrina on the bayou," Ruby said. "That was a bureaucracy hurricane."

There had always been skepticism of outsiders along Grand Bayou. Now Ruby feared that developers would try to convert the place into expensive fishing camps. An uncle had once warned her, "Those sportsmen you are taking out fishing will one day invade your territory and one day you will regret the day you took them out."

"It's happening," Ruby said.

She had ordered her daughter Gabby not to sell the family land under any circumstances. Carolyn Sylve said someone could offer her five hundred thousand dollars, and the answer would still be no.

"This is home, the only home my husband knows," she said.

Ruby had lived in the FEMA trailer park in nearby Diamond after the storm. It felt as if she had died and gone to hell, all those people fussing and cursing day and night. The life on Grand Bayou was the only life he wanted, Paul Sylve said. The city was all cluttered up, even a small city like Belle Chasse. Out here, he loved the smell of the air and the enveloping of nature, and he felt safer in a boat than in any car. Only a few years earlier had Jeremy agreed to use a cell phone. He still did not like computers.

"I like to do things myself," he said.

Paul stood atop the steps on his storage shed and pointed to ridges in the marsh that were Indian burial mounds. The pirate Jean Lafitte had also plied these waters, perhaps stashing his plundered lucre in the nearby swamps and bays. Everything necessary was in arm's reach on the land and the water, Paul said. He could grab a couple dozen oysters from his dock. He could lower a twenty-two-foot net into the bayou and catch shrimp as the tide ran out. He could grind up meat from the hind legs of a nutria and mix in a little beef fat and make a burger as tasty as anything at McDonald's or Burger King.

"The Arabs, they wash their hands in oil," Paul said. "Farmers, they wash their hands in vegetables. We wash our hands in shrimp and crabs."

For his Thanksgiving meal, he mixed celery, mushrooms, potatoes, smoked sausage, and crab boil in a burner with his boiled ham. Rice was cooked in a microwave, hooked to a generator. Inside the storage shed, the picnic table was covered with a table cloth, and paper plates were set out. Paul said grace and read from First Corinthians and took Communion. Before Katrina, he had been the assistant pastor at the Grand Bayou Light Tabernacle Church. Many people on the bayou felt anchored there by faith.

"As long as they have people here, as long as one person is going to give his heart to the Lord before God calls him, it'd be worth it all to stay here," Paul said.

The family ate and laughed and told stories about bayou life: Coco Reyes's trawler towed the young and the old in inner tubes on the Fourth of July. The bayou froze once, and kids were pulled along using blankets for sleds. Carolyn Sylve dressed in a bunny suit and hopped from house to house on Easter. Paul translated for his French-speaking aunt when politicians came around. Their daughter Julia once kissed the head of a pig in the refrigerator. Bridegrooms had money pinned to their tuxedos and were thrown overboard at wedding parties. Ruby Ancar flagged down a Vietnamese fishermen when her father caught a heart attack, so she could use the pay phone at the community school to call an ambulance. The Sylves finally got running water when Jeremy was a baby and were among the last to get a phone, holding out until ten years ago.

In Belle Chasse, Paul had been miserable, his wife said. Living in a FEMA trailer was like living in a Pepsi can. It had been a while since Carolyn had seen her husband so relaxed and happy.

"This was the best Thanksgiving, the best," she said. "That's all we asked for, to go home for Thanksgiving."

The sun appeared in late afternoon, and Jeremy drove his boat a short distance to the mouth of Secola Canal. Redfish were heading for deeper water as the tide rushed out. The water roiled where it met the bayou, and the redfish hit the shrimp bait with ravenous insistence. How did they know the bait was there? Jeremy wondered aloud. Did they see it? Smell it? "I can't see under that water, me," he said. Quickly, he replenished the ice chest whose contents the raccoon had devoured. At sundown, the sky turned a vivid pink, streaked with gray like the latticed crust of a pie.

Jeremy baited another hook.

"It's like this every day," he said.

21

"KNOCK SOMEBODY OUT!"

THERE WERE NO CLASSES THE DAY AFTER THANKSGIVING, but Cyril Crutchfield told his players to arrive at school at nine in the morning. He didn't want them running around on the day of the state quarterfinals. Some brought sleeping bags to the trailer where they dressed on Fridays. The Hurricanes watched movies, listened to music, caught part of the LSU–Arkansas game on television. In late afternoon, Crutchfield sat in the dark of his office, hand on his chin, staring ahead. South Plaquemines' opponent in the quarterfinals was St. Edmund of Eunice, a Catholic school located in the Cajun country of southwestern Louisiana. In 1979, Port Sulphur High had defeated St. Edmund 3–0 to win the Class 1A state championship. Paul Lemaire, now the Plaquemines Parish school-board president, had kicked the winning field goal. That game was played in Eunice and, according to Port Sulphur fans, their victory celebration was met by police dogs on the sideline. Some fans said they were kept off the field entirely. Others said they broke down a fence and overwhelmed the threat of the dogs.

Tom Andrus, the St. Edmund coach, had been an assistant in 1979. He later left coaching for twenty-five years, then returned for the 2007 season. His team was big and disciplined. Quarterback

271

Wesley Richard had thrown for 2,416 yards and 29 touchdowns. Defensively, the Blue Jays hustled rapaciously to the ball.

"What's Crutchfield like?" Andrus asked before the game. "I hear he's half crazy."

Andrus said he had also heard that South Plaquemines was jumping to Class 3A in 2008. He was repeating a rumor making the rounds on the Internet that the school had a surge of new students this year. The rumor was untrue. South Plaquemines still had only two hundred students in grades nine through twelve. Apparently, some fans of other teams had come to believe the Hurricanes' success was due more to bulging enrollment than to skill and coaching.

Crutchfield's game plan was to throw deep on St. Edmund. He knew the Hurricanes had more speed than the Blue Jays. And he had a surprise waiting. In the first two play-off games, the opponent had scored first. Tonight, the first time South Plaquemines received a kickoff, it would run a reverse.

"Nothing deflates a team more than they score and we stick it down their throat," Crutchfield told his players.

St. Edmund won the toss and, surprisingly, elected to kick, giving the ball to Louisiana's most explosive offense. Lyle Fitte lined up at the thirty-five-yard line, near the South Plaquemines bench. He circled back to the fifteen, took a handoff from Cantrelle Riley, and sprinted toward the right sideline. The St. Edmund players seemed confused, hesitant in their white helmets and jerseys. When Lyle sliced back across the middle, four of the Blue Jays, shoulder to shoulder in startled futility, changed direction at once, like a school of fish. It was already too late, and Lyle was past them, shifting the ball from his right arm to his left, only one man between him and the goal line. This last defender kept backpedaling, hoping to slow Lyle or force him into a betrayal of intent, a giveaway of the head or shoulders, a signal that he would remain along the sideline or cut yet again toward the middle. But the boy ran out of time and room and he was hit and he tumbled into a backward sprawl. Lyle strolled into the end zone. He had run eighty-five yards without anyone touching him.

Other teams might have succumbed after such a startling disadvantage, but St. Edmund struck back. Its halfback took a hit and disappeared into a pile but spun and kept his feet, emerging again and running twenty-six yards for a touchdown. The extra point put the Blue Jays up 7–6.

"What's going on?" Crutchfield screamed. "Y'all are not wrapping up. Those white boys came to play. Y'all better step your fuckin' game up."

Ridge Turner threw thirty-three yards over the middle to Seth Ancar, then Lyle ran a counter to his left, following Jeremy Sylve and Jordan Ancar into the end zone from three yards out. The Hurricanes went ahead 14–7, but during the drive, Ridge banged his biceps muscle against a helmet. He came to the bench in pain.

His throwing arm hung limply by his side, but if he was badly hurt, it did not keep Ridge out of the game. Two minutes later, he drifted slyly as a punt traveled to Lyle, then cut across the field and took a pitch and stepped around a freeing block by Seth Ancar. Ridge pointed ahead to his blockers, setting them into position. He stepped out of a low tackle at midfield and slipped past a hugging grab at his waist at the twenty-five-yard line, stumbling slightly but keeping his balance and scoring from seventy yards to put the Hurricanes ahead 21–7.

Still, St. Edmund did not concede. Its defensive line was powerful and smart, and blitzing by the Blue Jays' linebackers became obstructive. Lyle muffed a punt. Ridge was tackled for no gain on fourth-and-one at the St. Edmund eight-yard line. As the half neared, South Plaquemines was forced to punt for the first time in the play-offs. The game had come to a standstill, neither team yielding or able to impose its will.

Then, a break for the Hurricanes: Defensive end Beau Fitte blindsided the St. Edmund quarterback, and the ball came free, tossed sideways, a lateral. Seth Ancar rushed from his position at middle linebacker and recovered for South Plaquemines. The Hurricanes reached the Blue Jays' twenty-one-yard line and ran a sweep with Lyle on fourth-and-three, but he was trapped behind the line of scrimmage. He got to his feet and snapped off his chin strap in disgust.

A minute remained in the half. If the Hurricanes could stop the Blue Jays quickly, they might have one final chance to score.

"Seth, you've got to come harder!" Jody Ancar yelled from the stands at his brother.

And then again, "Seth, knock somebody out!"

JODY ANCAR WAS EARNING HIS APPRENTICESHIP AS A TUG-boat captain. This was one of his rare Friday nights off. He had been a freshman defensive end when Port Sulphur High won the state championship in 2002. After Katrina, he joined Randall Mackey and three other players who evacuated to Bastrop, winning a title in 2005. Jody said he had enjoyed his experience in Bastrop and did not feel the players had been exploited for their football skills.

"They treated us nice, and it opened a lot of opportunities," he said.

Even though that 2005 title had been stripped, and the players had been recruited illegally, Jody said, "They could never take the memories out of my mind. That was a magical season." At the same time, he added, "I'd trade everything up there to have played my senior season at Port Sulphur."

It saddened him, he said, to think things would never be the same again in lower Plaquemines and that there was a new school, with a new team name, sitting on the old campus of Port Sulphur High. Somehow, the new name, Hurricanes, didn't feel right.

"We went down in a hurricane," Jody said. "But I guess you have to let it go. It hurts me, but there's nothing you can do about it."

He had built himself to 225 pounds for his senior season at Bastrop. Afterward, he had signed a letter of intent to attend Grambling State University. But Jody never entered school, deferring his football ambitions, then surrendering them entirely. There was an unplanned pregnancy, and now at twenty, he was the father of a fifteen-month-old daughter. It was one thing Crutchfield had always stressed: Take care of your responsibilities. He could hear Crutchfield's words still ringing in his head from high school, now coming out of his own mouth.

"Every decision you make in life, there are consequences," Jody said. "The consequences of sexual activity are a baby."

Still, he felt the nostalgic pull of football. Not a day went by that he didn't think about what he might have accomplished in a helmet and shoulder pads.

"I didn't even scratch my potential," Jody said.

That's why he rode his brother so hard, yelling at Seth from the railing of the stands, cajoling him to pick up his grades and improve his practice habits. Seth was a sophomore, already perhaps the best linebacker in the state in Class 1A. Jody was determined that Seth would fulfill the opportunity that he had missed.

"I'm hard on him," Jody said, "but when he does good, I'm the happiest person in the world."

IN THE LOCKER ROOM AT HALFTIME, CRUTCHFIELD REminded his players of what he had said before the play-offs began: There would be one game that could go either way. This was the game. A 21–7 lead over St. Edmund did not appear safe. Only once, in the season opener against Belle Chasse, had the Hurricanes scored fewer points in the first two quarters.

"You better get it out of your mind that you're invincible," Crutchfield told his players. "They done stopped you. You gotta go out and make plays."

The offensive line wasn't blocking anybody, Crutchfield said. If the linemen could only hold their blocks, deep passing routes would open all night.

"They're blitzing a lot of people," Sal Cepriano said.

"I'm not ready to go home," Cantrelle Riley said.

"I got two more weeks in me," Sal said.

"Man, it's in the palm of our hands!" Seth Ancar said.

Ridge sat against a wall, holding his right arm, cursing, wincing.

"You sure you can go?" assistant coach August Ragas asked.

Ridge nodded.

As the Hurricanes walked down a ramp from their trailer, Jody Ancar approached Seth and clubbed him across the chest.

"Come on!" Jody yelled to his brother. "You gotta step your game up!"

THE BROTHERS SPOKE DAILY WHEN JODY WAS AWAY ON THE water. When he was home, Jody put Seth through grueling workouts, using equipment that he bought for his younger brother: an agility ladder to improve footwork, a medicine ball, a parachute to provide resistance during wind sprints. Sometimes the two brothers wrestled in the yard. At sixteen, Seth stood five foot ten and weighed 180 pounds, all of it appearing to be lean muscle, his narrow waist expanding in a V to a wedge of sculpted chest. He went about his weight-lifting workouts with a quiet diligence, but on the field Seth became a battering ram of a linebacker, blitzing through the middle, all strength and leverage and determination, shoving linemen backward, snapping their face masks upward in a way that made the eyes water. He was not content with simply tackling quarterbacks and running backs. He wanted to club and pummel and dominate them.

"I'm trying to hurt somebody," Seth said.

He played with a ferocity that reminded Crutchfield of himself. Earlier in the season, in a 58–6 rout of Ridgewood Prep, Seth had tackled a running back in the backfield, and a coach yelled, "Keep running." The dispirited back replied, "Where do you want me to go?" In a summer scrimmage against Edna Karr High of New Orleans, the Karr coach had said to his defense, "I'd trade all of y'all for number 2."

That was Seth's number. Yet he was hard on himself, shaking his head after a tackle or throwing up his arms as if he expected perfection from an imperfect game. The previous Saturday, when the Hurricanes watched Belle Chasse in the play-offs, Seth sat quietly in the stadium wearing sunglasses at night.

"I'm imagining myself knocking somebody out," he said.

It was nearly all he thought about, winning a state high school championship and going to college on a scholarship and then to the NFL. His brother Jody was his hero, and Seth hung on his every instruction. He did three hundred pushups each night and sometimes got up at six in the morning to run a mile. He ran sprints alone in the yard and jumped rope and dashed around cones. Jody wanted Seth to lower his time in the forty-yard dash from 4.7 seconds to 4.5, to improve his ability to catch the ball, to practice fifty punts and fifty extra points every day in the summer so that he would never have to leave the field during a game. Why waste your talent? Jody said. He had another idea, too, on how Seth could distinguish himself with recruiters.

"He wants to change the way I walk," Seth said. "So people will look at me and know who I am because I walk differently."

He took his brother to heart when Jody told him that only a coward let another player push him around and that he should hit linemen in the mouth to let them know that he was a man.

"You may get only one chance and you never get it back," Jody had told him about college.

Seth was determined not to miss this chance. He could be an indifferent student, though. Both Crutchfield and Jody reminded Seth constantly that he needed adequate grades and standardized test scores, not merely the numbers of catching and tackling, to earn a college scholarship. Seth had two years of high school left, but Crutchfield said repeatedly to his players that the seasons went quickly and before they knew it, their time would be finished and the recruiters would not call if they did not have the grades.

"I'm trying to get him to go to college, to better his life," Jody said of Seth. "The only thing I thought about was football, football, football. After it was gone, it hurt me. You've got to get your education. That's the number–one thing coach preached."

If these were lessons Jody had learned too late for himself, perhaps he could teach them more urgently to Seth. Jody treated his brother the way Crutchfield had treated him, heavy on the criticism, light on the praise. This is what had driven Jody, trying to gain Crutchfield's satisfaction, to prove him wrong, just as Crutchfield had done with his own father, who had called him "Dummy."

"If I turned my uniform in wrong, he wanted to fight me," Jody said of Crutchfield. "He was always all over me. It motivated me. I never played against my opponent. I was always playing against my coach. I wanted his congratulations. It taught me my work ethic."

He had watched on a recent day at practice as Crutchfield grumbled his way through a kickoff rehearsal, telling Jesse Phan, the freshman of Cambodian descent, "This is America. We only use eleven players on kickoffs, not twelve."

And to Leston Smith, another freshman: "We're going to do this one more time. If you're not lined up right, I'm going to punch you in the head."

Jody had smiled on the sideline. How many times had he heard the same bombastic threats himself?

"That's the coach I like," he said.

AS THE THIRD QUARTER OPENED, SETH ANCAR FLUSHED THE St. Edmund quarterback and wrestled a running back to the ground as if roping a calf. Ridge Turner intercepted a pass from his spot at cornerback. Still, the Hurricanes could not score. Ridge threw two interceptions, one at the Blue Jays' five-yard line, and Lyle Fitte dropped what would have been a seventy-two-yard touchdown pass, the ball slipping from his fingertips in the open field.

On the first play of the fourth quarter, at the St. Edmund twenty-three-yard line, Lyle redeemed himself. He lined up in the left slot, came in motion, and took the ball from Ridge on a speed sweep right, following his guard, slipping inside a block from the tight end. A linebacker came at him low, and Lyle slung him down with his left arm, as if closing a sliding door. He came to a near stop and then cut sharply to his left and the free safety's cleats skidded out from under him. Twisted awkwardly, the safety put his hand to the ground to keep from falling and Lyle trotted into the end zone for a 27–7 lead.

St. Edmund drove resolutely to the South Plaquemines' eleven-yard line, but Bradley Sylve stepped in front of a pass at the five, and there was no catching him. He was a freshman, and a year before, he had won the league hundred-meter title as an eighth-grader. This season had been frustrating. An eye infection kept Bradley out of the lineup for a handful of games, forcing him to have his eyes dilated daily and to wear sunglasses even in the dark. Finally, the infection was gone and he raced down the sideline and held the ball up triumphantly and the Hurricanes went ahead 35–7.

Bradley was soon to become Crutchfield's stepson. His mother, Mickey, was planning a wedding for late December. Crutchfield had repeatedly admonished the young cornerback to turn his head and look for the ball in pass coverage, and now as Bradley scored, Crutchfield laughed and said, "That's my boy!"

South Plaquemines scored twice again, and the game ended at 47–13. The Hurricanes were headed for the state semifinals. Roger Halphen was in attendance after missing four games upon his suspension. He was told by the school district that he was not barred from games, so he had sat in the stands tonight in a South Plaquemines letter jacket. During the game, he slipped a note of encouragement and instruction to Jordan Ancar. Afterward, he stood outside the team trailer, head lowered as he leaned on a wooden railing, crying. He went inside the trailer and congratulated the team. Some of the players who were also wrestlers—Little Wayne Williamson, Mike Barthelemy Jr.—hugged him.

"I never felt pain like that," Roger said later. "They thought I was happy; I was in pain. I felt like I had been swindled, double-crossed."

St. Edmund had played a gutsy game. Some of the Hurricanes believed it was the best team they had played all season. Still, South Plaquemines had scored forty-one consecutive points before a late, inconsequential Blue Jays' touchdown. That was not enough to please all of the Hurricanes' fans, who could be demanding, even irrationally so. And they were never hesitant to tell Crutchfield how they thought he had erred. Afterward, in the team trailer, Carlton LaFrance, a school-board member, criticized the calling of shovel passes near the St. Edmund goal line.

"You lucky you have a job," LaFrance told Crutchfield. He was joking, but disagreement was evident in his words.

There was a bluntness about football in lower Plaquemines, a directness and brusque candor that came with the territory. The next morning, it became evident that James Ragas, the team's equipment manager who filmed games from the press box, had missed Bradley Sylve's interception, inadvertently pressing the "off" button on the video recorder. Crutchfield yelled at him, saying, "What did you do with the film?"

During the film review, Crutchfield admonished his players to quit listening to people who told them how great they were. They would have to play with more self-control to win in the semifinals. He noticed that Seth Ancar had seemed overly eager sometimes at middle linebacker, trying to anticipate the center snap, jumping offside a couple of times, drawing a flag for grabbing the St. Edmund quarterback's face mask.

"Pure garbage," Crutchfield told Jody Ancar, who also came to see the film.

"Coach, I tell him that all the time," Jody said.

There was not a more fearsome linebacker in Class 1A, as far as Crutchfield was concerned. But discipline won football games.

"Sometimes I get disappointed in myself," Seth said later. "I expect so much. Hey, you try not to mess up, but this helps me keep my focus and motivates me to work hard. If you work hard, you should get what you deserve."

22

AN OPPONENT NAMED DESIRE

AFTER THE CROWD HAD CLEARED FROM THE ST. EDMUND game, Cyril Crutchfield walked a block to his trailer. "I really ain't gonna sleep now," he said. He wanted to watch video of South Plaquemines' semifinal opponent. Desire Street Academy, once situated in the Ninth Ward of New Orleans, had been devastated by Katrina. Its players had experienced the same catastrophe as those from lower Plaquemines. The school had relocated to the Florida panhandle, then to Baton Rouge. Desire Street's players had a strong incentive to reach the state-championship game. It would be played in the Superdome. They would be going home to New Orleans.

In 2006, South Plaquemines won its inaugural victory over Desire Street, 24–21. That game would have little reflection on this one. Both teams had been unsettled from the storm. A year later, Desire Street was playing with much greater purpose. It had forfeited two games at the end of the regular season, for using an ineligible player, and had entered the play-offs seeded twenty-third among the thirty-two teams in Class 1A. But the Lions had the skill of a much higher seed. Six of Desire Street's seniors would sign Division I scholarships, two with LSU, a third with Auburn. Three of its starting linemen weighed 300 pounds, a fourth weighed 280, and a fifth weighed 270.

"Those dudes, they from the projects," Crutchfield said. "They smell the 'Dome. They might come out like gangbusters. Guess what, we're gonna come like gangbusters, too."

BY THE NEXT MORNING, A BLEARY-EYED CRUTCHFIELD HAD begun to formulate his game plan. He figured that Desire Street would probably try to spread the Hurricanes' defense, luring everyone out of the box, then pound away with a three-hundred-pound fullback named LaVar Edwards, who was headed to LSU.

"It all starts with the defense," Crutchfield told his players. "Seth, you've got to bring your A game."

Privately, Crutchfield said that Edwards had the skill to become a terrific player in college. But he told his team that the Desire Street fullback did not run hard, that he looked for contact and a chance to fall.

"He's a cupcake," Crutchfield said. "Big Puddin'."

Crutchfield would counter with his Bandit defense, using three linemen instead of four, and he would pressure Desire Street with five linebackers. South Plaquemines would attack from so many angles, the Lions' quarterback and linemen would grow confused and frustrated. Trey Stewart, South Plaquemines most agile linebacker, would play single coverage on the Lions' star receiver, Deangelo Peterson, who was also headed to LSU.

Defensively, Desire Street was athletic but not disciplined, Crutchfield believed. The Lions would blitz, but without much direction and restraint. And their cornerbacks seemed vulnerable.

Maybe the players would hang their heads if they fell behind early. South Plaquemines would attack with screen passes, turning Desire Street's aggressiveness into a liability.

"Big week," Crutchfield told his team. "Desire Street is in our fuckin' way. We gotta get 'em out of the way."

THE NEXT NIGHT, SUNDAY, A LIGHTNING STORM KNOCKED out the power from Port Sulphur twenty miles to the north. In the darkness, using the glow from their cell phones, the players made their way from the gym, where they'd been lifting weights, to Crutchfield's classroom. The emergency exit sign provided the only illumination as Crutchfield addressed his team.

"Our goal is not to play in the semis," he said. "Our goal is to win the state championship."

There would be no tutoring after school this week. There wasn't time, Crutchfield said.

"But don't take advantage of the situation," he told his players. "We're here for education. Don't not turn in an assignment or not study for something you're supposed to."

Fear was mounting around Port Sulphur that the Hurricanes would lose to Desire Street. People were talking at the doughnut shop. Beneath the bravado of local fans was insecurity. Sometimes their confidence seemed as fragile as the recovery from Katrina. The Lions were too big, the Hurricanes too small. No way would they beat those boys from the projects.

Don't listen to any of it, Crutchfield told his players. Don't listen to anyone outside this room. Sure, it would be a difficult game. Things were certain to go wrong. So what? Don't worry. Don't start fighting with each other. Stay positive.

"When a teammate screws up a play, remember, the most important thing this player needs is a friend," Crutchfield said. "You gotta stick with it. If you drop a pass, you didn't mean to do it. If you throw an interception, you didn't mean to. If you do something wrong, we live to fight another play. I feel like you're going to dominate this game. They big, we fast. They fast, we faster. I'll take speed over size any day of the week. One thing I know they don't have that we have—we got heart."

His players sat in desks and Crutchfield walked back and forth, as if teaching a class. He told the story about how, six months after Katrina, he had recovered the autographed football from Port Sulphur's 2002 state championship. It had been in a locker in his ruined office, and he had busted the lock with a hammer, afraid of snakes, but there it was, in good condition. It was funny how life worked, Crutchfield said. Some of the players from that team were doing pretty well, others not too well. One had died in a car wreck.

"Let me tell you something," Crutchfield said. "If you think you're enjoying yourself now, I promise you, if you get to experience a chance to play for a state championship, it will forever change your life. Katrina did big-time damage, sure did, really did. But of all the things that Katrina took away, it couldn't take away that ball, that little thing that means so much. I promise you, if we get there, no matter what happens—another hurricane, a blizzard, a fire—that can never be taken away."

Thunder crackled and the rain came pouring down again.

"The game now is mental," Crutchfield said. "I'm not going to prepare for a loss. If we don't win state, I don't know what I'm going to do. I'm about to lose my mind now. We need to do that for ourselves, for our community, for your parents, for your peers. You deserve it. Look how far we've come in two years. Last year, no weight room, no practice field, having to travel back and forth.

"In society, people only see the end results. Do they really see how far we've come? They don't say, 'They doing damn good.' No, they say, 'If you don't win the game, you're garbage.' I still hear people criticize Ridge. They say he's not Randall. Hey, he's Ridge Turner. And I'm proud of him. Damn right. Hey, son, you can throw the damn ball."

South Plaquemines was going to win, Crutchfield said. Desire Street did not have the same dedication. Its players didn't run the river levee in the summer or lift weights in sucking heat or jump hurdles in weighted vests. The Hurricanes would win, and they would go to the Superdome, and they would come through the tunnel to practice before the championship game, and they would see the grass and all the seats, and it would change their lives.

"Y'all are my family," Crutchfield said. "What else can I do and be happy? I curse, I scream and fuss because I love the game. I love the game and I can't play the game no more. I can only experience it through your eyes. I promise you, when we win this one, you'll get to experience something great."

A generator was hooked up to the television and video machine so that the Hurricanes could watch video of Desire Street. Eventually, the generator ran low on gas and began to surge, and Crutchfield considered siphoning fuel from his SUV. Then James Ragas, the equipment manager, found a can of gas in the gym. The video session went on. Desire Street's quarterback did not like to be hit, Crutchfield said.

"Hit him and wrap him up and put him in the dirt," he told his players. "If they call it, they call it. We want him on the sidelines. But don't take no cheap shots."

Desire Street had won a slim victory in the quarterfinals after its opponent, Oak Grove, missed a field goal in the final seconds. South Plaquemines watched the video as the Lions ran jubilantly off the field.

"That's gonna be us next week, and we're going to the state championship," Crutchfield said. "I don't know about y'all, but I might get nekkid."

The power blackout continued for miles in lower Plaquemines, and Crutchfield decided to dismiss his players early. They could watch more game tape tomorrow.

"Y'all can go," he said.

Not a player got up from his seat.

"Y'all want to watch some more?"

For another half hour, as the generator hummed outside the classroom, the Hurricanes watched as Crutchfield explained how they would win. Desire Street shouldn't even be on the field with South Plaquemines, he said. How could people say the Lions would win? Crutchfield just didn't see it, but only if the Hurricanes worked hard and stayed focused all week.

"Y'all better come out like gangbusters," he said. "Those boys from the projects never been to the 'Dome. They gonna be ready."

That was the one thing he feared about Desire Street, an awakening by these huge, immensely talented, but vaguely underachieving players. A chance to go home, to play in front of family and friends, was alluring motivation.

"I'm worried that a light will go on and those boys will realize, 'I'm big, I'm fast,' and understand how good they are," Crutchfield said.

After the team left, Crutchfield turned the television to face the greaseboard in his classroom. It was still connected to the generator, and he used the blue light of the TV screen to copy Desire Street's plays and formations onto a notepad. Then he grabbed the video machine, a book bag, the generator, and the gas can. He would do more film study at home. As he walked outside, a cruise ship passed on the Mississippi like a floating bowl of light.

Then everything went dark again. Crutchfield had slept little since Friday, watching video, dozing for a few hours, then watching more video. He had a headache, and he hadn't eaten since breakfast.

"I've got to get those kids ready," he said. "Got to get 'em ready."

ON AUGUST 29, 2005, THE WATER KEPT CLIMBING IN EAST-
ern New Orleans, coming over the cars. Deangelo Peterson and
his family had not evacuated for Katrina. They stood in their
second-floor apartment, trying to ride out the storm. Deangelo
was looking forward to the inaugural varsity football season at
Desire Street Academy. It was only four days away. But now
floodwalls were collapsing and levees were breaching and 80
percent of New Orleans was going under. Deangelo decided it
was time to get out. He lifted his three-year-old niece over his
head, walked through water that surged to his chest, and
brought her to a nearby hotel. He was six foot three, a football
and basketball player, and he kept his head above water and
went back for his mother and his sister. Eight relatives gathered
in the hotel until a military boat rescued them, and they landed
at the New Orleans Convention Center, that televised hell,
thousands desperate for food and water, evacuees collapsing in
the heat, an elderly woman dead and covered in a wheelchair,
frantic voices pleading to cameras for help from a government as
broken as the levees.

Deangelo was afraid to sleep for three days at the Convention
Center. People were hungry and looking for food. There were
rumors of piled bodies and gang rapes and guns being fired. The
rumors turned out to be exaggerated, but they seemed real
enough on those anxious nights. Deangelo, only sixteen then,
was afraid to close his eyes.

"At night, you could hear people screaming for their children,"
he said. "I was scared. I didn't know when we were going to leave."

After three days, his family left on a helicopter for the New
Orleans airport. A plane brought them to a shelter in San Antonio
and later to Houston. Other students were scattered as far away as
Utah. Football season seemed lost. Unknown to Deangelo, though,
the officials of Desire Street Academy were determined to reopen
the school in some fashion. Staff members combed shelters in

Louisiana and Texas. The school's development director, Danny Wuerffel, winner of the 1996 Heisman Trophy at the University of Florida and a former quarterback with the New Orleans Saints, made appeals on television. Three-quarters of the school's 190 students were located, most in southern and eastern Texas. One student spotted the Desire Street principal on the road and ran up to him in a traffic jam.

The academy—which took the name of the notorious housing project in the neighborhood—had been founded in 2002 by Desire Street Ministries as a kind of lighthouse in the impoverished, crime-plagued darkness of the Ninth Ward.

"We try to salvage those kids that many say are unsalvageable," said Oscar Brown, the dean of students who said that his own errant life of selling drugs and boosting cars had been saved by the ministry.

Katrina had put eight feet of water into the Ninth Ward school, so it was relocated to the Florida panhandle, at a 4-H camp in Niceville. About eighty students made the transfer from New Orleans, sleeping in cabins. Four football games were played in that truncated 2005 season. Each week, the Desire Street players loaded onto charter buses, made a four-hour ride to play in the New Orleans area, then rode four hours back to Florida.

"I think we made a mistake," said Mickey Joseph, an assistant coach in 2005 and now the head coach. "We thought football would be therapeutic. But we almost lost some of them for the rest of their careers, losing like that. They were devastated."

These were brittle kids, separated from their families, their hometown. Most had lost everything they owned. And they had never played varsity football together. Desire Street's first game ended with a 50–14 defeat. The second and third games were equally hopeless. The season finale brought the lone victory.

"We didn't have any experience; some guys got their heads down," Peterson said.

In 2006, with the Ninth Ward still largely forsaken, Desire Street Academy moved to Baton Rouge, seventy-five miles upriver from New Orleans, inhabiting a former Catholic church and an abandoned elementary school. It was a boarding school, with 116 boys enrolled, 53 from New Orleans, including most of the football players, and the rest from Baton Rouge. Bus trips to New Orleans were available each weekend so students could visit their families. Deangelo Peterson traveled home after each game to see his mother, Deborah, who suffered from high blood pressure.

Desire Street's football team did not have its own field or a locker room or a weight room or even goalposts to practice extra points and field goals. Joseph, the head coach and a former quarterback at Nebraska, was living apart from his wife, a dentist, whose practice was in Oklahoma City. His two daughters were there, too. This might be his last season at Desire Street, he said, unless he could take a leave of absence in the off-season. But for now, his most urgent concern was the Class 1A play-offs. His Lions were one of only four teams remaining.

"In Florida, we didn't have a lot of discipline; everybody was doing his own thing," said Ronald Clark, a 270-pound tackle. "We would get down on ourselves and we ended up giving up. Now our coaches have brought us together. We believe in ourselves. This year, we're not losing."

In a little more than two months, Peterson and Clark and four other teammates would return to the old gym at Desire Street Academy in New Orleans to sign their letters of intent to play college football. The hurricane had been a transforming moment for Deangelo. Once he had been arrogant and disrespectful, prone to cursing people, and he had been kicked out of several schools, said Brown, the dean, with whom Peterson lived.

"Now he's humbled himself, he's a leader," Brown said.

Deangelo said he would be the first in his family to graduate from high school. "That will make my mom smile," he said. To be awarded a scholarship and an all-expenses-paid chance to graduate from college was "unheard of," Brown said, adding, "When he graduates, they'll have a party and it'll last for two weeks."

During his junior year, Peterson had written an English paper titled "Don't Wait for God to Do Something Before You Trust Him:"

Katrina was a bad experience for me and my family. Still to this day we're not close together. Life is so hard being away from your family. When you're still in high school, you miss them so much. I imagine that when I get out of high school, I will still miss them when I am away from them.

My trust in God confirms my family will be reunited. I miss all the things that my mother and I used to do. Sooner or later, God will make a way to bring us together. Before Hurricane Katrina, my mother came to all my basketball and football games. She even supported me during the track season. Sometimes, I can see her right here with me. I am desperately wishing for her to be here. I am trusting in God for our reunion. He has never failed me.

Against South Plaquemines, Deangelo figured to be a consequential figure. Aside from being a star receiver, he was also Desire Street's kicker and punter. The Lions couldn't afford to get into a "track meet" with the Hurricanes, Joseph said. He planned to try to slow the game down. The best way to stop South Plaquemines' offense was to keep it off the field.

"This is the post-Katrina Bowl," Joseph said. After the storm, "Kids on both teams didn't have a future, didn't know where they would be staying or eating, or if they would have shoes on their feet and shorts to wear. Some didn't take a shower for three or four days. You enjoy watching them. They've come a long way. They didn't have anything two years ago."

THE SEMIFINAL GAME WAS ONLY FORTY-EIGHT HOURS AWAY, and Cyril Crutchfield was growing impatient. At practice, Ridge Turner seemed to struggle to read the scout defense. Little Wayne Williamson appeared confused about his assignment at safety.

"Y'all see it falling apart, falling apart, falling apart, falling apart," Crutchfield told his players.

Ridge attempted to tackle Trey Stewart during a drill and reinjured the biceps muscle on his throwing arm.

"Damn," he said as threw a pass.

"What, your arm hurts?" Crutchfield asked.

"Yeah."

"Okay, you can't throw anymore."

Crutchfield called for Cantrelle Riley. He threw a wobbly pass. One was enough.

"I got it," Ridge said, coming back into the huddle.

He threw a slant pass and winced. Clearly he was in pain, but it was difficult to tell how severely Ridge was hurt. He was the leading passer in the state. South Plaquemines could hardly afford to play without him. But the team did not have a trainer. And the nearest specialist was forty miles away. Nobody seemed alarmed, as if ignoring the injury would somehow minimize it.

"Hey, don't worry," Crutchfield said sarcastically as Dylan Boutwell ran the wrong route on a crossing pattern with Lyle Fitte. The fans wouldn't blame the players for a defeat, only the coach. "Y'all got nothing to worry about," Crutchfield said.

"Get your heads right," he told his players as practice ended. College recruiters would be in the stands on Friday. "Put your name on the fucking map," Crutchfield said.

Off the field, at least, there had been some encouraging developments. Lyle's mother had finally received the keys for the family's new house from Habitat for Humanity. They hoped to move in by Christmas. And despite the sloppy practice, Corey Buie thought that the Hurricanes held a psychological edge over Desire Street.

"It's a difference in attitude between the city and the country," Buie said. "In the city, you have. In the country, you want."

ON GAME DAY, A SERIES OF HURRICANE WARNING SIGNS were posted along Highway 23 leading to South Plaquemines High:

You're Getting Closer: Winds 125

A Little More: Winds 135

Almost There: Winds 145

Category 5: Storm Warning

Ground Zero: 155+

"We are strong like the wind," said a sign festooned with blue and white and silver balloons. "We are unpredictable like the rain. We strengthen when we hit the field. We will shine like the sun when it's all done."

Still, many fans were petrified of Desire Street.

"I'm nervous," Big Wayne Williamson said as he barbecued at the concession stand. "I'm listening to the hype. They're big, strong, fast."

"I'm scared to death," Mike Barthelemy Sr. said. "Little Mike said he's worried about Ridge."

Crutchfield had grown so nervous by the end of the school day, he couldn't talk. Two hours before the game, he gathered his players in the end zone. The seniors would never play again on this field, Crutchfield told them. Leave no doubt about the outcome.

"If you're nervous, two things will happen," Crutchfield said. "Either you will fold, or you will get your back to the wall and fight your way out. Fight your ass off."

This was November 30, the last official day of hurricane season. It was unseasonably warm, and a parish insect-control truck again drove down the field, spraying for gnats.

Back in the dressing trailer, Crutchfield sat alone in his office. Ridge placed strips of tape around the heels of his cleats and wrote, "Comeback Kid." He rubbed some deep-heating balm on his sore arm. When he returned to the field for warm-ups, Corey Buie told him, "They got scouts all through here."

Alabama's chief scout was there. So were others, all looking at the half-dozen Division I prospects from Desire Street. Turner was only a junior, but this was the night to catch their eye.

"This is your time to shine," Buie told him. "This will start your senior year off. You blow 'em up tonight, they gonna forget who they came to see."

Desire Street sent its linemen onto the field first for warm-ups, along with Deangelo Peterson. Perhaps it was an attempt at intimidation. And why not? The Lions were huge, nearly as big as some NFL linemen. They outweighed some of the South Plaquemines' linemen by a hundred pounds.

"If something bad happens, we're still the better team," Crutch-field told his team one final time. "They are bigger, but we are better. Don't let size fool you. Leave no doubt. Bust they fuckin' ass."

Danny Wuerffel, who was now executive director of Desire Street Ministries, stood at midfield and watched the Hurricanes run through their pregame drills.

"Whoa," he said, "somebody can throw that ball."

THE HOME STANDS WERE FULL. THE CROWD OF NEARLY 2,500 spilled out along the end-zone fences. Before the kickoff, Stanley Gaudet asked for a moment of silence.

"We would like to thank all the people who couldn't be with us that would like to be with us," Gaudet said, "and thank both schools that have had such a hard go the last couple of years."

Desire Street won the coin toss and deferred possession until the second half. It was a mistake. On the game's first play, Cantrelle Riley split right and dragged a cornerback over the middle. Lyle Fitte circled out of the backfield, and there was a vacancy in the flat, no one within ten yards of him. Ridge Turner stepped to his left, stopped, and threw back to his right, a soft, arcing pass that hit Lyle in full stride. He ran alone to the end zone, sixty-three yards, a towel dancing at his waist. Fans along the fence whooped and waved as if calling for beads at a Mardi Gras parade. After sixteen seconds, the Hurricanes took a 6–0 lead.

Crutchfield had spotted a revealing eagerness in Desire Street's man-to-man defense, players rushing to one side, fast and determined but vulnerable to the counterflow. Ridge rolled to his right and found Lyle along the sideline with a forty-two-yard pass. Then, at the Lions' nine-yard line, Lyle lined up at wingback and sprinted to his left, but he was a decoy now, drawing the Desire Street defense toward him like iron filings to a magnet. Turner faked the sweep and kept the ball and ran to his right, a huge seam opening in the defense, an unimpeded path to the goal line. He raised the ball in the crook of his arm and hopped in the end zone. The game was not four minutes old and South Plaquemines had a 14–0 lead.

"I was looking up," Ridge told Cantrelle when he came to the bench. "Damn, I didn't think those boys were that big."

Big, but teetering. LaVar Edwards, the three-hundred-pound fullback, punched into the middle of the line, but Seth Ancar and Beau Fitte resisted, and Desire Street seemed to be losing its wind and its resolve.

"They huffin' and puffin'," Marcelin Ancar screamed on the sideline.

Ridge faked another speed sweep left to Lyle, keeping the ball on a counter to his right, following the blocks of Sal Cepriano and

Caileb Ancar, another hole opening impossibly wide. Turner ran forty-two yards to the end zone and no one touched him and the Hurricanes went up 20–0. "Gotcha," he said to Freddie Smooth, an imposing three-hundred-pound defensive tackle, as he ran past.

Nervously, Desire Street looked deep over the middle for Peterson, its star receiver, but Cantrelle Riley leaped and intercepted the pass, his left leg kicking high as he reached for the ball. While Peterson stood and looked toward his bench, annoyed, his palms upturned in complaint, Cantrelle returned the ball thirty-six yards to the Lions' fourteen-yard line. On fourth-and-goal at the eleven, Ridge faked another handoff to Lyle, trapped the cornerback in a moment of indecision, and threw a slant pass to Cantrelle for a touchdown. Fifty seconds into the second quarter, South Plaquemines had a 28–0 lead.

"It turned into a track meet," Mickey Joseph would say later, "and they ran the hundred-yard dash in record-breaking time."

By halftime, it was 36–6 after a twenty-eight-yard run by Ridge. The Hurricanes were on their way to the Superdome. They gathered in their trailer, and Crutchfield stomped around and urged them not to lose their intensity, saying, "Make them think we on some fuckin' dope. Snort that coke! Snort that coke!"

Peterson had one negligible reception for Desire Street, and the man covering him, Trey Stewart, flexed his arms: "He don't want it. They big, but I'm cut. I shut 'em down."

The Desire Street linemen were enormous, but they could not push South Plaquemines around. They were becoming tired, playing both offense and defense, forced to chase Ridge, who sapped their legs with screen passes and negated their charges with fake sweeps and elegant counters.

"They can't get no push," Seth Ancar said. "We stronger than them."

In the third quarter, Ridge performed more sleight of hand, hinting at a sweep to Lyle, keeping the ball and scoring from two yards to give the Hurricanes a lead of 43–6. "We want 50!" Crutchfield screamed, and Ridge threw a twelve-yard touchdown pass to Cantrelle, and it was 50–6. His seventh touchdown of the game gave Ridge sixty-four for the season, running and passing, and set a state record with 5,239 total yards.

"They giving up," Jordan Ancar said as he came to the sideline. "They tired."

South Plaquemines went ahead 56–6 and players poured water on Crutchfield. He began jumping and yelling, "I want some more! I want some more!"

Gaudet stood on the bench and danced with an umbrella, and the crowd chanted, "Whose field? Crutchfield!" The coach tried to calm his team, saying, "Our goal is not to get to the state championship," but before he could finish, his players yelled in unison, "It's to win the state championship!"

"And that's exactly what we gonna do!" Crutchfield said.

Danny Wuerffel said the Hurricanes had played "like a machine."

"A lot of teams have fast players; this offense was fast, everything moving in five directions at one time," Wuerffel said. "Incredibly talented. Very well coached. The quarterback did everything. Anytime you have a guy who can throw and run, you have a potential Tim Tebow on your hands."

Sal Cepriano undressed in the team trailer and said he would have never believed it possible to play for a state championship two years after Katrina obliterated lower Plaquemines.

"Finally, some good news comes out from down here," he said.

Outside the locker room, Jeanitta Ancar, Jordan's mother, hugged Cantrelle, who had collected three interceptions and two touchdown receptions, and told him, "We love you no matter where you're from."

In that exultant moment, there were no divisions or tensions, no small-town resentments and rivalries, no players from Port Sulphur and Buras and Boothville-Venice, only players from South

Plaquemines, a defiant little team headed for a state-championship game, teenagers telling adults that it was okay to come home, that a lost community had a chance to find itself.

"This is all we have," Carlton LaFrance, a school-board member, said as he stood outside the team trailer. "This is it. Friday-night football. The fish are still biting and you can rebuild your house and deal with FEMA, but this is the only positive thing going on. This is what we live for."

23

CRUTCH IN THE HOLE

THE CELEBRATION LASTED TWENTY HOURS. AND THEN IT ended abruptly with the turning of a doorknob. Late on this Saturday afternoon, as the orange ball of a sun began to set over the marshes, Cyril Crutchfield walked into his classroom. The excited chatter fell silent. "Crutch in the hole," the players often said in alert when he approached. Everyone knew to shut up.

"That's the one thing I'm worried about, everyone telling you how good you are," Crutchfield said to his players. "Everybody telling you, 'We got it, we got it.' Got what? We haven't done nothin' yet."

The Hurricanes had won ten straight games. Only once in that stretch had they failed to score at least fifty points. But the most important game was still to be played. Losing in the state-championship game was unbearable, Crutchfield said. He explained yet again how his Port Sulphur High team had three touchdowns nullified by penalties in the 2001 state-championship game and lost, 35–34, to Oak Grove.

"Sickening," he said.

In a week, South Plaquemines (12–2) would face West St. John High of Edgard, Louisiana, for the Class 1A title. The alluvial soil along the Mississippi River between Baton Rouge and

New Orleans seemed as fertile for football players as for sugar-cane. Six players from this area would participate in the upcoming 2008 Super Bowl game between the New York Giants and the New England Patriots. Glenn Dorsey of LSU, the 2007 consensus defensive lineman of the year in college football, also grew up in this region.

As South Plaquemines had, West St. John loaded the first half of its schedule against schools with higher enrollments. All five of its nonleague opponents had made the play-offs. The Rams (9–5) had won nine consecutive games. Their coach, Laury Dupont, was a legend in Louisiana, having won 208 career games, three state titles in Class 2A, and three runner-up trophies in Class 1A. Now he was retiring after thirty-five seasons in coaching, the last twenty-one at West St. John. Another title would serve as his figurative golden parachute.

Dupont and Crutchfield were friends. Before Port Sulphur's 2001 state-championship game, Dupont had warned him about the distractions of playing in the Superdome, how his players would stumble on the artificial turf and how he would have trouble communicating with his quarterback because of an echo in the building. It would be easier the second time, Dupont said, and it was, as Port Sulphur won the title in 2002.

In 2005, Crutchfield said, Dupont had offered him a job as associate head coach at West St. John, with a promise to become head coach upon Dupont's retirement in 2006. Crutchfield said he declined because he did not want to be an assistant coach. Now Dupont was leaving, and Crutchfield knew he would be a formidable opponent.

"We're better than them, but if any team can beat us, they can," Crutchfield told his players.

He reminded them again about their grades: "I've been telling you over and over again, but it's like the rain. For some, it soaks in. Others, it evaporates."

Still, there was not much to complain about after last night's 56–6 victory. Crutchfield began handing out rare compliments.

To Seth Ancar: "You were all over the field."

To Lyle Fitte: "At one point, I thought you were a selfish young man, but I think you've started to come around. Other people are starting to see it. At one point, I figured you could play Division I. Now, there's no question you're gonna play Division I. I would be surprised if you're not offered [a scholarship] in the spring."

There was one potentially divisive moment ahead next week. After the South Plaquemines–West St. John game, Bastrop High and Randall Mackey would be seeking their second consecutive Class 4A championship, against Archbishop Shaw of suburban New Orleans. If not for Katrina, Randall would still be the quarterback at Port Sulphur, which might have won a string of state titles by now. Ridge Turner would have remained a cornerback. But the hurricane came, and everything was turned upside down. Now it was Ridge who held the state record for yardage in a season, having passed for 3,529 yards and 41 touchdowns (against 5 interceptions), and having run for 1,710 yards and 23 touchdowns. He fit the South Plaquemines system better than Randall as a runner/passer, Crutchfield believed. If Ridge threw accurately in the championship game, he could establish a national record for completion percentage in a season, set at 75.1 percent in 1994 by Tim Couch of Hyden, Kentucky. Couch later became the number 1 pick in the 1999 NFL draft. Through the semifinals, Turner had completed 213 of 281 passes, or 75.8 percent.

"Right now, I'm seeing a complete quarterback, probably one of the best in the state, easy, in all classes," Corey Buie said. "If Ridge sets his feet, he makes every pass."

Inevitably, though, Ridge and Randall would be compared on performances in their respective championship games. If South Plaquemines lost and Bastrop won, Port Sulphur would be morose with thoughts of what might have been. The best outcome would be victories by both teams. Ridge and Randall had spoken earlier today and had talked about winning titles and rings together.

"My concern is with Ridge, not Randall," Crutchfield said. "If Randall plays well and Ridge doesn't, I'm not gonna sleep. If Ridge plays well and Randall doesn't, I'm gonna sleep like a baby."

SUNDAY, DECEMBER 2: CRUTCHFIELD READ TO HIS PLAYERS the rules of conduct for the state-championship game. No dumping of Gatorade or water would be allowed on the artificial turf at the Superdome. The fine was five hundred dollars. The team would leave for New Orleans on Thursday, two days prior to the title game. Three or four players would share each hotel room. Cell phones would be confiscated. Family and friends were not allowed in the hotel. No distractions and no misbehavior would be tolerated. Crutchfield had sent a player home before Port Sulphur's 2002 title game. When it was time for curfew, he said, the lights had better go out.

"It's the room lights or your lights," he said.

Again, he reminded the Hurricanes not to celebrate prematurely.

"Nobody says congratulations for taking a test," Crutchfield said. "First, you have to pass the test."

It was okay to be nervous, he said. But being nervous didn't mean being afraid. The championship was there for the taking.

"Tomorrow isn't guaranteed," Crutchfield said. "We don't know what will happen when the Gulf water turns warm and the wind starts to blow. We don't know when your parents will decide to move away to Texas or Nebraska, or God forbid, if He takes one of you home with Him. We've got to take advantage of the situation."

The Hurricanes were the superior team, Crutchfield said. If both teams played their best, South Plaquemines would win. Losing, he said, "would put a sick feeling in me that's going to last all through

Christmas, all spring, and all summer. It would be hard for me to let go of certain things. Some of y'all gonna catch hell. It's one thing if Trey Stewart fucks up in the weight room on March 15 if we're the state champions. If we lose and he fucks up on March 15, I'm not gonna be responsible for my actions."

Make no mistake, Crutchfield said, some people wanted the Hurricanes to lose. Some people in Belle Chasse. Even some people in lower Plaquemines. And the teams the Hurricanes had beat. They, too, would probably be pulling for West St. John.

"They say I'm cocky, arrogant," Crutchfield said. "Yes, I am. I like that. We tell everybody we gonna kick your ass and then we kick your ass. That makes me happy."

There was nothing to fear in the championship game, he said, but fear itself.

"A famous man said that," Crutchfield said. "The only thing to be scared of is being scared. We're better than them. I haven't prepared myself for losing. Hasn't crossed my mind. Let's be ready to make plays and be smart about making them."

West St. John would play deliberately, running trap plays and play-action passes, Crutchfield told his players. Defensively, the Rams shed their blockers, ran enthusiastically to the ball, and tackled ferociously, just like the Hurricanes. But many of them played both ways. Crutchfield thought he could tire West St. John by running wide and throwing deep. He had used forty different formations during the play-offs, thinking ahead to this moment. He could run just about any play out of any formation. West St. John wouldn't know what was coming.

"They got something to play for, but so do we," he said.

He dismissed his team and grabbed his video machine out of his classroom. Crutchfield had slept little the night before. It would be that way all week, just as it had been for the previous four play-off games. He worked until one or two in the morning, slept on the sofa for a few hours, and watched more tape before he left on his morning bus route. Exhaustion was starting to come on. He could feel it in his eyes.

MONDAY, DECEMBER 3: ELEVEN HUNDRED TICKETS WERE sold in two hours at school. South Plaquemines ordered 2,100 more from the state high school association. A sign on the school marquee said, "There's no place like 'Dome."

TUESDAY, DECEMBER 4: THE TEMPERATURE WAS IN THE LOW fifties and dropping, leaving a chill in the destroyed gym as the players lifted weights. Only a few splotches of sun remained on the bleachers in late afternoon.

"Turn on the heat," Sal Cepriano joked.

Not only was there no heat, but the front door was gone and most of the windows were broken out.

"We in nature," Lyle Fitte said as he sat on a weight bench. "That's why we play the way we do. Only the strong survive."

On the practice field, Crutchfield looked toward the river and saw an unfamiliar red truck outside the end zone.

"Who's that?" he asked his assistant coaches.

"Yo and Froggy," Anthony LaFrance said.

Okay, Crutchfield said, turning back to business, convinced the men in the truck weren't spies for West St. John.

Everybody in lower Plaquemines seemed to have a nickname. They were so common that many people's given names seemed to have been forgotten.

"You don't want anybody to know your real name," LaFrance said with a laugh. "The bill collector comes around. The police. 'Who you talkin' 'bout? I don't know nobody by that name.'"

After the sun set and the stadium lights had been turned on, a truck stopped on the road that circled the field. An oil-field crew boat was hitched to the truck. In the rear of the boat, a man set up a tripod. This was getting suspicious, Big Wayne Williamson said as he stood in the stands. He told Rod Parker, one of the assistant coaches, to find out what the men were doing.

"Probably just a seismographic survey crew," Big Wayne said. "I guess we'll know if practice shows up on the Internet."

Crutchfield wondered whether Bob Becnel, the Belle Chasse coach, would attend the state-championship game. Probably not, he figured.

"I know what he's thinking," Crutchfield said. "He wants us to lose because he's afraid he'll lose some kids to us [next season]."

There were supposed to be a lot of Bastrop fans cheering for South Plaquemines at the 'Dome, he said.

"In case there's another hurricane, they can scope out who they want," he snickered.

WEDNESDAY, DECEMBER 5: LYLE FITTE AWAKENED AT FOUR in the morning to study for a chemistry test. At five fifteen, under a crescent moon, with the temperature in the low forties, he headed out of his grandmother's FEMA trailer wearing a watch cap, sweatshirt, gloves, sneakers, and pajama bottoms.

"My grandmother told me, if you don't wear it on your head and hands, you'll wear it on your nose," he said.

He walked across the street to the Mississippi River levee, past a clump of trailers, some of which had Christmas lights on in the windows. The rumble of a passing ship could be heard on the river, and muscular swells slapped into the shoreline.

Several mornings a week, before school, Lyle ran sprints up and down the sixteen-foot levees. As he stretched in the dark, he said he didn't want football season to end. Still, he was feeling exhausted, beat up. Through fourteen games of his junior season, he had rushed 193 times for 1,836 yards and 22 touchdowns and had caught 70 passes for 1,546 yards and 18 touchdowns. He had returned 6 kickoffs for touchdowns and 1 punt return.

The only time he had to sleep, Lyle said, was during free periods in school.

"I need a break," he said.

An honor student with a 3.9 grade-point average, he worried about falling behind in algebra II. His teacher, Jamie McQuarter, was considered a top math instructor, but she was also South Plaquemines' athletic director. With all the preparations for football and the logistics of lining up buses to transport the basketball and volleyball teams, Lyle said, "It's hard for her to teach."

"I think we're behind," he said. "Some of my friends in Belle Chasse tell me that. After the season, I'm going to get them to help me catch up."

A season earlier, while playing at Belle Chasse, Lyle had hurt his left elbow. Two pins had been inserted during surgery, and now his arm sometimes ached when it was cold. He windmilled his arms to warm up and then began his sprints up the levees, five at a time, then a short rest, then five more, breathing lightly, only slight hisses and grunts announcing his exertion, until he had run twenty times up and down the grass-covered embankment. His footprints were visible in the dew.

The kids in Belle Chasse probably had mixed feelings about South Plaquemines reaching the championship game, Lyle said on the walk back to his grandmother's trailer.

"Half want us to lose, the other half want us to win so they can say they beat a state champion," he said.

He went next door to another family trailer to shower and dress for school. Debra Fitte, whom everyone called Gram, gave a wake-up call to her other two grandsons, Beau and Evan. Both were freshman starters on the team; they were staying with their mother in a FEMA trailer park in Belle Chasse. Then Gram phoned Lyle.

"Hey, Hollywood, you fell asleep," she said.

A few minutes later, Lyle returned in a sweatshirt and long khaki shorts. He retreated to a back bedroom to resume studying for his chemistry test. Neighbors and friends began to drop by. They sat on the bottom bunk of the trailer's bunk beds, or stood at the door and smoked cigarettes, while they drank coffee and ate a piece of Gram's pepper tot—a sweet-potato pie without the crust.

She had ordered more than ninety tickets for friends and family, and about five dozen T-shirts bearing photographs of her grandsons. Someone had dropped by with the money for eight more tickets. Her brother, John Sylve, stopped by with two copies of the *Times-Picayune*. The all-metro football teams were supposed to be in the morning paper. Gram flipped through the pages. Not a word.

"I'm gonna call and fuss at them," she said.

Her brother said that a psychologist had called him, offering fifty dollars if he would agree to be interviewed about whether he was struggling or depressed after Katrina.

"I said, 'I'll take fifty dollars for beer; that'll cure my depression,'" he laughed.

The talk turned to the priorities of football and education. If anyone was certain to receive a scholarship offer at South Plaquemines, it was Lyle. He may not travel as far as the University of Hawaii, which had expressed interest, but he was going somewhere to continue his education and his football career. His grandmother joked that she was going to college with him. Who else would take care of him? She dreaded his leaving, but she knew it was important not to stay.

"I don't know if people get too comfortable down here or what," Debra Fitte said, explaining why others didn't leave. "The security; everybody has family around. You know if you get a job and it doesn't work out, the door is always open. Maybe they fear leaving. Some just don't want to learn."

IN LATE MORNING, LAURY DUPONT SAT IN HIS OFFICE AT West St. John High School, located west of New Orleans among the chemical plants and cane fields along Highway 3127. Football had been every bit as important to the identity of West St. John as it had been to South Plaquemines. "We don't have malls or movie theaters," Dupont said. "Our show is Friday-night football. They sell jambalaya and fried chicken. All we need is a Ferris wheel and we'd have a festival."

Thirty-nine years earlier, Dupont had been an all-state quarter-back, leading E. D. White Catholic High of Thibodaux, Louisiana, to the 1968 Class 1A state championship. He had intended to become a lawyer, he said, but he struggled with the foreign-language component of prelaw in college. One of his professors had told him, "Dupont, you've got a French name but you're no Frenchman." So he stuck with football and became one of the most respected and successful high school coaches in Louisiana. On Saturday, he would coach in his seventh state-championship game. At fifty-six, having survived testicular cancer, Dupont was white-haired, balding, and self-deprecating. From what he could see on film, he said, there were two teams that could match South Plaquemines on offense: "Arkansas and Florida."

"Turner is phenomenal," he said. "He's got a rocket for an arm. We picked him up a couple times throwing flat-footed, and he threw forty yards. I call him a throwing running back. He plays like [Dar-ren] McFadden of Arkansas. You think he's gonna throw, he runs. You think he's gonna run, he throws. Fitte causes all kind of prob-lems. He can run out of the backfield, or they put him in the slot, or they motion him across and clear out. They put you in a bind."

Of course, his own team had won nine straight games. And just as Crutchfield had noticed about West St. John, Dupont had noticed about South Plaquemines: A number of starters played both ways. Maybe he could tire the Hurricanes out. And he had a 230-pound fullback named Romell Howard who ran like an asphalt paver.

"Everybody knows he's getting the ball," Dupont said. "Stopping him is the problem. If they load the box, maybe we'll catch 'em with play-action passes. No one has put them under adversity. Maybe we can put them in a situation they haven't seen. But you get down twenty-one points and it's hard to come back. They have so much speed. I'd rather play against big, fat kids. They're aggressive, they gamble, put a lot of people in the box. If you score, their philosophy is, 'So what. We'll score on you.' That's a scary philosophy."

THURSDAY, DECEMBER 6: CRUTCHFIELD SAT IN THE BACK OF his free enterprise class, entering his game plan into a computer as his students worked or talked quietly. A pep rally was scheduled shortly on the football field, then the team would make an hour-long drive to its hotel in the New Orleans suburb of Metairie. Micquella Sylve stood in the back of the classroom. The night before, Crutchfield had sat on the sofa with his head back, and his fiancée asked, "What's wrong? What are you thinking?"

"I have to do this for my dad," he told her.

Cyril Crutchfield Sr. had been in decline from Alzheimer's disease when his son won a state title at Port Sulphur in 2002.

"He wasn't in his right mind," Cyril Jr. said. "Now he's in a better place. I feel he can enjoy it."

"It's good to do it for your dad, but you've got to do it for yourself," Micquella said to Crutchfield. "You deserve it, working 'til four in the morning."

As she stood in the back of the classroom, Mickey said that she became aggravated sometimes. "Football or me, I think he chose football," she said. "But I've got to deal with it."

She wanted to get married by the end of the year.

"After football, he's all for me," she said.

At the same time, she knew that Crutchfield would be devastated if South Plaquemines lost the championship game.

"He won't talk to me for a week, maybe two," she said. "He may not come to school."

It was sixty-five degrees and overcast as the South Plaquemines students gathered in the stands at the football field for a pep rally. Stanley Gaudet wore a Panama hat and told the kids that there would be a mandatory Hurricane evacuation on Saturday from South Plaquemines, with all evacuees asked to report to the Superdome. The anxious flight from Katrina had been reshaped into a football battle cry.

"Nothing is going to be as important as this victory we're going to have on Saturday," Gaudet said. "This is for the community. Our football team does a great job of representing our community. They gave us the strength to show what can be done. We will rebuild. We will show the rest of the world how strong we are."

The players gave Gaudet an umbrella, decorated with footballs and tinsel, to celebrate with a second-line Mardi Gras strut in the Superdome.

"Let's hope he can dance," Sue Cook, the guidance counselor, said.

After the pep rally, the players, wearing slacks and ties but no jewelry, began to gather with their relatives near the charter bus that would take them to New Orleans. The cheerleaders wrote "Hurricane Season Never Ends" on the windows. Ridge Turner stood with his arms around two of his aunts. One of them, Evelyn Rose, told him, "I want two touchdowns just for me. That's all I ask."

Elouise Bartholomew, with whom Ridge lived, had missed the semifinal game against Desire Street while on a cruise to Mexico. Nervously, she had been out of cell phone contact at the start of the game. "They had to give me a shot," she said.

She hugged Cantrelle Riley and said, "Go get my ring."

Before the bus pulled out, the players held hands in one end zone and Crutchfield told them, "A chain's only as strong as its weakest link." They walked the length of the field and back again and gathered in a circle. Crutchfield began crying. He covered his eyes with his right hand and stepped out of the circle, then stepped back in.

"In today's society, life is uncertain," he said. "We need to take care of business on Saturday."

The Port Sulphur fire trucks blared their sirens in appreciation as the bus pulled onto Highway 23 for the trip north. Tiny paper footballs bearing each player's name covered a window at the doughnut shop and a wall at the Cajun Kitchen. At St. Joseph Lane, where Ridge lived, fans stood on both sides of the road, holding balloons and waving umbrellas. In Diamond, two banners were stretched across the highway, one of them declaring, "Hurricanes '07 State Champs." The bus slowed and pushed right through the signs. Dozens of people stood on the shoulders of the road and waved, or sat in their cars and honked their horns. Up Highway 23, signs were placed in the median: "Let's Go Canes." "Leave No Doubt." After about thirty miles, the bus passed citrus groves on the outskirts of Belle Chasse and went by the home of Bob Becnel.

"He's not standing on side the road?" Crutchfield asked in mock surprise.

In Belle Chasse, sheriff's deputies shielded the intersections so the Hurricanes would not have to stop at any red lights. In the neutral ground, or median, workers had been planting flowers. The beautification project was part of a state grant awarded before Katrina. But it drove the residents of lower Plaquemines crazy. How could they plant flowers in Belle Chasse when so much trash and debris still needed removal down the road?

"I'm so glad we gotta ride through this mother," Crutchfield said. "They should be standing outside, bowing to us."

THE HURRICANES CROSSED THE CRESCENT CITY CONNECTION toll bridge into New Orleans at rush hour. The skin of the Superdome seemed bronze at sunset, its white roof hardly visible against the hazy sky. Traveling west on Interstate 10, the bus finally reached the team hotel, off Causeway Boulevard in Metairie. Four days after Katrina struck, some five thousand people had squeezed under the overpass here, seeking shade in the ninety-degree heat, dropped off by helicopters to wait for buses that never seemed to come, separated from loved ones and from their medications and from any certainty about where they might be going and when. One man climbed off a helicopter, clutching a backpack full of framed photographs, and he tripped and fell and shattered the only keepsakes he had taken from his home. Another woman cried as she attended to a niece who was autistic and a son who was blind and had cerebral palsy. Thousands waited patiently without much food or water or answers to their questions. Some of them couldn't wait any longer, and they began walking down the interstate, going nowhere but away from where they were. There were no cars on the road, just mattresses and shopping carts, a discarded shoe, discarded people.

More than two years later, plenty of people still needed help. In Plaquemines Parish, 2,500 residents were still living in FEMA trailers. Four hundred and thirty trailers were corralled in six trailer parks. A story in the weekly *Plaquemines Gazette* said that the six FEMA parks would be closing by May 31, 2008. No more extensions would be granted. FEMA had announced months earlier that the flimsy white trailers—they resembled inhabitable toasters—were available for purchase, most for five hundred or six hundred dollars. Residents would also be able to purchase full-size mobile homes from FEMA, for about thirteen thousand dollars, and have them placed on their private land.

The parish was also considering various housing options, including so-called Katrina Cottages, small, inexpensive, quickly built, but sturdy emergency homes. Rental assistance would be available from FEMA, but beginning in the spring or fall of 2008, residents would be expected to pay fifty dollars per month toward their rental costs. The tab would rise an additional fifty dollars each month until residents paid their entire housing costs, or until the program ended in March 2009.

"There's gonna be a lot of people, fussin' and fightin' and not wanting to leave," Rodney Bartholomew Sr. said in the lobby of the hotel as the players placed their luggage in their rooms.

Surely, the Plaquemines parks would not close by the May deadline, said Anthony LaFrance, an assistant coach.

"It ain't possible, no way," he said.

FEMA should not have wasted four hundred million dollars to store thousands of trailers and mobile homes in Hope, Arkansas, LaFrance said. Instead, he believed the agency should have cleaned up homeowner property in lower Plaquemines and assisted in building new homes or said, "'Here's your trailer, be happy.' That would have been the end of it."

Now, once the FEMA parks closed, some people needing rental assistance would surely have to be placed in apartments. There were few, if any, in lower Plaquemines. This meant some people would have to relocate to Belle Chasse, or even to suburban New Orleans, creating daily commutes of fifty miles or more to school in lower Plaquemines.

"Parents who want their kids at South Plaquemines, where's their apartment gonna be?" LaFrance asked. "How are they gonna go to school?"

He was growing weary talking about Katrina, LaFrance said. Why did anyone have to keep commemorating its anniversary, anyway?

"They don't want to put that woman behind them," he said. "They need to. If you're gonna do something, you need to keep it in your head. Don't celebrate it."

"That's what they did with Betsy," Bartholomew said of the 1965 hurricane. "They let it go. The only time you ever heard about it was when the old people talked."

PLAYERS BEGAN DRIFTING DOWNSTAIRS TO THE LOBBY, and Crutchfield took them, as he always did, to a buffet-style restaurant. Traveling on the bus were his three children from a pair of previous marriages—Cyril III, Maya, and Casey. The kids lived with their mothers. The youngest, Casey, sometimes came to games, but Crutchfield was so private about his personal life that even some of his assistant coaches did not know that he had a daughter. At the restaurant, he got a surprise when he looked up to see his sister, Shanna Crutchfield, who had flown in from Seattle. He had not seen her since their father's memorial service sixteen months earlier.

"Don't cry, coach," Trey Stewart said. Everyone laughed.

The usual no-talking rule had been relaxed tonight, but as soon as Crutchfield got up from his table, the room went silent. Back at the hotel, Crutchfield pulled his dress shirt out of his slacks and walked barefoot around the lobby, addressing his players. Saturday's championship game would be played for respectability, he said.

"This is for the people who criticized us for starting our own school, for coming home to play when there was nothing down there, the people who told you that you couldn't get a scholarship if you came down there," Crutchfield said in a reference to Becnel, the Belle Chasse coach. A lot of people are coming back. Dorothy of Kansas said it best: "There's no place like home."

"Let's not listen to all that 'Katrina destroyed all this and that.' Yes, it did. It destroyed us two years ago. But look where we're at now. It should teach you a lesson after football. If you can make it through all that despair and destruction and heartbreak, nothing in this world can defeat you. Sometimes, things don't go right. Your marriage fails. You lose a job. You lose a loved one. We don't like when it happens, but it's not the end of the world. If you keep plugging, good things are going to happen. You get back up. Guess what? We are about to get on top of that mountain. I promise you, when we get on top, we're gonna stay on top.

I hate that Coach Dupont is leaving. One thing I hate more is that he's going to leave a loser. It's only one game. He's got the rest of his life to live. But let's send him home a goddamned loser."

24

BIG STAGE RIGHT THERE

FRIDAY, DECEMBER 7: AT NINE THIRTY IN THE MORNING, IT was overcast as the team bus pulled up to the Superdome, which resembled an extraterrestrial mushroom. As the Hurricanes walked inside, their eyes got wide and they looked to the ceiling. At 273 feet, it was nearly as high as a football field.

"Ooh, boy," Lyle Fitte said. "Big stage right there."

Seth Ancar peered up at the catwalk.

"It would take you thirty minutes to fall from there," he said.

The far goalpost seemed distant in the cavernous building.

"That field's longer than a hundred yards," Bradley Sylve said.

Beyond the fact that it was indoors, the Superdome was different from the South Plaquemines' field in another significant way: It had a locker room, not just one, but many, covered in carpet, with nice wide metal lockers and equipped with that rarest of commodities: electricity.

"I had a rat jump out the other day," Lyle said. "Freaked me out."

"That was your pen pal, Stuart Fitte," Seth said.

"They got power in here," Caileb Ancar said.

"You don't need a generator," Seth said.

"No raccoons," Little Wayne Williamson said.

"I'll take home any day," Sal Cepriano said. "Room temperature, 24/7. When you want a shower, just go inside when it's raining."

"They got security for us," center Blake Espadron said.

"We got possums," Sal said. "That's our security."

The players dressed in their uniforms for a team picture and individual photographs. Many of the Hurricanes had played in the 'Dome in Bantam League football. Two of the players, Jesse Phan and Anthony Huon, had never been inside the building, even as spectators. Even those who had visited seemed distracted during this morning's hour-long practice. Unlike high school fields, where lights were mounted on poles along the sideline, the 'Dome lights ringed the ceiling in a halo. Cantrelle Riley and Lyle Fitte, the state's two leading receivers and the team's punt and kickoff returners, both wore visors. They appeared to be having trouble adjusting to the ball in the lights. Somehow, Lyle said, visors created an illusion that the ball arrived quicker than it actually did.

"You notice something, that they're not all here?" Crutchfield asked about his team. "Like they're overwhelmed?"

After practice, Crutchfield reminded the Hurricanes to drink plenty of fluids to avoid dehydration. Their adrenaline would be pumping, and even with air-conditioning, it could be hot and humid in the 'Dome.

"Are y'all acclimated yet?" Crutchfield asked. "It's a different environment, there's a lot at stake. We're the better team. We're supposed to win. But it's not the best team that always wins. It's the team that handles the environment and makes plays. If you're not used to a visor, or gloves, why change now? Why do anything different?"

Despite this awkward practice, he sensed that his players were prepared. He could see it in their eyes. If any team deserved a championship, it was this one, he told reporters. As he began to leave the field, the players from Bastrop walked into the end zone to have their pictures taken. Crutchfield spotted Randall Mackey. He seemed taller, maybe six feet now, and bigger. Crutchfield asked Brad Bradshaw, the Bastrop coach, if he could walk over and give Mackey a hug. Bradshaw muttered something that seemed to be a reluctant assent.

"Boy, you better let me kiss you," Crutchfield said.

Randall smiled and Crutchfield kissed him on the cheek.

Later, Crutchfield seemed incredulous that Bradshaw had not bothered to shake his hand and congratulate him when their paths crossed.

"He needs to realize he's only winning because he got kids from somewhere else," Crutchfield said. "He's never won with his own kids. Imagine if we got kids sent to us?"

In late afternoon, the Hurricanes returned to the Superdome to watch John Curtis Christian School win its twenty-second state championship with a 28–13 victory over St. James High in Class 2A. The South Plaquemines team sat behind one end zone, and as the Curtis players began to celebrate, Marcelin Ancar pointed to the field and said, "That's gonna be us tomorrow."

As the Hurricanes waited outside for their bus back to the hotel, Lyle began to dry heave near a set of barricades. He bent over and his whole body seemed to shiver. After a week, the wait for the Class 1A championship had become excruciating. Crutchfield and some players seemed exhausted. Others had threadbare nerves.

"I don't understand," an amused Ridge Turner said. "Straight to sleep for me. Nothing to worry about."

At the hotel, Crutchfield summoned his players in the lobby for a final team meeting. There was a Christmas tree in one corner, bookshelves along one wall, chairs and carpet the color of a wine stain. Wearing jeans and a windbreaker, clicking a pen in his hand, spitting tobacco into a cup, Crutchfield began to pace. Glen Campbell music played in the background.

The fun was over until game time, Crutchfield told his players. It was time to concentrate. The most focused team would win.

"To me right now, it's not a game, it's war," Crutchfield said. "It's kill or be killed. As the commander in chief, it's my job to make sure you're ready to draw your weapon. It's up to the individual. You can have your weapon, but you may not want to draw your weapon. If you don't, we will be defeated.

"What we need are some soldiers, some mercenaries, some assassins. Assassins are high profile. Guess what? The Superdome is a high profile environment. Some of you kids want to go to college. That's where you put yourself on the map. Some of you don't really care about college. All you care about is a state championship. That's okay, too. But guess what? We can't wake up tomorrow morning and raise our pillows and be like the tooth fairy and find a ring under our pillows. West St. John is not going to give it to you. You have to go out and earn it. You gotta demand it. You gotta go out and make plays. Let's make sure we ready to play. Let's not go back to South Plaq scratching our heads, like 'damn, damn.'

"Seniors, you're running out of time. Ten, eleven, twelve, fifteen hours, your high school career is over. Never again will you experience this. Let's make sure we take advantage of this. Everybody in the state of Louisiana, we got 'em by the balls: How can South Plaq be devastated by a hurricane and field a team and in two years be playing for a state championship? If you win, that's gonna boost you up a little more.

"We gave you the strategic plan. Now it's time to get some rest and go out tomorrow and execute the plan. Regardless of how good or bad that plan is, it's going to boil down to you executing better than the guy over you. If you can't, we'll be stuck with,

'South Plaq had a heck of a year, went to the state championship but they lost.' There's nothing good about a 'but.'"

Everybody had better be up at seven thirty in the morning, everything packed, ready to get on the bus, Crutchfield said. And there had better be no laughing or joking.

"Because the joke's going to end up on you," he explained. "Because I'm the fuckin' joker and I'll give you a fuckin' riddle."

Then he opened the floor to the seniors for any last words.

Sal Cepriano had been speaking on the phone from New Orleans to his sister, Jenna, back in Port Sulphur. To her, Sal seemed more sad than excited. Win or lose, this was going to be his last football game. Football had inspired him, had rescued him from a jagged life, and after tomorrow, he would never play again. Before the season, he told his sister that he might consider failing in school, just to get one more year. It was only a joke, but that's how much the game meant to him. And now in a matter of hours, it would be gone.

"This is all I got," he told his sister.

"You can play in the street," she told him.

"It's not the same," Sal said.

Now he sat on a sofa between his teammates and said, "Thank y'all for giving me the season we had. I love all y'all. We got to get that victory tomorrow and bring it down home. They need it. We gonna give it to 'em."

"What Sal said is true," Crutchfield said. "You right. We do need it. Everybody down the goddamned road needs it. They deserve it. So do y'all."

The team prayer was said, and then the room grew silent, except for the clicking of Crutchfield's pen. Coaches sniffled and wiped tears from their eyes. Jordan Ancar covered his face with a towel. Caileb Ancar sat in a chair, staring at the carpet. Seth

Ancar drew his sweatshirt hood tight over his face. Sal put his head in his hands and his shoulders heaved.

SATURDAY, DECEMBER 8: THE SOUTH PLAQUEMINES BUS pulled out of the hotel for breakfast at seven forty-five a.m. Music played over the intercom, both rap and Phil Collins: "We ready" and "We some headbusters and we'll knock a hater out" and "I've been waiting for this moment all my life."

The championship game was five hours away, but already fans were making their way from lower Plaquemines to the Super-dome for tailgate parties of Crown Royal and sausage and venison and "slap yo' momma" spaghetti. If there was a day to rob the lower end, this was it, Stanley Gaudet said.

"They turned off all the water, all the electric," superfan Boo Landry said by phone as he made the forty-five-mile drive. "The doughnut shop ran out of gas and Fremin's ain't sellin' no more liquor. Call Ray Nagin and tell him to stop the tolls on the bridge."

If the fans were excited, Crutchfield was withdrawn like an oyster into his usual game-day shell. After a prayer, the players walked silently through a buffet line, and Devin Dykes, an eighth-grader generously listed at five feet tall, made the mistake of putting a cinnamon bun on his plate. This was considered frivolous food to eat before a game, and Crutchfield walked over to Dykes's table and crumbled the bun in his face. Lyle Fitte wiped the crumbs from the front of Dykes's sweatshirt, and Dykes walked into the bathroom, crying.

"He shouldn't do that," George "Miguel" Sylve, the team's equipment manager, said later about Crutchfield in the parking lot. "I feel bad for the kid."

Dykes should have known better, assistant coach Rod Parker said. Crutchfield had his rules.

It was a hot, humid morning with a mottled sky. Fog shrouded the New Orleans skyscrapers and engulfed the top of the 'Dome. At 9:20, three and a half hours before game time, the South Plaquemines bus pulled into the stadium. The field was occupied by a cheerleading contest, so the players milled about the locker room, getting their ankles taped, dressing in their dark blue game pants. Wearing khakis, a white mock turtleneck, and a blue vest, Crutchfield paced back and forth, holding his arms behind his back. His six-year-old son, Casey, walked alongside, impersonating his every step.

Big Wayne Williamson watched the kindergartner and began to laugh. After nearly two decades escorting the team bus, he had decided to give it up after this season. Little Wayne was graduating. Big Wayne had a house three hours away in Opelousas. He'd like to visit there more often on the weekends. But, slowly, he had begun to change his mind about escorting the Hurricanes. He wanted to see Ridge Turner and Lyle Fitte through their senior years. And he had received a touching request at the team hotel from Chaz Savoy, a sophomore who suffered from muscular dystrophy and was confined to a wheelchair. Chaz followed the team to every game, his family's van part of the escorted convoy. He even wore a jersey on the sideline.

"You not gonna stay with the Hurricanes until I get out of school?" Chaz had asked Big Wayne the night before.

"I'm trying to find someone else."

"Suppose when we drive they don't let us follow the bus?" Chaz asked.

So Big Wayne made a deal with him: "If we win, I'm in."

Lyle knelt at his locker and said a prayer. As usual, he wrote "564" on his patches of eye black, the dialing prefix for Port Sulphur. Crutchfield walked outside the locker room, beneath the stands, twirling his whistle around his fingers. Two hours before kickoff, the players joined him, their cleats clicking on the cement.

If West St. John won the toss, South Plaquemines would begin with an onside kick, Crutchfield said. Beware of West St. John trying the same thing, he said.

"On offense, I've got two letters: E and O—early and often," Crutchfield told his team. "Let's put it in the goddamned end zone. If we don't score early, stick with the offense. We're gonna run the piss out of them. If it's not working in the first quarter, it'll work in the fourth quarter.

"Our defense is predicated on speed to the ball. Pound their ass. Let's get some turnovers. Knock 'em on the ground and strip 'em."

His six seniors gave Crutchfield a pair of gloves bearing their names. He put them on.

"There's nothing else to talk about, men," Crutchfield said. "This is what we worked for. Demand nothing less than a state championship. If you don't win, you don't get a ring. If you win, you get a big rock. Let's go rock their ass."

An hour before kickoff, the 'Dome gates opened, and fans from South Plaquemines began streaming to their seats. The Class 1A championship was the first of three games today, and eventually the crowd would swell to 39,383. The Hurricanes' fans wore white T-shirts emblazoned with the names and pictures of the players. They were mothers, fathers, brothers, sisters, aunts, cousins. Big Wayne spotted people he hadn't seen since Katrina. For once, everybody in the parish seemed to be pulling together. Or as together as they could ever be.

"What do you call pissed-off fans in the stands?" someone asked outside the South Plaquemines locker room. "Belle Chasse Cardinals."

Crutchfield laughed and said, "Bobby Becnel, I bet his stomach's got butterflies."

The South Plaquemines fans rushed to the railing behind the Hurricanes' bench. Millette Williamson, Little Wayne's mother, waved a decorated white umbrella. She chanted with Andria

Barthelemy, the mother of eighth-grade tackle Lorne Barthelemy: "Who dat? Who dat? Who dat say they gon' beat them 'Canes? Nobody."

Andria leaned over the railing and shouted, "Katrina came and took everything from us. All we got is right here. We waitin' for the trophy. That's all we want is this trophy. We lost everything, everything we lost. But we comin' home with it, though. We happy. We happy."

Jeanitta Ancar held up a sign that said, "Katrina couldn't, Rita didn't, West St. John Won't Stop Us!"

Sal Cepriano's short speech last night had seemed to galvanize the team, but it did not conquer all the nerves. When the Hurricanes came out for warm-ups, David Merrick, a junior running back, vomited on the field.

Finally, South Plaquemines gathered in the locker room one final time. "We worked too hard to have this taken away from us," Sal said. "We gotta come out there and play balls out!"

The players held hands. Crutchfield told them to close their eyes and imagine making a play to help win the game. Then, bouncing on his feet, he told them to close their eyes again and imagine celebrating a championship.

"The whole year we have worked the hardest, therefore we deserve it," Crutchfield said. "When we get out there, leave no doubt."

One of the West St. John coaches told Corey Buie that after a week of watching video, the Rams still couldn't figure out the Hurricanes' complicated offense.

"We don't know what y'all are going to run," the coach said.

Immediately, though, the Hurricanes became careless, self-destructive. They had been so precise and meticulous through a month of the play-offs. Now, dressed in blue pants and white jerseys and silver helmets, they seemed anxious, perhaps overwhelmed by the moment. A delay penalty sabotaged the first play of the game. Then Lyle streaked down the left sideline, past the cornerback and safety, and Ridge arced a perfect pass for what could have been a sixty-one-yard touchdown. Instead, the ball skidded off Lyle's fingertips. He came to the sideline and bent over in disbelief. On the next play, distracted by a blitz, Ridge fumbled a snap in the shotgun. He had laughed the night before when Lyle dry-heaved outside the 'Dome, but now he, too, was feeling nervous. "That shocked me," Ridge said later.

West St. John recovered the fumble at the Hurricanes' twenty-eight-yard line and moved purposely toward the end zone, dressed in blue jerseys and pants and blue helmets. Three plays later, Ridge dived futilely at cornerback as West St. John's quarterback, Dray Joseph, faked a handoff and threw for fifteen yards over the middle, giving the Rams an 8–0 lead after a minute and a half.

"Calm down," Crutchfield admonished his players. "There are four quarters left. Calm down."

Ridge's next pass was wide and short and West St. John intercepted it. The Rams then punted, an awful shank, and Felix Barthelemy saw nothing but thirty open yards to the goal line for South Plaquemines. He grabbed at the high bounce but he was too hurried, trying to catch and run at the same time, and he lost the ball, and the Hurricanes committed their third turnover in less than four minutes.

"We're killing ourselves!" assistant coach Anthony LaFrance screamed.

West St. John tried to run wide, then up the middle, but something began to change, abruptly, inexorably, the way an arm-wrestling match shifted when a contestant, in danger of being pinned, began to raise his hand against suddenly failing resistance. The Hurricanes switched to their Bandit defense, with three linemen and five linebackers, and Felix Barthelemy and Beau Fitte and Seth Ancar began to subdue the West St. John offense. All of them converged roughly on a running back behind the line of scrimmage. Seth charged low and grabbed the back's legs and Beau pulled from up high and everyone tumbled to the turf. Seth hopped to his feet and flexed his arms in theatrical domination.

"We have so many people coming, they don't know who to block," Beau Fitte said. "They're confused."

This defensive stand seemed to lend muscularity to the South Plaquemines' offense. The early nervousness disappeared. On first down at the Hurricanes' forty-four-yard line, two receivers and a tight end bunched on the left side and Lyle Fitte jogged in motion toward them. The West St. John defense shifted instinctively that way, expecting a sweep, but Ridge put the ball into Lyle's stomach and pulled it out and slashed into the line. He found a tunnel and his blockers sealed him inside and Ridge accelerated beyond the reach of the linebacker and the cornerback and the safety. One instant he was in a jumble of players, and then he was free, tucking the ball and sprinting with elegant resolve, his heels clipping the back of his pants and his pads rising above his knees. He looked back and saw no one near him and he raised his left hand as he reached the goal line. South Plaquemines 8, West St. John 8.

Everything began to shut down for West St. John. There was no place to run or throw, no time to make decisions. Seth Ancar sacked Joseph, the Rams' quarterback, then Beau Fitte shouldered him down for another loss. Beau would make thirteen tackles during the game, six of them behind the line of scrimmage. Three times, he spilled the quarterback for a sack. He was only a freshman, six foot one, 210 pounds, but already Crutchfield said, "He'll be the best thing ever to come out of here."

Before the first quarter expired, Lyle Fitte ran left on a counter, ducking inside from the two-yard line, a defensive end grabbing his waist but unable to bring him down until he spilled into the end zone, putting the Hurricanes ahead 14–8. Beau Fitte recovered a fumbled punt, and South Plaquemines threatened again. From the four-yard line, Ridge faked another sweep to Lyle and knifed toward the end zone. A lineman hit him at three, but Ridge lowered his shoulder, gaining leverage, not a sprinter now but a fullback, his feet churning, dragging two more tacklers ahead, falling short of the goal line but reaching his right arm over with the ball and increasing the margin to 20–8.

Trey Stewart intercepted a pass for South Plaquemines, and Crutchfield drew up a play on the sideline. Lyle split right as a receiver and threw up his hands. Ridge pumped but held onto the ball, and Lyle broke down the sideline as the cornerback chased futilely, never looking up for the pass. The ball reached Lyle at the West St. John forty-five-yard line, and the cornerback seemed to close on him, but Lyle dashed evasively to his left and the cornerback faded. Crutchfield ran down the sideline jumping and shimmying as the sixty-six-yard touchdown pass put the Hurricanes up 28–8.

Beau Fitte blindsided the West St. John quarterback, and the ball came free. The half was nearing, but there was still time to score, and Lyle Fitte swept left into the end zone from two yards. Three tacklers fell away like bowling pins, and South Plaquemines took an indomitable 35–8 lead.

"They're not finished," Crutchfield told his players in the locker room. "They didn't make it to the state-championship game to lay down after the first half."

West St. John was finished, though, and the Hurricanes felt a sense of inevitability. The Rams were arguing with each other, ready to capitulate, left with only the impotent ruse of play-action passes. "Lord, please spare my life," Crutchfield said as he walked back and forth in the locker room. "My heart hurts. I gotta make it through these next twenty-four minutes. If I'm gonna die, let me die after we get that trophy."

Early in the third quarter, Ridge faked another sweep to Lyle, found Dylan Boutwell free on a crossing route, and threw a thirty-two-yard touchdown pass. This was Turner's sixty-eighth touchdown of the year, a state record. When he took off his helmet, Crutchfield kissed him. His sixty-ninth touchdown came on a counter early in the fourth quarter, after a seventy-one-yard pass to Cantrelle Riley, and the Hurricanes took a 48–8 lead.

"I guess we stopped being nervous," Ridge said on the bench. Nearly a quarter remained, but there would be no more scoring. Ridge glanced at all the cheering faces in the crowd and said, "Look around, everybody's coming home."

Stanley Gaudet opened the umbrella the team had given him and danced on the South Plaquemines' bench. Devin Dykes, left crying in the early morning, now stood on the bench, waving his arms, urging the crowd to its feet. Sal Cepriano thought about how impossible this all seemed, the 2005 season lost to Katrina, players scattered all over the Gulf Coast, and the 2006 season played with no hot food for lunch and no home field and a sixty-mile round-trip drive to practice, three bitter rivals merged into a new school, still without a locker room and a working gym, electricity coming from a generator and light from a few bulbs, nothing back to normal except for football.

"This is everything," Sal said. "This is all we have, the best thing that happened to anybody in two years."

Billy Nungesser, the president of Plaquemines Parish, stood on the sideline and said that a team rebuilding itself gave hope that the entire lower end might be able to rebuild itself.

"This is what people needed," he said. "Katrina money has been coming slow. We keep telling them we're going to rebuild, be patient. We've been telling them that for two and a half years. This will take people's mind off it for a while. The last month, that's all anyone has talked about, South Plaquemines. These guys came back against all odds, kind of like the people in lower Plaquemines did."

When it was over, and the championship was won, Crutchfield knelt and said a prayer and pointed toward the sky. "This one's for you," he said to his deceased father. "I know you're watching." He called his mother from the sideline. He walked hand in hand with Eva Jones, the parish school superintendent, to accept the trophy— a wooden shape of Louisiana and a running back in that familiar stiff-arm pose. Players collected around the trophy at midfield, some standing, some kneeling, some lying on the artificial turf, everyone smiling and raising an index finger, signaling number 1. Back in the dressing room, Lyle Fitte kissed the trophy. Some players said they were ready to start practicing again on Monday, but even Crutch-field said, no, that was too early, wait until after the New Year.

"The first one was memorable," Crutchfield said, referring to his 2002 state title at Port Sulphur High, "but with all these kids had to go through, all the adversity, this is the best. You don't always get what you want, but you always get what you deserve. They stayed strong and started getting better and more confident. A lot of people could have folded. They stayed strong."

Laury Dupont had not wanted to finish his sterling career with a tarnish like this. West St. John gained only eighty-nine total yards, a mere thirty-four on the ground. But he was gracious in defeat, saying, "I think we could have played ten times and they would have beat us ten. Speed kills. They spread you out and we couldn't make up for their speed. And we underestimated their strength. They controlled the line of scrimmage. We knew they were fast, but we didn't know they were that strong."

In this dominant, curative season, the Hurricanes had twice scored more than 70 points in a game, had once scored 60 in a quarter, and had averaged 51.5 points while allowing only 12.8 points per game. When Crutchfield finally left the locker room, he stood in a hallway at the 'Dome in a kind of fog. People passed and congratulated him, but he seemed stunned, distant.

Keven Smith called to offer congratulations and said, "Coach, you seem overwhelmed."

"Son, I am," Crutchfield said.

Randall Mackey and his Bastrop team were playing next in the Class 4A championship game, but Crutchfield did not take a seat to watch. He stood on a concourse with Micquella Sylve, as August Ragas held the championship trophy. Crutchfield had his own title now and there was no more need to watch Randall and wonder what might have been.

At halftime of the Bastrop game, Crutchfield rounded up the players who wanted to leave, found the team bus, and began the hour-long trip back to lower Plaquemines. People kept talking about Randall, Crutchfield said aloud to himself on the ride home, but he had another quarterback, Ridge Turner, and Ridge was a state champion. Passing through Belle Chasse, Crutchfield said, "I wonder how Bobby Becnel feels; I wonder if his stomach is churning."

(He felt fine, Becnel said later; "We had beaten a state champion. I thought that was a feather in our cap.")

As the bus approached Port Sulphur, the stadium lights at South Plaquemines shined in the distance. Several dozen fans had come to congratulate the players, to pick up their sons, and to talk about next year. The Hurricanes had only six seniors. The heart of the offensive line—Caileb Ancar, Jordan Ancar, and Sal Cepriano—was graduating, but Ridge Turner and Lyle Fitte were returning on offense. Seth Ancar, Beau Fitte, Trey Stewart, and Felix Barthelemy would be back to anchor a strangling defense. South Plaquemines seemed certain to be ranked number 1 in the 2008 preseason polls.

"I'm going to church tomorrow to pray for what we have, and for what we gonna have," Boo Landry told Crutchfield.

"That's right," Crutchfield said. "Hurricane season never ends."

Ridge remained at the Superdome to watch Randall play his final game. They passed each other as South Plaquemines left the field and Bastrop appeared for warm-ups. "Now it's y'alls' turn to watch me," Randall said. He scored early on a fifty-yard run and did a somersault into the end zone. He would run for 139 yards and throw for 259 yards in a 38–14 victory, and for the third year in a row, he would be named the most valuable offensive player in the Class 4A championship game.

Ridge, too, was named the most valuable offensive player, in the Class 1A game, having rushed for 108 yards and three touchdowns and having passed for 197 yards and two touchdowns. What were the chances of that, two kids growing up on the same street, their lives overturned by a hurricane, ending up at separate schools and being named the most valuable players in adjacent state-championship games?

No one had ever had a greater season as a high school quarterback in Louisiana than Ridge Turner. Not Terry Bradshaw or Bert Jones or Peyton Manning or Brock Berlin or Ryan Perrilloux. Nobody. The numbers were stunning: 5,554 total yards and 69 touchdowns passing and rushing (2 other touchdowns came via a punt return and an interception return). He completed 219 of 298 passes (73.5 percent) for 3,726 yards and 43 touchdowns with 6 interceptions and rushed 195 times for 1,818 yards and 26 touchdowns. Only four high school players around the country had ever gained more total yardage in a season, according to the National Federation of State High School Associations. Only a six-for-seventeen throwing performance in the championship game kept Ridge from surpassing the national single-season record for completion percentage.

After collecting his MVP plaque, Ridge sat in the stands, and a man approached him and asked, "Are you Ridge Turner?" Yes, he replied, and the man asked, "*The* Ridge Turner?" Yes sir, Turner said, and the man looked disbelievingly at his five-foot-ten, 175-pound frame and asked, "Where's the rest of you?"

Later that night, Ridge and Randall passed each other on Bourbon Street, and the next day they spoke by phone. Why did you do a flip in the end zone? Ridge wanted to know.

"To prove to Crutchfield that I'm better than you," Randall said.

When he got back to Port Sulphur after the game, Ridge was asked by his aunt, Elouise Bartholemew, if he understood the magnitude of what he had accomplished. He shrugged. "Records are broken every day," Ridge told her.

In the weeks after the game, his aunt sometimes sat alone in Ridge's room. Elouise had saved him when his mother, her sister, struggled with drug addiction. She kept him in the church and in sports, and he had discovered greatness on a football field. She found it hard to believe, even then, sitting there with all his awards and newspaper clippings on the wall as proof. Most of the time Ridge had seemed so timid to her, except when he played football and his eyes grew so wide that he seemed to look right through you. One minute he was there, amid the light and noise and roar of a game, and then it was over with. Like a thunderstorm, she thought. Or a hurricane.

EPILOGUE

IN MID-JANUARY 2008, ELOUISE BARTHOLOMEW MET WITH her sister, Roslyn Turner, for lunch at the Ground Patti restaurant in the New Orleans suburb of Gretna. Four days before the state-championship game, Roslyn had been released from jail, where she had remained since mid-August for a parole violation. She did not attend the game, she said, because she did not have enough money. Later that December night, she said, she was watching television at a friend's house when the sports news came on. On the screen was her son Ridge.

"That's my baby," Roslyn told her friend.

"He looks like you," the friend said.

"That's my baby for real," Roslyn said.

She said she called Ridge the next day to congratulate him.

"You're in the paper, bro'."

At forty-five, Roslyn had soft, plump features. She was full of pride for Ridge, she said. She carried an Internet story about him in her purse. And she couldn't thank her sister enough for raising him while she battled her addiction to cocaine. It was best that Ridge continue to live with Elouise while she tried to cobble her own life together, Roslyn said.

"He's doing well," she said. "He's where he wants to be."

They had talked several times by phone since her release, Roslyn said. She also said that she had watched tapes of Ridge's games at the home of Ethan Barthelemy, her nephew, Elouise's son. She hoped to see Ridge in a few days.

"She tells me she's proud of me," Ridge said.

She had an interview the next day for a job at a supermarket, Roslyn said at lunch. She had not used drugs since 1999, just before going to jail, she said, and no longer drank alcohol.

"I don't even want a root beer cold drink," she said.

She had changed the people and places and things in her life, Roslyn said. If she got a job, and her recovery continued on course, she said, perhaps she would consider moving back to lower Plaquemines. Maybe get a trailer near Elouise and Ridge.

"What those boys did," she said of the Hurricanes, "gives me courage that I can do something. Gives me hope."

In mid-March, though, Elouise said she had not heard from her sister since that lunch two months earlier. On occasion, Roslyn called Ridge, but not lately, Elouise said. Nor had mother and son seen each other, Elouise said. Roslyn Turner did not return a call seeking comment.

Ridge had been named the offensive MVP on the Class 1A all-state team by the Louisiana Sportswriters Association. Cantrelle Riley had also been named all-state at receiver, along with Lyle Fitte at running back and Seth Ancar at linebacker. Since his junior season ended, Ridge had begun receiving recruiting feelers from such schools as LSU, Alabama, Tulane, and the University of Louisiana–Monroe.

"His momma don't have a clue," Elouise said.

If Roslyn had wanted to see Ridge play in the state-championship game, all she had to do was ask, Elouise said. She would have been happy to buy her sister a ticket.

"That would have meant the world to him," Elouise said.

If Ridge earned a college scholarship, his aunt only hoped that it was someplace nearby. Of course, she would support him wherever he went. She always had. If she had to work two or three jobs, pick up cans, she didn't mind. She just wanted him to make something of his life.

"I get overwhelmed," Elouise said of Ridge's accomplishments. "I'm just amazed at what he went through and where he came out. He's been through hell. There's a lot more he could tell us that he's not telling us. He's a private person. Maybe as he gets older he'll discuss it."

AFTER A REST OVER THE CHRISTMAS BREAK, LYLE FITTE IM-proved his bench-pressing ability beyond three hundred pounds. In mid-February, he rated first among nearly five hundred players in running and jumping and throwing tests administered at a combine in suburban New Orleans. He listed LSU, Miami, Alabama, and Texas among his prospective college choices entering his senior season at South Plaquemines.

"I think he can play in the SEC," Cyril Crutchfield said.

INSTEAD OF CELEBRATING MARDI GRAS ON FEBRUARY 5, SAL Cepriano and Jordan Ancar took a recruiting visit to Benedictine College, a Catholic liberal arts school of 1,250 students in Atchison, Kansas. A scout from Benedictine, which played with other small schools in the National Association of Intercollegiate Athletics (NAIA), had spotted the two Hurricanes during the Class 1A championship game. He was impressed with their mobility and athleticism. On his recruiting visit, Sal saw snow for the first time. Jordan had never seen so much of it, and he dived headfirst into a big pile.

Before the trip, Sal had been convinced that, at 190 pounds, he was too small to play college football. He was not the most confident of kids, and he wondered if Benedictine expressed interest "because they feel sorry for me."

It didn't work that way in college, he was told. Talent won over compassion. Benedictine offered Sal a scholarship that would pay all but $1,000 of the school's approximately $23,000 annual fee for tuition and room and board. Jordan would have to pay $3,000 yearly. Weeks later, both players accepted. They were excited to learn new positions in the fall, Sal at linebacker, Jordan at fullback. They hoped to room together.

Sal had longed to get away, to leave behind an orderless home life, to get away from an uncertain existence on the water. He would be the first in his family to graduate from high school. And now he would have a chance to get a college degree while doing the thing he loved most, the thing that had saved him from despair: playing football.

"I never thought this opportunity would present itself," Sal said. "They're all about the academics. None of us are gonna make it to the NFL. They'll give us free tutors. They say it's impossible not to graduate. I'm ready to go. It's a good opportunity. I'd be miserable right now if I couldn't play football anymore. Down here, there's not too much for a person. It's wonderful to get out and experience something other than Plaquemines Parish."

RANDALL MACKEY CONCLUDED HIS SENIOR YEAR AT BAStrop High by being named the most valuable offensive player on the Class 4A all-state team and the top overall high school player in Louisiana. He was also one of fifty-seven players nationwide named to the Parade All-America Team after throwing for 3,103 yards and 33 touchdowns as a senior, while rushing for 1,087 yards and 17 touchdowns.

On Christmas Day, though, Bastrop coach Brad Bradshaw was quoted in the *Times-Picayune* of New Orleans as saying that Randall had "come up short academically" in his attempt to play major-college football in 2008. He would first have to attend junior college, Bradshaw said.

During the holidays, there was talk about whether Randall would leave high school immediately and enroll in junior college or remain at Bastrop. He spoke with Crutchfield, who advised him to make sure he graduated if he remained in high school, preserving his chance to play college football at some level.

In early February, Randall reversed field and signed a letter of intent to attend Ole Miss, a lower-rung SEC school, but one with a rich history in what was widely considered the top football conference in the country. He planned to take correspondence courses and an ACT preparatory class in an attempt to gain eligibility to play in the fall of 2008. That effort fell short, and Randall signed in the spring to play at East Mississippi Community College.

"My dream was to go to Texas and go pro," Randall said. "What happened? I think it was just grades. That's my fault. I should have taken care of business when I had a chance."

Crutchfield felt that Randall had been exploited at Bastrop. "I think he did the right thing, but I also think he got used," he said. "They weren't worried about his books. They wanted him to win games."

Randall said he disagreed. "They didn't use me," he said. "They were nice to me. I had so much assistance up here."

Yet after two and a half years, Randall still seemed conflicted about his decision not to return to Port Sulphur after Katrina. In Bastrop, he said, "The football was the best thing I've seen." Everywhere he went, people asked for his autograph. Everyone knew who he was. Even so, he said, contradicting himself from a year earlier, if his mother had let him, he would have returned home to play for South Plaquemines.

"She thought it was better for me up here," Randall said of Bastrop.

In the end, things had worked out for both Randall and Ridge, his former neighbor. "That's why I'm happy I came here," Randall said. "Ridge got his time. That's my boy. Every single day we played football together."

Still, he missed Crutchfield.

"The old Crutchfield, the one who used to curse and beat us up all the time," Randall said with a laugh. "He probably still does it, but not like back in the day. He's changed."

CANTRELLE RILEY, LOUISIANA'S LEADING RECEIVER, SOUGHT another year of eligibility but was denied by the state high school athletic association because he would turn nineteen before the 2008 season began. "They did the best they could," Lisa Riley said of school officials.

AFTER HIS FOOTBALL CAREER ENDED, LITTLE WAYNE Williamson finished second in the state wrestling tournament in the 171-pound division. He joined the South Plaquemines baseball team and hoped to play the sport at one of the smaller colleges in Louisiana. If that didn't work out, he planned to enter the navy.

"Having gone through Crutchfield's boot camp, I'm sure he can do it in the military," said Big Wayne, who agreed to escort the team bus for another year.

ROGER HALPHEN HAD ATTENDED THE STATE-CHAMPIONSHIP game in a kind of daze, sitting in the stands, moving from section to section to find the best view. Afterward, he came onto the field at the Superdome and shook hands with Crutchfield. Then he went into the dressing room and congratulated the players. "See what you missed for hitting that kid," he remembered one of the players telling him. Or was it something less stinging? He later forgot that Sal Cepriano had embraced him, saying, "A lot of what we know, you taught us." Everything was a whirlwind.

The Hurricanes had played more games without him than with him. Roger had spent the play-offs in a fog, wounded, dislocated. "Like I got my heart yanked out of my fucking chest," he said. After the title game, he celebrated on Bourbon Street with other teachers from South Plaquemines. He felt proud and terrible at the same time. The kids had handled themselves like champions. Marcelin Ancar had done a commendable job replacing him as line coach. He wanted to be there with them. The next morning he felt cheated, empty.

Roger planned to return to South Plaquemines to teach P.E. for the 2008–2009 school year. He was not supposed to coach anymore, but even if school officials changed their minds, he was not sure that he wanted to. He thought it might be best to limit his contact with students to class time. He would keep his head down, do his job, go home. Maybe he would catch a few football games, maybe not.

"I've got to try to survive one more year," he said.

And then he would be eligible for his pension.

ON NEW YEAR'S EVE, CYRIL CRUTCHFIELD MARRIED MIC-quella Sylve. He wore a purple vest with his tuxedo and had purple roses on his wedding cake, the team color of Port Sulphur High. In early January, conditioning drills began for the 2008 football season. Having lost only six seniors, with the state's leading passer and one of its top running backs returning along with an insatiable defense,

Crutchfield believed the Hurricanes should repeat as champion in Class 1A. Asked to name the top challengers to South Plaquemines, he said, "It doesn't matter."

He had seen a cardiologist about his chest pains. He had a slightly enlarged heart and elevated blood pressure, but his stress test had come back fine, he said. There were no blockages, and he did not have high cholesterol.

Such was Crutchfield's anticipation for the coming season that he began getting up early on Sunday mornings and designing his new offense before leaving for church, Micquella said. On weekdays, he stood atop the Mississippi River levee across from school and urged his players as they ran up and down, frontward, backwards, sideways. By late January, the levee was already carved with dirt trails that resembled stripes on the sides of sneakers. On the football field, players ran sprints and jumped over hurdles, and Crutchfield barked at them with a coach's timeless and theatrical discontent: "Go see the Cowardly Lion and get some courage! Go see the Woodsman and get some heart!"

He also coached the track team. His stepson, Bradley Sylve, a freshman, won state titles at 100 meters (10.6 seconds) and 200 meters (21.85 seconds). Ridge Turner finished second in the 300-meter hurdles, and Cantrelle Riley took third in the 110-meter hurdles. Bradley was scheduled to join Lyle Fitte at running back in the fall. The state results were remarkable, given that South Plaquemines had no track, and Crutchfield trained his sprinters and hurdlers on the football field.

A temporary gym was built on campus, and a weight room was still in the planning. Yet, the future in lower Plaquemines became a little more uncertain in January, when the U.S. Army Corps of Engineers said it might offer voluntary buyouts to residents of the parish who would be at high risk in another destructive hurricane. One question loomed, according to the *Plaquemines Gazette:* Do we stay, or do we go?

Meanwhile, Billy Nungesser, the parish president, traveled to Washington to sell his plan on pumping sediment from the river through pipelines to rebuild wetlands and barrier islands.

"We can't let the Corps or FEMA or anybody else tell us what parts of Plaquemines are important or not important to save," Nungesser said.

If another devastating hurricane ever hit, Crutchfield said, he and all his players would transfer to the same school. "Somebody in north Louisiana will be loaded," he said.

As Katrina's third anniversary approached, so did another football season. For Crutchfield and his team, another storm was less of a concern than a more familiar adversary. Encouraged by his older brother Sal's achievement, Phillip Cepriano, who was sixteen, decided to try out for the Hurricanes. The day after spring drills began, Phillip asked his mother, "You think we gonna beat Belle Chasse?"

ACKNOWLEDGMENTS

THE DAY HURRICANE KATRINA STRUCK, I GOT A PHONE CALL from Kristin Huckshorn, then the deputy sports editor of the *New York Times*. Get to New Orleans, she said, there must be a good story about high school football in the storm's aftermath. By the time I arrived, though, it was clear there would be little or no football played in southeastern Louisiana in the fall of 2005.

A year later, I reminded Kristin of her assignment, proposing a story about a newly-formed school, South Plaquemines High. The paper had a glut of Katrina anniversary stories, Kristin said. Instead, she and two other editors, David Firestone and Mike Abrams, suggested that I follow South Plaquemines for the 2006 season and write a series upon its conclusion. Once I returned to Louisiana, Kristin decided that we should begin the series right away. A planned three or four stories became nine stories. For that I am eternally grateful. This book grew out of that series.

Having grown attached to the players, I returned to South Plaquemines in the spring of 2007 to attend their graduation and to watch the school's spring football game. At the time, Coach Cyril Crutchfield Jr. told me that he was sure the Hurricanes would win the upcoming state championship. So I returned week after week in the fall of 2007 as it became clear that South Plaquemines might actually win the title.

I want to thank my editors at the *Times*, Tom Jolly and Jason Stallman, who allowed me the freedom to continue following South Plaquemines High. And I want to thank Alex Ward and others at the *Times* for permission to reprint material in this book.

I grew up on the Cajun prairie of southwestern Louisiana, but had never visited Plaquemines Parish before Katrina. The people I met were as generous and open as they were resilient. Coach Crutchfield and Stanley Gaudet, the principal at South Plaquemines, granted me complete access to the team and the school. I was allowed into the locker room and the classroom and was given carte blanche along the sidelines. I rode the team bus, interviewed players in the middle of games and even joined the huddle during timeouts. Players and their parents took me hunting and fishing, shrimping and oystering. They invited me to pregame meals and had me over for Thanksgiving. Many got to know my name; others simply called me "New York." I had long wanted to write a book about my home state; unfortunately much of the area below Interstate 10 had to be wrecked for me to get that opportunity. Nevertheless, South Plaquemines was an irresistible story.

David Black, my agent, indulged my passion and kept pitching the book when it seemed unlikely that anyone would buy it. I want to thank Susan Weinberg, the publisher of PublicAffairs, for taking a chance, and David Hirshey of HarperCollins for mentioning the book to Susan. Lindsay Jones, my editor at PublicAffairs, provided smart, patient guidance.

I'd like to also thank the members of Coach Crutchfield's staff for their time and insight: Roger Halphen, Marcelin Ancar, Corey Buie, Rod Parker, August Ragas, Anthony LaFrance and Buddy Veillion. Wayne Williamson Sr. and Rodney Bartholomew Sr. were generous with their friendship and knowledge of the history of football in lower Plaquemines.

For their counsel, I want to thank Billy Nungesser, the president of Plaquemines Parish; Eva Jones, the school superintendent; Rod Lincoln, the parish historian; Darryl Bubrig, the district attorney; Jiff

Hingle, the sheriff; and Norris Babin, co-owner of the *Plaquemines Gazette*.

Paul Atkinson, a documentary producer, provided invaluable access to his video collection, along with his unstinting encouragement. For their support, I'd also like to thank Jeff Duncan of the *Times-Picayune* of New Orleans, along with William Kalec and Trent Angers of Acadian House Publishing.

As always, the selflessness of Deborah Longman, my wife, and the consent of Julie-Ann, our daughter, allowed me the extended time away from home to research the book.

Finally, I'd like to thank my parents for their bottomless supply of love and seafood gumbo.

BIBLIOGRAPHY

Alvarez, Louis and Kolker, Andrew. *The Ends of the Earth: Plaquemines Parish, Louisiana*. Documentary, The Center for New American Media, 1982.

Atkinson, Paul. *A Season with the Hurricanes*. Documentary, Versatile Productions, 2007.

Brasseaux, Carl. *French, Cajun, Creole, Houma: A Primer on Francophone Louisiana*. Baton Rouge: Louisiana State University Press, 2005.

Byrnes, Donia. "A History of the Louisiana Sulphur Industry." *The Student Historical Journal*, Loyola University of New Orleans, 1985.

Conaway, James. *Judge: The Life and Times of Leander Perez*. New York: Knopf, 1973.

Duncan, Jeff. "Displaced Ninth Ward Students Struggle to Play On." The *Times-Picayune* of New Orleans, December 13, 2005.

Jeansonne, Glen. *Leander Perez: Boss of the Delta*. Jackson: University Press of Mississippi, 2006.

Kane, Hartnett. *Deep Delta Country*. New York: Duell, Sloan and Pearce, 1944.

Kolbert, Elizabeth. "Watermark: Can Louisiana Be Saved?" The *New Yorker*, February 27, 2006.

Manning, Susan. *Riding out the Risks: An Ethnographic Study of Risk Perceptions in a South Louisiana Bayou Community*. Master's thesis, Louisiana State University, 2005.

Marshall, Bob. "Last Chance: The Fight to Save a Disappearing Coast." The *Times-Picayune* of New Orleans. March 4, 2007.

Pierce, Janice. *Grand Bayou: Seasonal Activities in a Louisiana Marsh Community*. Master's thesis, Louisiana State University, 1979.

Spitzer, Nicholas. *Mississippi Delta Ethnographic Overview*. New Orleans: Jean Lafitte National Historic Park, 1979.

White, David. *Cultural Gumbo? An Ethnographic Overview of Louisiana's Mississippi River Delta*. New Orleans: Jean Lafitte National Historic Park, 1998.

INDEX

Jeré Longman, a sportswriter for the *New York Times* who has written about sports for more than thirty years, grew up on the Cajun prairie in Eunice, Louisiana. Jeré is the author of the *New York Times* bestseller and Notable Book, *Among the Heroes: United Flight 93 and the Passengers and Crew Who Fought Back; The Girls of Summer;* and *If Football's a Religion, Why Don't We Have a Prayer?* He lives in Philadelphia.

PublicAffairs is a publishing house founded in 1997. It is a tribute to the standards, values, and flair of three persons who have served as mentors to countless reporters, writers, editors, and book people of all kinds, including me.

I. F. STONE, proprietor of *I. F. Stone's Weekly*, combined a commitment to the First Amendment with entrepreneurial zeal and reporting skill and became one of the great independent journalists in American history. At the age of eighty, Izzy published *The Trial of Socrates*, which was a national bestseller. He wrote the book after he taught himself ancient Greek.

BENJAMIN C. BRADLEE was for nearly thirty years the charismatic editorial leader of *The Washington Post*. It was Ben who gave the *Post* the range and courage to pursue such historic issues as Watergate. He supported his reporters with a tenacity that made them fearless and it is no accident that so many became authors of influential, best-selling books.

ROBERT L. BERNSTEIN, the chief executive of Random House for more than a quarter century, guided one of the nation's premier publishing houses. Bob was personally responsible for many books of political dissent and argument that challenged tyranny around the globe. He is also the founder and longtime chair of Human Rights Watch, one of the most respected human rights organizations in the world.

·   ·   ·

For fifty years, the banner of Public Affairs Press was carried by its owner Morris B. Schnapper, who published Gandhi, Nasser, Toynbee, Truman, and about 1,500 other authors. In 1983, Schnapper was described by *The Washington Post* as "a redoubtable gadfly." His legacy will endure in the books to come.